POEMS

AND

PROSE WRITINGS.

BY

RICHARD HENRY DANA.

IN TWO VOLUMES.

VOLUME II.

NEW YORK:
BAKER AND SCRIBNER.
M DCCC L.

CAMBRIDGE:
STEREOTYPED BY METCALF AND COMPANY,
PRINTED BY EDWARD O. JENKINS,
114 NASSAU STREET, NEW YORK

CONTENTS

TO

VOLUME SECOND.

ESSAYS.

REVIEWS.

ESSAYS.

OLD TIMES.

"The world is empty, the heart is dead surely!
In this world, plainly, all seemeth amiss."

It went to my heart when they cleared the old parlour of the venerable family furniture, and stripped the oak panels of the prints of the months, — July with her large fan and full ruffles at the elbows, and January in her muff and tippet. They would have pulled down the panels, too, to make the room as smart and bright as paper could make it; but placing my back against them, I swore by the spirit of my grandfather, that not a joint in the old work should be started while I could stand to defend it. And I have my revenge when I see how pert, insignificant, and raw every thing looks, surrounded by the high and dark walls of the apartment. But the old furniture was huddled together topsy-turvy in the garret. The round oak table, which had many a day smoked with the substantial dinners of former times, lost one of its leaves by too rough handling; but an old oak desk, at which my grandfather in his days of courtship was wont to pen epistles and sonnets to my grandmother, escaped the violence of the revolution with only a few scratches. I have had the dust wiped off its black polish, brought it down by my study fire, and placed before it the old gentleman's arm-chair, which I found standing calm and stately upon its four legs, amidst the disordered rubbish of the garret. The mice have made a hole in the smooth leather bottom, which, however, I have never mended, as I keep it to remind me of the neglect and ingratitude of the world. It does not make you hate the world: no man could sit in my grandfather's chair and hate his fellow-beings. I am seated in it this moment; and with my pen fresh dipped in his leaden inkstand, shall scribble on till my mind and heart are eased.

To this corner I retire at the shutting in of day for self-examination and amendment. It is here that I sit in the shadow of a melancholy mind, and see pass before me, in solemn order, my follies and my crimes, and follow them with trembling into the portentous uncertainty of the future. It is here I learn that we must not lean on the world for comfort; it is here that I give myself up to the visions of the mind, and fill the space about me with beings from distant regions and of other times. Here, too, have I looked, with a dream-like contemplation, upon the shadows sliding over the wall, silent as sunlight, till they seemed to me as monitors from the land of the dead, who had come in kindness to tell me of the vanity of present things, and of the hastening on of another and an enduring world.

It is natural, in these lonely musings, to brood over the heartlessness and noisy joys of the world. There is at bottom a feeling of self-complacency in it. Our calmed reason sets us above the beings about us, while we forget how many, at that very moment, are as meditative and rational as ourselves; and how few there are, amidst the multitude that cover the earth, who have not their hours of solitary contemplation too.

It was in this cast of thought, in which the heart is made sad for want of communion with some living thing, when the tasteless character of what surrounds us hurries the mind forward to the excitement of hope or carries it back to dwell for a time amidst the softened but deep feelings of the past, that the fresh and thoughtless joys and the pure and warm affections of my boyhood came over me like a dream, and the cares of years, and the solemn and darkening scene about me, gave way, and I stood in the midst of the green and sunshine of a child. I felt again the wrinkled cheek over which my baby hand had a thousand times passed in fondness, entered into all the plays of children, and then remembered the quaint customs, the individualities of the age of strong character and warm feeling, which marked the times of our fathers, when the old sometimes mingled with the young, and the young bowed in reverence to the old. That was the age of feeling. Would that this over-wise age had something of its childlike simplicity, something of its rough and honest manliness, which dared at times to be a boy. But the age has changed; and those amusements in which we were all children together, and which made the heart better without weakening the understanding, are at an end.

There are no April-Fool-Day's tricks in this period of decorum, no "merry Christmas," no "happy New-Year." I feel the blood move quick again at the recollection of the glad faces I once used to see, when every body was running to wish you "happy New-Year." I can remember when, hurrying from my chamber, with my fingers too stiff and cold to button my little jacket, I burst open the parlour door, that I might be the first to "wish." Though, on this morning, I was sure to be up an hour earlier than usual, I always found the family standing round the new-made crackling fire, ready to break out upon me in full voices with the old greeting. There was something restoring in it, which made me feel as if we had all awaked in a new world, and to another existence; and a vague, but grateful sensation, that new and peculiar joys were in store for us, went warm and quickening to the heart. I was filled with kindness; and eager as I had been but a moment before to surprise every one in the house, the laugh of good-natured triumph at my defeat made it dearer to me than a victory.

But old things are passed away; all things are become new. Not only those customs, which now and then met us in our dull travel over the road of life, are gone; even the seasons seem changing. We no longer gather flowers on May-Day; and our last New-Year's morning, instead of rising upon the crusted snow and fields glittering with ice, spread itself with a sleepy dankness over the naked earth. I awoke with an ill-foreboding languor upon me, and with a weighed-down heart sauntered into the silent parlour. The brands had fallen over the hearth, and by their half-extinguished heat seemed to doubt their welcome. I knew not where to sit or stand; the fireside looked cheerless, and there was an uncomfortable, ill-natured chill at the window. The vapour was passing off from the withered grass; the freshness of every thing about me appeared deadened, and the beauty of nature faded. In the midst of this dull decay and solitude, a sense of desertion overshadowed me. The world's inhabitants were as strangers, and even the objects of nature, with which I was wont to hold discourse, seemed to shut me out from communion with them. The family at last came in, one after another. I was about wishing them the New-Year's blessing; but the memory of the heartfelt sprightfulness of old times came across my mind, and brought along with it those that were at rest in the grave. I gave a loud "Hem!" (for my throat was full,) and bade a cold "Good morning." I would not have uttered the old wish if I could have done it; — there was a feeling of proud resentment at the neglect of ancient customs which forbade it. I did not care to wipe off the dust, which is fast and silently gathering over them, to bring them forward to the ridicule of the affected refinement and cold rationality of this enlightened age. They would as ill sort with our modern laboured artificiality of manners, as our grandmother's comfortable arm-chair and worked cushion in a fashionable drawing-room with distressingly slender fancy-chairs, and settees, on which ladies crowd and elbow one another. No, these good-natured and homely observances are passed away, and I have a sacred attachment for their memory, which, like that for a departed friend, forbids mention of them to strangers.

Amidst this neglect and decay of old customs and characters, when every thing is brought to a wearisome level, and all is varnish and polish, so that even the roughness upon the plum is held to be disgusting, — when the utterance of strong feeling is ill-breeding, and dissimulation wisdom, — it is well for the world that there are beings not mindless of the past, who live with ages long gone by, and look upon the characters of the present time as light and artificial, who bring back and keep alive amongst us something of the wild and unpruned beauties of the earth, the ardent and spontaneous movements of man; so that the forest and rock, the grass-plot and field-flower, are yet about us, and some few walking in the midst, who are mighty and awing, kind and like a child.

In that period of the world when the ignorance which had settled down upon the mind of man was passing off, and his understanding and heart were turned up and laid open to the day, there was a morning, earthy freshness in all he saw and felt. The dust and hot air of noon had not dimmed the colours, or killed the wholesomeness of all about him. The relentless curiosity of modern times had not broken in pieces the precious stone, or soiled and torn asunder the flower. Man was the worshipper of the works of God in their simple beauty and grandeur; not the vain inquisitor, eager to learn their structure, that he might prate of what he knew. All was rustic and unforced; "a generous nature was suffered to take her own way to perfection." The cottage seemed a shelter for earth's children, from which they might look out upon, and learn and love, her beauties. They dwelt in the religious twilight of her woods, and mused by her water-falls on the passage of years. The universal puttings-forth of spring quickened the pure spirits of the young; and the yellow leaf was the moral companion of the old. It was, indeed, nature without doors and within. Man walked abroad upon the green sod, and sat him down upon rushes by his fireside. The mind was as full of motion, various and creative, as the earth about it; and, like hers, its productions were its mere relievings, effortless, but plentiful. Its images were not formed in a daintily finished mould, or finically chiselled out; but like fairy frost-work, or the wavy sweep of a snow-drift, though ever beautiful, yet always seeming accidental. It was the poetic age. Growing up in the absence of a false elegance, and not educated to the cautious and constrained politeness which crowded society has forced upon us, men were left to an independent individuality of character and conduct. Without the excitements of the pleasures and distinctions of the city, the mind spread itself out over the beauties about it; felt and nursed their truth; perceived a fitness and kindly relation in all things; not only gazed upon the lofty works of God, and walked by his still waters in the valley, but looked untired upon the flat sand-waste or the long stretch of a rough heath. The taste was not pampered and vitiated by ill-assorted prettinesses, turning the unnumbered beauties, the simplicity and outspread grandeur of this gigantic earth, into the huddled and offensively contrasted crowd of a garden; but the rock, fringed and scattered over with its green or silvery moss, was looked upon, though not seated in a bed of roses, violets, and pinks; the wholesome perfume of the pine was grateful, and the crisp tread over its fallen and matted leaves pleasant to the foot.

In this age of improvements, when multiplied inventions have rendered useless many acts to which individuals were once called in the common concerns of life,—when one traverses a kingdom, without the touch of its breezes upon his cheek, and now and then takes a hasty peep, through his carriage window, at the scenery about him, as if he were a stranger to it and would not be unmannerly,—we may boast of the facilities and harmless luxuries of the world we live in. But though it gives us facilities, it works into the character a sameness, and an indifference to particulars. The object we sought is turned out finished to our hands, without our labour or observation; it is attained without effort, and possessed without delight.

This mechanical moving on of things may aid the politician, but will not benefit the man. To the mathematician, who holds the daily cares and heart-helping relations of life as so many interruptions to the solution of his problem, it may be pleasant visioning to suppose himself moved about without the aid of his troublesome but faithful beast, and his within-door concerns carried on by well-ordered machinery, and not self-willed servants; to think that his only perplexities in his domestic establishment would be the grating of a wheel or breaking of a cord: — Not rusty, like "my father's hinge," but well oiled, how smoothly all would go on! But to the man of heart and poetry this would be like the house of the dead, where the cold and stiffened bodies of the departed were raised up and charmed into careful and silent motion, acting unknowing, and obeying without sense.

In old times it was not so. Artificial aids were few and uncouth. Worked out in the rough and cumbrous, and requiring strength in the handling, they drew the attention; and lasting long, they became a part of the family, and held their place in the still and kindly-working associations of our homes. The old chair, in the very character of the age, looking so companionable and easy, yet with its comfortable arms protecting its good-natured occupier from the too near and familiar approach of his neighbour, stood in the snug corner of the ample fire-place, as by prescriptive right. It was no new-fangled thing, bought yesterday because in fashion, and set up for the gibes of the smart auctioneer to-day because out. It had been adorned by the patient industry and quaint fancy of our mothers, and had the honour of having sustained the weight of our ancestors for a century or more. Putting it away would have been neglecting our fathers, and the unkindly cutting off of remembrances that had taken root and grown up in the heart. Each piece of furniture had its story to tell, and every room in the antique mansion made the mind serious and busy with the past, and threw a sentiment and feeling, softening but cheerful, over present times. This converse with the inanimate kept the heart warm and the imagination quick; and the inly-workings, various and constant, found much to study everywhere, and something to love in all things.

The better feelings were kept in motion by the old relations of master and servant; the servant watchful of the master's wishes, humble in demeanour, yet proud in his fidelity; the master trustful in the other's good-faith and careful of his comforts in the reposing time of age. This long-tried service brought about a mixed but delightful sensation, when he who had tended us in our playing days had gone down into the still vale of years, while we stood on the open hill-top in our vigour and prime. It was a kind of filial reverence, touched by the sense of the humble and dependent state of him whom we protected and upon whom we looked down.

> "But we have bid farewell
> To all the virtues of those better days,
> And all their honest pleasures. Mansions once
> Knew their own masters, and laborious hinds,
> Who had survived the father, served the son."

Along with such softening influences, there was much of the wild and adventurous starting up in the midst of the common objects of life; at one time throwing over them mysterious shadows, and casting them into strange and awful forms; at another, pouring upon them a dazzling light, in which they flitted gay and fantastic. Surrounded by ideal shapes and untamed nature, the imagination was constantly widening and ever creative. Men could not leave their homes, the proper dwellings of the heart, without travelling into the regions of the fancy. Moving on alone through silent and unpeopled paths, winding round dusky rocks, and through tangling brush-wood, and overhung by gloomy woods, the traveller held converse with some spirit of the air, or, in the superstitious workings of his mind, saw some being of evil, darker than the night that had gathered round him.

Journeying far on horse or afoot, common to the times, fording rapid streams, toiling over rugged mountains and through wet low-lands, begat perseverance, healthful spirits, ready, cheerful, and self-trusting minds, acquainted with difficulties and used to overcoming them. Diversions, too, partook of the violent and daring; so that with all there was a combination of the natural and tender, the imaginative and the manly, in the characters of former days, which calls up within us an intense and restless desire to know them entirely, to live back amongst them, to warm us in their cheerful sunshine, to sit by their fireside, listen to their stories, mingle in their domestic games, and learn of their stern sense.

This is an exhaustless theme; but I have talked long enough, perhaps too long; for to many it may all seem childish conceit, or the strange fancies of a tired spirit impatient of reality. But he of wide and deep thought will not so look upon it, or hold this view of things false because it is sad. Now that every thing rude and irregular is cut down, and all that remains is trimmed up and made to look set and orderly, he will not forget how much there was of exquisite beauty, of loftiness and strength, in the one, how tame and unsatisfying is the other. Though there was a deep and subduing tenderness, an ardour and sway of passion, in the men of former days, sometimes uncontrolled and not always aimed aright, yet he will see that, with little of softness, man is still weak, and, without the extravagance of feeling, still erring: — The absence of passion is not always reason, nor coldness judgment.

THE PAST AND THE PRESENT.

> "O that he were thus pervaded
> With the Past! were thus persuaded
> Of his proper sphere and powers!"

> It will secure you from the narrow idolatry of the present times and fashions, and create the noblest kind of imaginative power in your soul, that of living in past ages;—wholly devoid of which power, a man can neither anticipate the future, nor even live a truly human life, a life of reason, in the present.
>
> COLERIDGE.

THAT distinguished divine, John Owen, said, long ago,—"The world is at present in a mighty hurry, and being in many places cast off from all foundations of steadfastness, it makes the minds of men giddy with its revolutions, and disorderly in the expectations of them."

If this was a truth in the days of Owen, it is equally a truth now; if men in his time tore themselves violently off from old associations, and went wild after change, no less are they ridding themselves of all that is old, and quite as wild are they after alteration, in our day.

There is nothing new under the sun, said Solomon. Men seem resolved upon bringing the time speedily about, when they may look around them, and, reversing the declaration of the wise man, be able to say, There is nothing *old* under the sun!

What a spirit is there in that word *old!* Who would live in a world where there was nothing *old?* Experience would not, could not; nor sedateness, nor reflection, slow and thoughtful. Fancy might, perhaps; but not imagination, that deeper power of the soul. And could the heart let go all its old attachments, and yet live? And hope, even beautiful hope, though the future be its nourisher, is the child of the past, and waits by the bed of weariness or sorrow: —

> "A woman-saint, who bare an angel's face,
> Bade me awake, and ease my troubled mind.
> With that I waked, —
> And saw 't was Hope."

And how large would be the discourse of reason, looking before, and never after? What would prospect be to us, without retrospect? A strange land without a guide. And what is the present to us, without a lingering feeling for the past? A state of self-complacency, strangely blended with restlessness, and an impatient desire to be something we are not, no matter what, to gain something we have not, no matter how.

If this be indeed the age of change, it may be well to stop awhile, and ask ourselves whether all we have cast behind us is quite so useless as we have presumed; whether that which we may have retained is only to be tolerated for a time, and soon to be thrown by as worthless; whether the present, in comparison with the old and despised past, is every thing, and, compared with the vague but exciting future, nothing.

It is not, however, my present purpose to go into the question of the relative merits of past and present times; but to speak, first, of the influence which a respect for the past has upon the mind; and then of the influence which an exclusive attention to the present has upon it.

I must not be understood as confining myself to the remote, when I speak of the past; but as coming down and including both that which has more lately gone by us and taken its place in the memory, and sometimes even that which may still remain within us, but bearing the marks of age and the aspect of the past. This subject lies broad and deep in human nature; but all I can now do is, to set down a few of those thoughts which such a subject must call up in every reflecting mind, and to give utterance to only a part of those feelings which grow from it, and which are dear to me, because of my inward conviction of their truth.

The question naturally arises, in the outset, Is change, in *itself* considered, a good, or an evil?

Existence may be so unvaried, as to bring a sluggishness into the feelings, and a sleepiness over the intellect; uniformity may settle down into dulness, and content be the mere absence of sensibility. There may also be a pertinacious adherence to what is old, growing out of a morose pride in it, rather than out of a kindly love of it; a sulky rejection of the new, merely because it is new, and not from a heart-sense that "the old is better";—there may be more of surly dislike of the one, than of considerate esteem or mellowed affection for the other. Age sometimes bears you a grudge, because not itself possessing that of which youth is full,—buoyancy of spirits, hopefulness, and health.

Nevertheless, after all that may be said about old-fashioned notions, obstinate prejudices, a stupid indifference to improvement, or a provoking unbelief in it, there is no less of clear-headedness, and quite as much of true-heartedness, in this clinging to things as they were, as will be found at work in our eagerness after so-called improvements, in other words, change.

Through a long acquaintance with any thing, no matter how insignificant in itself, it becomes imperceptibly inwrought with our accustomed associations of feelings and thoughts, and thus partakes of their common life, and, by sharing in it, adds to it. How much is there in the term, *wonted* to a thing! We cannot utter it without being conscious of a gentle stirring among the affections. It is something that took life early in our hearts, and grew up, unobserved, it may be, branching in among our gentler feelings and quieter meditations, till the whole shoots up into a beautiful tree-top; and when the air of some outward circumstance blows upon it, how easily it swings back and forth, all together, and what a melody there is in its low murmur! Look at it! Listen to it; for I know you are not so lost in the present, as to be no longer able to see it, to hear it, ay, to feel it.

The past, having thus grown up in and with us, is become a part of ourselves, or rather, may it not be said? is become very self; not the whole self, but so in and of self as to take away the thought of parts or portions, and thus has acted in the way of increment, without breaking up the integrity of the man. Nay, the unity of the character is the more perfect for it; for where unity does exist, its perfectness will be according to its intensity, and its intensity will be according to that which goes to make up its one simple element of living consciousness: the more life, the more perfect oneness.

So it is that the past, resolved within us into the

principle of self, and thence taking form early in us, becomes a constituent of our inward growth; and our enlargement has an all-pervading unity, and our variety is harmony. There is consistency in the man; and there has so long been a blending of the thoughts and feelings, that they are, as it were, elemented of one, and the result is a whole man.

Hence comes strong individuality; for the growth being mainly from within, it partakes of the character of that from which it springs, and all the nourishment it absorbs from without is transformed into this individuality, and then transfused through it to invigorate and expand it, but not to change it. The branches of this spiritual tree may grow broader and stronger, but will keep their old shapes; its leaves may be fresher, but you will not be shocked by an unnatural putting forth of various sorts upon the same boughs. With variety there will be singleness of kind; for they are of one family, the children of their common parent trunk, not adopted ones; and thus all will be beautiful congruity.

As this spirit of the past gives congruity and oneness to the character, all that share in this oneness must, as was said, in partaking of it, add so much to its life, and not lie like detached masses upon the mind to be moved by it, but, on the contrary, be converted into the living energy of the mind itself, and so be an increase of that mind's moving power.

The past gives strength to the living principle in still another way. One who is not dead to old associations never has his thoughts go back to the past, without a softening emotion of the soul. There is something in the past (I will not stop here to inquire what it is) which moves our better affections and makes us thoughtful, in a manner that neither the present nor the future ever does. Nor are these thoughts and affections confined to that which once had life. The commonest material object to which we had once been used has this same moving power over us. And just in proportion to our interest in the past and what is old will be this life of the mind. And it has this characteristic; — the intellect is kept alive by the suffused, mild warmth of the affections, and is all over tinted by them. Here, the principle of love is the spring of the mind's action. But we cannot have our affections drawn out towards a material object, in its mere material character. To have our affections excited towards it, to have our thoughts gather about it, we must impart to it affection and thought, and thus bring it into sympathy with ourselves. We must quicken its insensibility, and infuse into it consciousness and life.

Even where a material object is not endeared to us from a long acquaintance with it, — for instance, where we take it up for the first time, and find it to be some little relique of one whom we loved, and a thousand emotions towards the departed are immediately awakened in us, — even here, with all this power of association and remembrance upon us in regard to another, which one would think enough to draw us off from the thing itself that put them in motion, — even here, that trifle which has called up this train of recollections is not a mere thing to us, but becomes instinct with life from our feelings; and the soul converses with it, as with a being conscious of what had once passed between us and the departed object of our regard. Here, again, we see the soul, as if surcharged with life, giving out life to the commonest material objects around it. A cross-beam in an old ceiling, a decayed post, an old walking-stick, is endowed by us with feeling, and sentiment, and power of converse, and every thing around us becomes to us life: we move amid nothing but living things. As in Ezekiel's vision, "When the living creatures went, the wheels went by them; and when the living creatures were lifted up from the earth, the wheels were lifted up:—for the spirit of the living creature was in the wheels."

If it be the nature of this spirit of the past, moving within us, to give out life to material things, we must remember, that the very act whereby the mind imparts life and consciousness is an increase of the intensity of that mind's own life,—that the emanations from this spiritual sun do but raise in it a light still brighter, and a more cheering warmth,—and that it is also the blessed constitution of our spiritual natures, that to whatsoever we give, from the same we shall receive seven-fold, and that the poorest thing on earth towards which our hearts go out shall make us rich returns.

That this *spiritualizing* power belongs in a peculiar manner to "the retrospective virtues," as Wordsworth calls them, no one doubts who has read his own heart, and, along with it, the hearts of others. And we may, with Godwin, say of the man who is so endowed, "The world is a thousand times more populous, than to the man to whom every thing that is not flesh and blood is nothing."

Beside the vigour thus given to the life of the mind, beside this power by which, when it looks out upon the world, inert, material things start up into consciousness and life, endowed with associations and affections like the mind's self,—this state of affectionate thoughtfulness multiplies the mind's inward enjoyments from itself, and there is born a countless progeny, beautiful and like the first parent emotion of the soul. For, as Butler profoundly remarks, "Human nature is so constituted, that every good affection implies a love of itself; i. e. becomes an object of a new affection in the same person." Thus the birth of emotion upon emotion is begun in the soul, of which, though it has a beginning, no one can so much as imagine to himself an end: a creation is commenced which shall go on through eternity.

Not only has the past this life-giving power, by which, through the according action of heart and mind, the being grows up and expands with a just congruity throughout; it also imparts stability to the character; for the past is fixed: to that is neither change, nor the shadow of turning. We may look back along the shores of that sea, and behold every cliff standing in its original, dark strength; we may hear the solemn moving of its waves, but no plunge of a heavy promontory, tumbling from its base, startles us: what hath been in the soul cannot cease to be. Every secret thought of all the races of men who have been, all forms of the creative mind, put forth in act, still live. Every emotion of the heart that beat away back in time may sleep, but is not dead: it shall wake again. The hands that moulded the images first embodied in the mind may be dust now; the material forms of art may have fallen back into shapeless earth again; castle and fane, pyramid and column, may have come down; but the forms in the *mind*, of which these were but the outward show, still stand there perfect. True, a veil may hang before them for a while; but when the angel, that standeth upon the sea and upon the earth, shall utter the voice, "Time shall be no longer," that veil shall be rent from the top to the bottom.

O, it seems to me that I can look even now into this temple and its chambers of glorified imagery, and behold these spirits of the past in all their aspects,—of mysterious thought, subduing love, passionate endeavour, and lofty aim, and forms beautiful as the angels and noble as the gods! How populous is the past! Yes, not a passion, not a thought, not an image of the minds that have been, has perished: the spiritual cannot die. What mean we by that we call death? It is but the seal of eternity.

If the past, in its spiritual constitution, has this character of durability,—if it comes before us having put on the form of eternity,—its influence upon us must be to impart the permanent to our own characters. For between us and whatsoever we love, a secret, confluent process of assimilation is going on, till the two become, as it were, homogeneous. That which we much dwell upon, through a mystical intercommunion, we, in time, resemble: the aspect of our soul becomes like that spiritual countenance on which the mind's eye most rests itself. When Moses descended from Sinai, "and when Aaron and all the children of Israel saw Moses, behold, the skin of his face shone; and they were afraid to come nigh him." Moses had come from standing before the brightness of the Most High God!

Another effect of the past upon us, and a much needed and elevating one, is to beget in us the spirit of reverence. As it is unnatural for the mind to think of what has once lived as now utterly extinct, and as even material shapes, the representatives of the mind's forms, though lost to us in their material, still live to us in their spiritual shapes in the mysterious world of forms, the past comes shadowing over us with the calm awe of eternity in it, and man beholds and reveres. Eternity is present with him, not as an intellectual abstraction, but in the images of whatever has once been; it spreads out visibly before the mind's eye; and as in the clouds of evening twilight with the bodily eye we see figured

> "A towered citadel, a pendant rock,
> A forked mountain, or blue promontory
> With trees upon 't, that nod unto the world," —

in a higher and truer sense rises upon the mind's eye the vast, the crowded, the eternally living world of the past. The spirit is filled with it. Eternity has now a meaning and feeling in it, and the soul, awakened by its all-surrounding presence, stands awed at its own conscious immortality. With what solemn grandeur comes up before it the spirit of the past!

It is not in connection with the eternal alone, that the past awakens reverence in us. So long as we suffer our minds to have their natural play, that which existed long before we came into being will call out something of filial respect; the past will be reverenced as our great ancestor. Nor is this an unmeaning emotion. For whatever has been touches on whatever is; the present would not be as it is, had the past been different from what it was. As the peculiar gestures of the father are acted over again in the child, and as on the lip of the little one is still playing the mother's own smile, though she herself be gone, so the past, by wonderful communication, infuses something of its own character into whatever follows it. He who has no reverence for the past is an unnatural son, mocking at age, and forswearing his own father. And should this reverential feeling die out, and the children of this or the coming time make light of it, we may depend upon it, in its stead, passions will break into their social state, which shall rend them like the "two she-bears out of the wood."

Again, power raises more or less of admiration in the mind. When we look at it as an object of the mind's contemplation merely, and not as operating immediately upon ourselves, it makes itself felt. And this it does, however remote in time or place, and however used, whether for a good or bad end. For use changes not its nature, — it is still power; and we acknowledge it, from its infinite perfectness in the Almighty, down to its most tortuous acts in the worst of his creatures.

Aside from moral and intellectual power, in its lowest form, that of brute strength, power calls out a kind of admiration, I had almost said respect. We may have seen, in the countenance of a pallid book-man, a sort of scornful pity at the exhibition of muscular power in a hale day-labourer. But had we looked into the man's heart, we should have found that it gave his face the lie. It was an uncomfortable sense of another's superiority, (no matter in what,) driving him home to his misgiving self-complacency, his only hiding-place at such times.

If power awakens a sense of admiration, every circumstance that puts it, not only out of our check and direct control, but beyond our direct or indirect means of influence, also increases our sense of its greatness, and our consciousness of our own inferiority; and the more we dwell upon it, the more these impressions act and react upon each other; the more our admiration of it rises, larger pomp attends upon it, and we bend in reverence before it.

What a grandeur, then, is thrown round the powers

of the past! How they expand on our vision, till their height becomes terrible! Look, for they still live, — awful, mysterious powers! But we can only look and adore, not reach them, — even uncared for of them! Amid their vast thoughts, amid their great stir of passions, amid the proud structures they raised on earth, and which are now sublimated into ethereal domes and temples, amid all these, what one thought there is of us? what one standing-place there for our feet? what cathedral arch or clustering column there can we lay an altering hand upon? Time cannot crumble them now. A hand, like that which came out upon the wall, has written on them, Changeless as Eternity! The past has touched them.

To think of a power so at ease in its own strength and ever-during nature, as to take no concern for our opposition or favour, or even to heed that we exist, has something in it most humbling to our proud natures. But such to us is the past. Let any one who has stood under a heavy-based rock, and strained hard against it to give himself some sense of the immovable, call to mind his sensations at the time. Did he not feel, at his poor effort, how feebler than a very child he was? — so feeble that strength and weakness could not express the difference between him and that he strained against? And was he not conscious of a wonderful diminishing of his importance at the time? And so in the higher relation, — that between us and our fellow-man, — we have felt, not angered alone, but mortified, too, at an unreturned regard. Did not our anger spring from our mortification?

To be conscious, then, that we stand so related to any thing, as to be without influence or notice, lowers pride, and leads to a moderate estimate of self. In the present, however, who is so insignificant as to be self-persuaded that he is altogether without influence, or that there is no way in which some man may not be the better or the worse, the merrier or the sadder, for him? And who has never been in a mood to say to the future, "This shall be so and so?" But who shall say to the past, "I will it thus?" Try it. Are we not dumb? Call to it. Sounds any voice from the present, through its deep recesses? Do its barred gates ring to our blows? Let us be still, then, and be humble; and be content to reverence the glorious and the good, in which we cannot share.

Cannot share! O, be humble, and we shall share. Revere, and we shall enter in. Humility is the golden branch which shall open to us, as at a touch, its heavy doors; and we shall go in, and talk with the spirits of old as with familiar friends, and come back into the present more thoughtful men, and look forward, wiser discerners, into future time.

We shall stand in a true relation to the present and the future, by standing in a right relation to the past. For he who has been back into the past comes down again into the present, and is prepared to travel on into the future, laden with the experiences of ages gone, and made wise by the observation of principles in their beginnings, their workings, and their remote results. He is able to bring into contact early causes and their distant effects, and, tracing the former through their intricate windings down to the latter, to learn how it was that purposes so often produced their contraries, — hope despair, and despair hope. He has learned this truth for the consolation and strengthening of his soul, that, sooner or later, evil recoils upon itself, and that, if indirectness and wrong be not visited upon the father, it will be upon the children; and through his wide view, he is enabled to see how

> "from good still good proceeds,
> Direct or by occasion";—

a truth, stale, indeed, to the apprehension, but realized and let into the life of only a few hearts. He has found out just how short-lived and little worth are expedients and contrivings, and that, in the main, even temporary and particular ends are best reached through permanent and general principles: he has, in fine, been let into the true meaning of that "great word," as it has been well termed,— "Simplicity."

Having seen, also, that man is a creature of excess, blindly indifferent where worthy occasions open upon him, and straining with exhausting effort against that which, if let alone, would go harmlessly by of itself, a spirit of waiting composure is begotten in him, and over his actions is spread the great calm of thought.

An hour's reflection is worth a life's experience. To have studied and meditated upon the past is better for a man than if he had been born of Adam and had only lived along his centuries of years down to this day. For then he would have been always in the present, agitated by its excitements, ever changing with its shiftings, and so crowded before and behind, as neither to look back on what he had left, nor forward into that towards which he was going. What a motley, inexperienced, short-sighted, short-lived creature would be your present man of six thousand years!

Contemplation has also taught him the spiritual uses of material things, and how, from the outward acts of mere outward men, to draw vigour for inward action, and nourishment for the inward life. His mind is become an universal solvent, letting out the residuum of things, and taking up their essences into his own clear spirit. And see, again, how he has put the present all away from around him; and there he stands alone. No, not alone; for by him stands the great spirit of the past, as stood the angel of God by Adam. And he is lifting up before him, in vision, time to come. O that we would but stop and hear this seer tell unto us what he doth see!

There are many other aspects in which the past might be put. If, however, the influences of which I have spoken be admitted as true, they are enough. If they are disputed, nothing which I could add would be likely to gain for me an assent.

It may be that I have not made myself entirely understood by some, though what I have said seems to lie clearly enough before my own mind. For I deny the frequent assertion, that whatever one sees distinctly, he may, of course, make distinct to another. There are apt handlers of particulars, who observe all their minute differences, their numbers, their forms, and store these up in the memory, who never once think of considering them in their comprehensive whole. While generalizing minds, which catch just enough of particulars to answer their main purpose, and then forget them, may have powers so unlike, though equal, and associations of thoughts and moods of mind so differing, and may look at things from such opposite points, that one may not see at all, or see but dimly, what lies before the other in the light of day. The human mind can hardly conceive an unassociated truth. To communicate to another, therefore, a perception of a truth in its fulness and clearness, there must be sympathizing movements between two minds, which, at a touch from the one, shall put in motion in the other sets of associations, which shall answer, like for like, in both minds; for there are not only different orders of minds, but each mind, also, hath its several sphere.

Let us now turn to the influences of a too exclusive attention to the present upon the mind.

One influence is, to impart a materializing character to man. Present time constitutes, in a peculiar degree, a state of sense. He who is interested singly in the present lives mainly in a material world. He perceives only things, and he cares only for things. Even man is little more to him than a complex frame of head and trunk, legs and arms, endowed with animal life, and sets of thoughts and affections, to fit him to keep in motion, as a part of that great piece of machinery, the social state, and when he wears out, that is, dies, to be laid by in that vast lumber-room, where all old machinery is stowed away, called the grave. This is an extreme view of the matter, I acknowledge. But in proportion to an undue concern in the present will be the tendency to this state. There is so constant a pressing upon the senses by the surrounding present, that the remote, which requires effort from within to be an object of the mind, becomes quite ineffectual; the intuitive dies of mere neglect, and the outward and visible are all that are real to the mind, because they are all about which it is occupied, or disposed to be intent.

This materializing operation has a narrowing and deadening influence over the soul. Living in the present alone, the imagination is bounded by the visible and actual, its combinations are lessened in number, and its creative power held in check, and it can no longer go out into the invisible, no longer expand and exalt itself by the loftier and purer excellences of the ideal, or call into being creations around which the affections may gather, and be made indeed alive with conceptions and emotions, speaking of a higher original, and prophesying a return up thither, through infinite love. Thus it is that the soul is kept unconscious of its finer powers, and loses even its longing after something better and nobler than any thing that *is.* Instead of being limited by the ideally possible alone, it is tethered down to the actual, the ordinary, and the poor, and learns to be satisfied with the secondary, instead of having prime objects before it, and its prime faculties made strong in the earnest reach after them. The present! — the soul has no empyrean there!

As a necessary consequence from this, true sentiment goes out of fashion, and the romantic is held up to ridicule; for these cannot live long, if the air of the ideal world breathe not on them, and sweeten the atmosphere of our daily life.

And what, asks the self-complacency of worldly wisdom, what do we lose, in losing these, so long as we retain the real and the useful? The real and the useful! Let me tell him who asks this, that these longings after something not attained to here take hold upon higher realities and uses than ever moved his soul, and speak a brighter truth than ever shone in upon his mind; and that to be without them is to be ignorant of the past, lost to the better uses of the present, and blind to times to come.

However these qualities may have been perverted, along with all else that belongs to man, even now they make the "unbought grace of life." And if they never can be found in their perfectness here, the soul that feels its want, and goes out in painful search after them, is wandering up and down for that which flowered beautifully once, and though it drooped when the curse fell upon the earth and upon man, yet did not wholly die. He who has these longings abiding in him seems as if he had not lost "all his original brightness," as if gleams of it still played about him, and he would fain get back again into the day. He may not take the right path to it, and may go on craving and unsatisfied; but even then he shows the deeper workings of his nature. And I would rather struggle in vain, than live on effortless; I would rather pine my loss, than not know what I had lost.

Connected with the foregoing is a tendency of the present to weaken our powers of generalizing. For it holds true, that in the proportion we contract the circle round the objects of the mind's observation, we diminish the mind's power of generalizing, even upon what falls within that circle. By not habituating the mind to go at large, and run up towards the origin of things, and thence down through time, following out causes and effects, it loses its power of far-reaching; the effort soon becomes painful to it, and it relaxes, and falls back into the present and obvious; the atmosphere of abstraction is too rare for it.

And again, the present has a paralyzing effect upon the imagination and a faculty necessary to pure reasoning is becoming unfit for its use. We all know that higher reasoning can no more exist without the forerunning of the imagination, than poetry can live without it. Thus reason is deprived of its head serving-man, and with whom shall it work?

What some are pleased to call reason may go forward and backward, guessing at this and fancying that, and blundering on from one errour to another;

not to lose its self-confidence, perhaps, — for there are those who from mistakes gather only assurance, — but arguing, it may be, that the more mistakes they have made, the fewer there are left for them to make; not considering that use in any thing renders one the apter at it, that errour is endless, and that he has a long way to travel who thinks to come out clear of it by this road. We here see how the faculty for generalizing is weakened by the influence of the present, and in what way the mind loses its clear and wide vision, and how its action, in its higher processes, comes to a stand.

Even take a philosopher, in the large sense of that word, — one who has learned this great truth, "that the end of philosophy is the intuition of unity," — and stand him up in the present; then draw the small circle of that present around him, and bid him philosophize upon that, and that only, which falls within the circle. He looks and sees a multitude of things, but where the principle of unity? A crowd of things are around him, but where their origin? A huddling of all manner of things together, but where their relation to each other? A close pressure, but where the connection? Can he call up within this circle any first principle, to which to trace unity and relation? No! for the root of the present runs off into the past, and it is here cut off by his circle. As there is no uncaused present, and as "effect comes by cause," as Polonius says, so does effect exist in agreement with the character of its cause, and the purposes and foreseen relations wrapped up in it from the beginning; and all that now exists is but the branching out of it; and all that shall be will be but the further unfolding of this seminal principle, and series of effects be nothing more than the results of one continuous causation, — the first moving power, moving still through all the forms, varieties, apparent differences, influences, and relations.

We must not think, then, to understand the true nature of any thing, scrutinize it as we may, so long as we examine into it as something belonging only to the present. This would be cutting it off from its original, from that whence came its character and life; leaving it no longer a portion of the great whole, but changing it into a detached, lifeless mass, unrelated to the past, and, in its more significant sense, unrelated to the present also. For, in the higher meaning of the term, things can hardly be said to be related to each other, when looked at only in the present, and standing, as it were, upon a plain, the only communication between them being across in horizontal lines. Relationship must be followed up to its source, and thence back, in order to find whence the life-blood flows, and where, and through what it runs. In common parlance, we talk of brothers and sisters as related. But how? Immediately, one to the other? No, but mediately, through the parent stock. So we speak of the family of mankind, and of men, as brethren. But we do not think of them as a multitude of individuals, starting up by simultaneous and independent impulses into life, but as the children of one great father, Adam.

Here let me just notice the mystery of this principle of unity, as it appears in the sacred history of the creation of man. God did not make simultaneously a pair, — man and woman; but first the man, and thence the woman: Behold the One! And if I might, without irreverence, call the created, in a lower sense, by that name which, in its first sacred sense, belongs to the Increate alone, I would say, Behold Our First

Cause. There he stood, on this broad world, the only man. But what a man! The world is populous enough now; but since he fell and "brought death into the world, and all our woe," not a human being that has lived, but had his life in that man. And not a desire, not a thought, not an act of all who now are, or of all who have followed him through the gates of death, but has been the unfolding of what was in Adam, and had its principle in him. The history of the thousands of years which are passed, and of the countless thousands of men who have died, is but the history of the First Man. Wonderful is the mystery of unity! One, yet in and through all; many, yet one. But what shall we say of myriads of unrelated existences? Are these a mystery? No; for it is the oneness of the all-pervading, unseen power in the mysterious, which awes us so, — felt, though not understood. But unrelated existences! It is all folly and confusion!

If the character and influence of the present be such, that even the philosophizing mind, when confined to it, can no longer work by first principles, what shall we say of one so shut up, who has passed all his days in and for the present, and made it his be-all and his end-all? The effect in kind has been partially stated, the degree of it no man can reckon.

The man who habituates himself to the particular and the limited loses that master-power whose range is the limitless, which always sees in particulars the universal, and in the universal the one. As the more obvious view of present things is in their parts, and not in their unity, such a one's mind becomes fragmentary, — it has no whole; and wanting this, lacks that extended and well-ordered apprehension of things, which gives to each, truly and at once, its place, its due power, its relations, and its present and future uses and ends. Such a man fancies that which is apparently large to be greater than it really is, and what is apparently small he lessens; and thus is disappointed where he trusted, and is overwhelmed by that which he had despised. Knowing nothing of the workings of first principles, he of course foresees not their sure though slow results; soon becomes perplexed and bustling, and the more bustling for being perplexed; and having no single and generally operative truth to look to, runs into expedients, and is borne along in the series of ever-shifting events. In the rush of present things, stability of character is swept away, and the man gets overheated by the friction of close, grinding circumstances, and giddy in their whirl. Shut out from the calm past by the thronging of the exciting and urgent present, and standing too near to objects to take in their outline, they grow gigantic to him; then the spirit of exaggeration possesses him, disproportion follows, and the end is monstrous deformity. And this is the natural, nay, necessary termination; for, as old Bates well remarks, "To proportion, excesses as well as defects are opposite." And hence it is that we are all of us so besotted with the spirit of the age; and that men and women are perpetually set astare with some nine days' wonder. It all comes of the short-sighted, unstable, exaggerating present.

Are there not moral evils involved in these influences? Is not he who sees truth partially and limitedly less likely to reverence it singly, than if he knew something of its silent, but deep and wide-working power? Will he not be more likely to resort to contrivance to gain an immediate end, than to wait quietly upon some great principle, of which he can but poorly discern the tendency, the certainty, and the strength?

Besides, there is a certain impatience attendant upon the present; and as errour is rapid, and truth slow, and nature, though working wider than art, moving so evenly and all together as apparently to move scarcely at all, the creature of the mere present will consort with his like, and be in sympathy with errour and art, rather than with nature and truth.

Association with the present, making it difficult for the mind to extricate itself from the near and the visible, and withdraw apart for meditation and abstraction, the consequence is, a want of true self-acquaintance, and from this, again, an over-estimate of the good in us, and an under-estimate of the ill. More familiar with the outward world than with that more important world within, our rule of judging is not a simple, permanent principle of perfectness and truth,—which is not hard of apprehension to the inward-turned mind,—but it is the outward, the changeable, the mixed,—that which chances to go current for the time, under the blessedly vague and comprehensive appellative, the respectable. The way being thus made easy, each man comes to judge himself, with the subtle purpose of justifying himself; and to this end will, when hard pressed, even turn to justifying his neighbour, and so shelter himself under his charity for another. With finite to regulate the finite, with fallible the fallible, he soon becomes content with the secondary, seizes upon some convenient particular, and losing the apprehension of the one great motive power to all good, fails of that fulness of moral tone, that nobleness of inward impulse, which are his who sees truth in its vastness, and feels it in its steady, and harmonious, and eternal goings-on.

Meditative abstraction is not only necessary to a right self-judging, but to that well-disciplined composure which shall preserve self-thoughtfulness amidst the changing activities and exciting influences which every man must go out to meet, when he goes into the world. It is true, that it will not always help him to meet foreseen particulars; but what is better, it will help him to go with a prepared spirit to bear them. But what preparation has he to whom abstraction is pain, and not a delight, because not habitual? And how predisposed does he go to take the shape and hue of the surrounding present, who thinks too little of the past to draw from it experience, and whose extravagant notions of the present impart new power, to react upon himself, to that which has already too much, from being visible and near?

A particular bent of mind not only strengthens, upon the principle that inward power increases with action, and also from a sympathetic association with that of the outward, which resembles it in tendency and kind, but as it strengthens, so grows its distaste to that which is the contrary of itself. And the man in whom the present once becomes predominant retires more and more reluctantly and infrequently into the past and the reflective, into the unseen but conscious state of being within. Principles lose possession of his mind, and things take their places; and not seeing far or justly, he would rather see much and many than think much and deeply. The action of his mind is outward, outward; and observation justles aside reflection. He may attain to a certain sagacity which will give him a ready mastery over present things, as to present uses; but he will not be aware the while, that there is a secretly pervading power in what he is managing, which is making him servant to that over which he thinks he holds rule.

Knowledge, or the immediate and obvious uses of knowledge, rather than its final purposes, being his aim, acquiring takes the character of an indiscriminating passion, or, more properly, appetite; and so the mind be well filled, he thinks not to ask himself, Why all this jumble of things here? The near or remote, the like or the unlike, is all the same to him; and if not adapted to his nature, he has only to adapt his nature to them. And this his process of working does for him speedily. For the objects of his mind lying in accidental juxtaposition, and not being united by any permanent relationship in the nature of things, the weak principle of unity within is soon broken up, and he sees only parts, and thinks only of parts. There is truth, in more senses than one, in the term applied to a clever man, — a man of parts; for we scarcely think of him as an individual whole, — a unit. Indeed, the term, a man of knowledge, does not describe him; for the singular, knowledge, gives the impression of oneness. So, seeing that we now have the plural, literatures, why not have another plural, and call him a man of knowledges?

This certainly is the tendency of the present upon the character, so that he who lives mainly in it has but little acquaintance with the intuitive, the principle of spiritual life not having been awakened in him. In that life are included inward growth and action; but his action is outward, and his increase not that of a single internal expansive principle, growth, but that of accretion; and he is little better than an aggregation of unchanged, foreign bodies, adhering to him and to one another, not so much by any elective affinities as by some external propulsion.

I know not how better to illustrate the two orders of minds, than by a piece of variegated marble, in which the delicately tinted branchings seem but the veins and arteries of one original body, the issues of its own life; and next, by an uncouth, dead mass of pudding-stone. Here it is! bulky enough, to be sure. But where its unity? A mere heap of stones, tumbled together by some rolling flood of fire or water, and left to cool down, or thicken, into this shapeless, loose mass, from which one may take out piece after piece, without marring their beds. But can you unvein the marble?

The present, by diminishing the inward life and action, and, of course, the sources of individual internal enjoyment, soon makes seclusion inert and wearisome, and drives men out to congregate for the sake of sensation and action. This brings about, not a social, but a gregarious state. For the life of the social principle springs not from inward vacuity, but from inward love, — a living and a life-imparting quality of the soul. So that the more gregarious a man becomes, the less a social creature is he. He mixes not with men to make friendly interchange of rich things, or to bestow of the affluence of his own soul, but because of the poverty at home. He leaves his door a beggar of his daily bread, and hears said unto him, "Be ye warmed, and be ye clothed," and returns colder, emptier, and nakeder, than he went: He goes, not to give, but to get; and the root and the offspring of this is selfishness.

Going forth without a strong individuality of character, the growth of retired meditation and few and close attachments and habits that have worked into the constitution of the mind, men assimilate carelessly and unconsciously with the circumstances, views, and notions which happen to be in fashion at the time. A conventional uniformity gathers over the multitude; manners take the place of character; and how to bear one's self, and how to express one's self, and not how to think and feel, become the object of life: — conventional gratulations, conventional regrets, conventional indifference, conventional ecstasies, conventional smiles, and — conventional tears? O, no; that would put one out of all conventions!

It is thus easy to see, that, to be a social creature, in the true sense of the term, a man must be the creature of seclusion for the larger portion of his time; so that what makes him to differ from other men, and constitutes his individuality, may be allowed to expand and strengthen from its own living energy. Else, that variety which breathes spirit into intercourse must be tamed down into an insipid sameness, and that inanity of which men complain, and wonder why it is, must be the necessity and not the accident of such a state. To think of passing day after day in the world, and being doomed, in every face we look upon, to behold our own likeness; in every act of recognition to see repeated our own smile and our own bow; and from every mouth to hear echoed back our own remarks and our own turn of words! Would not the hermit's cell be more patiently borne with than this?

True it is, that nature is stronger than art, and being essentially various, art will never be able to bring society quite up to its notion of perfect similitude; yet the artificial is a process of assimilation, and as the social state departs from nature, it will alway be approximating a sameness. Besides, where the resemblance in character does not exist in reality, it does in appearance, and real difference is hid under a seeming likeness; so that to the tendency toward the former evil is added that of deception, and means and ends are both alike cursed.

True society — that which awakens life within us, and warms the heart, and stirs the intellect; that which is perpetually setting before us something to give healthful diversity to our thoughts, and something fresh to carry home with us for reflection — is made up of distinctly marked individuals, with just enough in common to understand one another, but with all else each man's own, and such as he, and he alone, would have thought of at all, or, at most, would have thought of or said in that particular way.

To draw good or pleasure from a man, he must have that in him which, in form or matter, we had not been conscious of in ourselves, yet not so far the contrary of what is in us but that it shall touch some chord within us, and call out sounds which had slept silent there, from the time the hand of God first strung the instrument. To adopt Coleridge's distinction between the words, while *contraries* repel, *opposites* combine. To be a social creature, then, man must be a solitary creature too; to fit men for each other, each must be much alone.

These evil effects seem to grow, not only naturally, but unavoidably, from absorption in the present, and a consequent hankering for herding together in multitudes. And what a blight it is upon the heart! And with all its excitements, how joyless life is made by it! For, pray, who is the better off? He who has his thousand friends, or he who chances not to have one? Why, in very deed, the latter; for he has no part to play; and it may be that he has a heart yet for a friend. But the other! — his heart! Why, he has quite forgot what has become of that; some one, or all, of his thousand friends must have it, — somewhere.

Truly, one would think that the end of coming together was to give no offence, and to produce an impression, as it is termed. And what are called the courtesies of life require such looks of interest and concern, such protestations of sympathetic sorrow or delight, that should a tithe of them ever reach so far as the heart, it could not but burst with its emotions. The observing man, who mixes only occasionally with the world, sees at a glance this farce, or rather this tragi-comedy, of life, in which they who have parts have nigh forgot they were acting, so long have they played in it to and upon one another. But the effect is a sad one upon just penetration, free-heartedness, and a discriminating moral sense; and the looker-on goes home, with a melancholy shake of the head, repeating to himself the words of good Bishop Hall, "I would fear that speaking well, without feeling, were the next way to procure habituall hypocrisie!"

If we follow out the influences of the present, it is plain enough how they should turn us to physical pursuits, and thus strengthen the power of the outward over us, rather than lead us to those operations which relate more inwardly to men; for there is something tangible about the former, and easy of apprehension to him who lives in the sensible, more than in the abstract. And if it be true that the present produces a love and a feeling of power, and out of these, self-satisfaction, physical pursuits, more than the abstract and unseen, gratify and strengthen these feelings, for they bring the result of our efforts distinctly before our eyes. Chemical and mechanical principles, carried into act by us, give out new and visible forms and combinations; and lo! there are standing before us the works of our own hands; and the feeling arises, that the moving power is in ourselves, and that we work upon the mere servants of our will, the unresisting subjects of our control.

From the way in which the man of the mere present views the outward, his employments furnish no correctives to his pride; for he is not the person to search out their relation to the infinite, nor will they themselves remind him of it. The study of the moral and intellectual touches on every side on the infinite and unsearchable; and according to the expanse of the mind so occupied will be its consciousness of an infinite unseen. For the larger the circle of the mind's thoughts, the larger the apprehension of things beyond it. And although this state hath its dangers, — for pride, through the absence of tangible limits, may find room for self-inflation, and has done so, — yet, from the very enlargement which a sense of the infinite imparts to the spirit, and from the awe which the mystery of the unseen has a tendency to throw around it, there may, in time, spring up the conviction of an independent power, greater than the soul itself, which shall lead it back to humiliation and trust. Only awaken a vivid consciousness of a soul within us, and after the mind has wearied itself with upward, downward, sidelong, hard-strained flights, must it not at last cry out on God, and return to its rest in him? But action directed towards the physical, while it tends to make us feel our power over it, contracts the mind, through its engagedness with the near and limited, and, by its intercourse with the seen and tangible, renders it forgetful and inapprehensive of the unseen and intangible, and thus contains no corrective of the evil by awakening within a sense of the soul's wants. So far as the inner world is concerned, man has quitted that and gone and taken up his abode in a world without:—in an age of mechanical inventions and chemical discoveries, Steam-Power has more worshippers than Spiritual Power.

Absorption in the present, leading to an over-estimate of it, naturally runs again into an over-estimate of self. The sense of nearness is one cause of this; for nearness produces a feeling of rights in common, not only in ordinary interests and privileges, but even in distinguishing qualities and endowments sometimes. Being next-door neighbour to a great man imparts self-importance; and to laud or to defend him, why, that is standing to him in the relation of an acquaintance, protector, and patron, all in one.

In this same present, which influences all, each one, as was a while ago said, however seemingly insignificant, has some influence in return, and a part that, in one way or another, acts upon what is going on. And therefore it is, that from palace to hovel, from the father to the prating young-one, we hear so much, even to very weariness, of the spirit of the age, the light of the age, the refinement of the age, and, last of all, of that march, to keep step to which every man, woman, and child is practising such contortions,—the march of the mind.

Yes, in the present, man feels his self-consequence; for he has an influence in it; and it is in his nature, that this self-consequence should grow in him, in the proportion that he magnifies that upon which he acts. The self-gratulatory manner in which men talk of this age in which we live verifies this, and shows, also, that we are under some strange illusion as to the advances of our times. For great truths, while they ennoble man, make him thoughtful, sober-minded, not thinking of himself more highly than he ought to think. And well they may; for complete truths, whatsoever they concern, reach into eternity and open immortality upon the soul. And shall not the spirit stand in awe, with eternity within it, and eternity round about it?

The thoughtful looker-on believes that all will finally work together for good. But he knows, too, that this spirit of vanity and self-satisfaction must first meet with some fearful rebuke; and that the spirit of pride, which engenders high things, is unwittingly engendering that which shall by and by dash them. If there be any one thing in particular which characterizes the age, it is overweening self-complacency. And this comes of living so altogether in and for the present; and it is this self-complacency, again, which keeps us so much in the present. For we may rely upon it, that it is this all-present which begets this self-complacency, and is again begotten of it.

How fatal is all this to the spirit of reverence! And what is created and finite man without reverence? But how shall he who is thronged by the changing, suffocating, every-day present enlarge himself to this spirit, that speaks of immortality? And how shall he learn to know its great nature, intent as he is on that where life feeds on decay, and death on life,—being and ceasing to be? A man of the mere present! he may be affable, obliging, generous; but the heart is not satisfied. We feel that there is a void in him; he wants the spirit of reverence. And the whole age wants it; all the earthly types of it are breaking down, and these are times of overthrow; and the spirit of overthrow is a hard spirit, and an arrogant.

There has been oppression enough on the earth, we

know. But what is so desolating to the spirit of a man, what makes him feel so an outcast from his kind, as the tyranny of the many? There is an impatience of gradations of ranks now shaking the earth, which springs quite as much from the decay of reverence in the minds of men, as from a spirit of resistance to wrong. Without setting up, in the commonly received sense, the old doctrine of the divine right of kings, may we not ask whether God has not purposed that there should be an analogy in the form of the political state, and an adaptability in it to the unfolding of the spiritual form of individual man in all its parts? and that one portion of it should develope the feelings connected with generous protection, and kind and condescending regard, and another portion teach contentedness, subordination, and respect? So far as God has deemed it well to unveil the higher world, there would seem to be orders there, and their unjarring movements, rank above rank, to make the harmony of heaven. The question is now trying, whether the nature of man can bear a form of state which sets this principle at naught, and whether it is not a form that must destroy reverence in the soul, and generate pride. This seems to be the working of the popular principle now; and it may turn out that a government founded wholly upon this latter principle is of too abstract a nature to be an *object* for the mind's easy and direct apprehension, or for the simple affections of the heart. It may appear that it wants embodying, and needs a visible head, something for the spirit of loyalty to look up to, and that for the want of this, in its place, comes in self. There is reason to fear that the sensitiveness of a man, upon all that touches the republic, is too often nothing else than self, and that it is he, in feeling, who stands for the body politic. And looks it not a little like it, when a lording spirit is already taking possession of him, and he will not consent to be ruled even by his own elected governours, — not he! — till they come, cap in hand, and own themselves his servants? And thus dies reverence!

This is a subject, however, which involves principles too important to be treated upon hastily, especially if considered in its bearing upon the religious character of man. We may go into it at some future time.

But even from the winning quiet of old age the present takes away reverence, while bearing, too, in his countenance, as the old man does, the aspect of the past. Where is that feeling for age, which Young so beautifully calls "tender reverence"? Almost died out. Yet what a delightful sensation it is to the soul; and how like is it to the kind respect a son bears a mother! Its blessed influences will abide in that heart into which it has once entered, and rest like soft lights on our spirits, even when we, too, are old: — Young man, if you would have a heart-blessing that shall go with you all your days, reverence age!

The spirit of reverence, and that which men revered in days past, were not all superstition. There was more in them than is dreamed of in your philosophy, more that was in accord with the wants, and the fulness, too, of the human heart. We must beware how we take for granted our superiour wisdom and our superiour light. A more various knowledge of the external, it may be, we possess. But that knowledge is not wisdom; wisdom is a more inward principle, and has somewhat to do with the heart of man. Let us take care, therefore, while we are learning a little of all manner of outward things, to "get wisdom," — that which shall turn them all to the soul's food. And for this end, bear in mind the words of old Baxter:— "Keep open the passage betwixt the head and the heart, that every truth may go to the quick."

Some one may here ask, whether there is no evil in looking exclusively to the past. The evil of such an excess was granted in the outset; and had this been an age of eremites and friars, I would have dwelt upon it.

And is there nothing good or great in the uses of the present? asks another. Much. And when it ceases to be over-magnified in our eyes, there will be still more.

But we are not living for the present alone, objects a third; we are not only auguring great things, but we are preparing great things, for time to come. Remember, that when pride augurs, that, of itself, is bad omen; and that in the spirit in which we prophesy shall things be fulfilled. Consider, too, that there is no setting bounds to moral influences, in time; no following them to their end, in eternity. As was awhile ago said, as "the present, however modified by long and complicated workings, would not be as it is, if the past had been different from what it was," so that which now is will make the future what it shall be.

One would think here was responsibility enough upon us, to make us put away too much confidence and overweening of self. Let us do so, and go about our work (for we must work) with firm yet humble minds, with hopeful yet dependent spirits. Let us be ready to take something from experience. Let us be willing to turn awhile to look upon the Great Past, to have our souls filled with its glorious, solemn vision. How still it stands on its foundations, laid in eternity! But see, there are faces there! And some of them are turned on us with a look surpassing earthly love; — the heavens have touched them! They are not all strange to us. There is one! — and there! We thought it dead; but it lives! And it shall live! And we, too, shall live, — we and the past; not one can perish. There is something awful in this truth; yet it may be a glorious truth to us, if we will but receive it. Let me leave it with you, reader, in the words of our fine poet, "To the Past": —

"Thine for a space are they, —
Yet shalt thou yield thy treasures up at last.
Thy gates shall yet give way,
Thy bolts shall fall, inexorable Past!

"All that of good and fair
Has gone into thy womb from earliest time
Shall then come forth, to wear
The glory and the beauty of its prime.

"They have not perished, — no!
Kind words, remembered voices once so sweet,
Smiles, radiant long ago,
And features, the great soul's apparent seat ——

"All shall come back —— "

LAW AS SUITED TO MAN.

> For government, though high, and low, and lower,
> Put into parts, doth keep in one concent;
> Congruing, in a full and natural close,
> Like music.
>
> SHAKSPEARE.

IT seems to be a principle of our nature, that one whom we love or dislike for any particular quality should be loved or disliked by us, not only in regard to that quality, but in respect also to whatever is essentially, or even accidentally, related to him. That love for a fellow-creature, which probably sprang from a single attribute in him, spreads itself over the whole character; his cast of thought, of expression, nay, his person, features, gestures, and even the commonest things which belong to him and are for his daily use, become objects of our attachment. Reverse this, and put dislike; and because of some hastily spoken word, perhaps, we come to dislike a man and all that is his; his face displeases us, however well in itself; his grace is awkwardness or affectation to us: we hate him; we hate his very dog. This springs from the quickly associating processes of the mind. Nature, it is said, abhors a vacuum; and it may equally well be said, the mind abhors a unit; and, for the very reason that it does so, it delights in unity. Check the activity of the associating principle, and cut off its result, unity, and the mere unit left becomes a dead thing; its generating powers cease; and the mind that fastens itself upon it gradually loses the power of thought.

I have alluded to this principle of unity and association, because I would say something of the different effects, upon the individual and the social man, of two forms of Constitution or Law,—of the form which bears more or less of resemblance to that of the country from which we sprang; and of that form which more nearly or remotely approaches our own Constitution. A further reason for alluding in the outset to this principle is, its being recognized throughout what is here said. If the associating principle spoken of acts upon us in relation to persons, so does it in relation to things, to modes and ceremonies, to forms of private connections, and to those enlarged and public forms of communities called Governments.

A new people, for instance, without simply considering what form of government would be best for them, would be likely to adopt that of the country from which they sprang, or the directly contrary to it, as love or hatred of the mother country might sway them. Had the Constitution of England, at the time of our Revolution, been a democracy,—had her mandates come from the multitudinous assemblies of the people, and not from the single-voiced throne,—had her troops been the people's, and not the king's,—might not the feeling of resentment at a rabble's insult and wrong have gathered us round a newly founded throne? Might not the hard, coarse oppression of the throng have refined us into a feeling of revolt against such an exhibition of power? And might we not have seen a glory around a single head, and decorum and grace and fair proportions in rank above rank? Might not a popular form have been offensive to our taste, and the thought of a ruling crowd have stirred in us pride and fastidious scorn?

One is aware that the first answer to a question such as this is likely to be only an incredulous, perhaps a contemptuous smile. But after we have thought upon it a little, we may begin to hesitate, and next, to acknowledge that there may be some meaning in what is asked. And, doubtless, the more we look into our natures, the more strength we shall allow to the principle upon which this question rests.

If this be so, it becomes important to us, that, in graduating the relative merits of different forms of government, we recollect what was the form of that government in our war with which we grew into an independent nation; and that we make full allowance, in forming our judgement, for our feelings of hostility at the time, and for that associating principle, which leads us to involve in one common feeling of dislike, or of love, all that in any way bears a relation to the objects of that feeling, whichsoever it be. If, then, the government to which we were opposed was of the monarchical form, we must be upon our guard as to our prejudices against that form, and cautious as to our partialities for its opposite, heightened as these will naturally be by those very prejudices. We must consider, too, the influence which mere names may have upon our minds, and how, in time, they move us to anger, or to love, while we know very little of the deeper meaning of the things to which the names belong. We must recollect, also, that our war of the Revolution was not a conflict about a difference of constitution, but a war growing out of what we held to be a violation of a certain Constitution.

In treating upon Government, or Law, (Law is here used in its most comprehensive sense,) the peculiar character of our times demands of us, as wise and good men, to lay aside such prepossessions, and to look the subject through and through, and to put the question to ourselves as thoughtful men, whether our dangers are transient and accidental, or whether they lie deep in the system itself, checked only by present and unusual circumstances, — our widely-extended, unsettled, yet fast-settling territory, and the many and various outlets for our activity, energy, and strong self-will; or whether, when this peculiar condition of things shall have passed by, from the very nature of man, our present form of government must not follow it, and another and opposite form take its place. As some things which will be here said may cross many associations and preconceived notions, I must ask to be listened to patiently, not for my own sake only, but for the reader's too, and above all for truth's sake, while a short time is given to the question, — What Form of Government, or Law, is best suited to the individual and social nature of man?

"Of Law," says Hooker, "there can be no less acknowledged than that her seat is the bosom of God, her voice the harmony of the world; all things in heaven and earth do her homage; the very least as feeling her care, and the greatest as not exempt from her power; both angels and men and creatures, of what condition soever, though each in different sort and manner, yet all with uniform consent admiring her as the mother of their peace and joy." And Coleridge speaks of "the awful power of Law, acting on natures preconfigured to its influences."

The answer to the question will depend, in no small measure, upon the way in which we are in the habit of considering Man, — whether we look at him as a higher sort of animal, or whether we are wont to think of him in his inner and more spiritual nature, — whether we are accustomed to regard him in his mere earthly, outward wants, comforts, connections, his clothing, his food, his making and spending of money, in his providing for the bodily wants and worldly condition of his family, — or whether, allowing their due place to these, we think of him as a being, who, having begun to live, must live for ever, — as a soul to which this body, with its many organs, is but an instrument for the use of a day, — as a being with capacities which shall for ever go on enlarging, and for which infinitude alone can make room, — as one with longings which earth cannot satisfy, and yet one who, in the proportion that these longings possess him, finds more and more, even here, for the soul's joy, — a being compounded of ethereal faith and hope, of imagination and sentiment, of sentiment which refines joy, and touches sorrow with a softening hue, — a being who looks upon the earth as indeed dust, and its toils as only the wasting of strength, further than as they minister to these inward sensations and powers, — and above all, and with all these expansive attributes, as a created, and therein a limited and ever dependent being, and truly realizing his nature only through an ever-abiding sense of limitation and dependence.

If we allow Law to have any influence over the character of man, it is evident that as we are habituated to look at him in the one or the other of these lights, so will be our views of Law. For we must first understand what it is which is to be operated upon, before we can determine upon the kind of instrument to be used.

Will any one say, that, granting this interiour view of man to be the true view, it is a matter with which Law has little or nothing to do? that Law takes cognizance of the outward, civil conduct only, not concerning itself with motives and feelings within? True, in its narrower sense, it must not call the thoughts into judgement; but there is a necessity upon it, grounded in the nature of things, to give a hue to those thoughts. For there is nothing without us which fails of reaching that which lies within. Through the countless varieties and differences of the material and moral world all stand related to all, — through the universe of God there is not one lonely being or thing. What falser view of Law, then, can there be, than that which looks upon it as a larger machine, regulating merely out-of-door intercourse, and, by its complicated motions and parts, only supplying conveniences and furnishing levers and springs to help on the more general purposes of man? Yet the greater part of men habitually speak of Law as a well or ill working machine. Nor do they think of it as acting upon the nicer moral and intellectual characteristics of man.

It is wonderful to observe the effect of this sensuous, external way of looking at things, and to see how, in the degree that we set the external above the internal, we necessarily limit the external itself, and take from it half its power: by it death enters the material universe to us individually, while it touches society, too, in all its forms.

And why is it thus? Because the material and external has no independent life. Its life proceeds from and returns into the spiritual and the internal; and just in the proportion that the latter is held by us as the dearer and superiour power, in the same degree the former, as dependent upon it, increases with it. As imagination, sentiment, and love reign in us, so does the outward become more and more alive from imparted life, and so does it return, to act, by multiplied and delightful influences, upon each thought and emotion of the soul; and there is no attribute of the inward man with which it is not brought into sympathy.

Would it not be strange, then, if Law, made for moral and intellectual beings, should not have an effect upon their internal moral and intellectual condition? True; but, it is again objected, it is only on these beings in their civil characters.

And have men double sets of faculties and affections, — individual or private, and public or civil ones, — the state or action of the one set having no influence upon the other? Or perhaps we must go still further, and ask, whether man has two souls, two consciousnesses, — in short, whether he is a kind of double being. If he has not, then Law must influence the same faculties and affections as are influenced by religion, family, books, occupations, the beauty, the grandeur, the variety of earth, sea, and sky. And do any of these come and go, and leave no hue, no impress, upon the soul? And must not Law, then, give form and pressure to every part of man? Why, not the thin shadow, from the quick cloud, gliding over the grain, leaves it what it was!

How superficial, then, have too often been our general views of Law. And what a gross, unmalleable substance have we held that to be, which touches and presses upon every part of the ductile spirit of man. Of the few writers on this subject whom I have read, it seems to me that, with the exception of Burke, scarcely one can, in the higher sense, be termed a philosopher. He traced the reachings of law into man's finer nature, and had that nicer sensibility wherewith to feel the delicate, electric *aura* which this individual nature gives back, and diffuses through every fibre of the great, general frame.

If there be this principle of unity binding together the intellectual capacities, the moral sensibilities and perceptions, and those multifarious qualities which go to make up what we call character, — and if every the least outward circumstance or condition has an influence upon some one of these, and, through their sympathetic connection with each other, upon all, and so upon their unity, or that which constitutes an individual, — it follows, upon every principle of harmony in God's universe, that there should be no jarring nor discordant influences within or without, and that the nearer man draws to his first, unfallen state, the more will be developed the resemblances and relations of things to each other, and the more plainly will order be traced out through all varieties, and a tending of the upper and lower, the inward and outward world to one great end, and the more will this world be found to contain, as it were, within itself, heaven, — a moment of time to involve eternity, — the greater, to speak with seeming paradox, to be contained in the less.

If the influences of this world reach into eternity, in order to fit man truly for either world, they must fit him for both, and that not partially, if they could, but in his whole mind and heart. But if there needs must be this family relation and likeness, which shall be taken for the original, — the form of this world, or that of the other? and by which, so far as he has the shaping of circumstances, shall man mould his condition?

He who made man, body and spirit, framed the material world for a spiritual as well as a physical use. He formed man a microcosm; and would teach him to know himself, not only by the revealed Word and by the influences of his Spirit, but by his providences, by the modes in which He has formed the ánimate and inanimate worlds, and by the ways in which He carries these forward to fulfil his great ends. Nor can this be barren knowledge, for its purpose is to bring man into the likeness of the pattern, and thus into conformity and union with the general ordering of God, and with God himself.

How prone are we to cut these relations right athwart; to consider, for instance, our religious character one thing, and our political character another: — One set of ties to God, another to man. Religion teaches humility, obedience; not so Politics: "We are *all* sovereigns!" cries the Christian speaker, and the religious assembly clap their hands! Was it the "Rights of Man," or the pride of man, that gave voice to the thought and returned the applause? This principle of severance will never do. The nerves we thus cut must grow together again, or just action will cease, and the man die. We must not think of going to God to learn humility and obedience, only to go back to Law again to throw them off. There are no such contraries in God's plan; and the rule of this world must be after the pattern of the heavenly, (imperfect it will be, but yet) teaching, in the main, the same lessons, and acting upon the same attributes of man.

This great principle of obedience, and the spirit of humility with which to obey, need be taught us in every thing; and Law, while allowing us due freedom, should be so formed as to be our schoolmaster in this lesson. It cannot be consistent, that what becomes so slowly the habitual state of the mind towards its Creator should not be intended by Him to find help in the forms of Law on earth, — that, on the contrary, Law should be at war with this principle, and should nourish pride and self-will; thus keeping man under opposing influences, and hindering his progress in that way which is to make him a meet subject for the order and sovereignty of heaven. Were it natural to man to live under an abiding sense of humility, and of obedience to his Maker, were it the first impulse of our hearts in honour to prefer one another, we might not stand in so extreme need that Law should meet us everywhere, with the air of supreme authority pressing upon our senses and rising up before our minds. Or rather, it would find us so assimilated to the condition, and recognizing it as so genial to our true natures, and so in harmony with them, as to constitute our perfect freedom, — indeed, the only real freedom of which man is capable.

If we look at Law in this way, as intended to fall in with the general plan of God, as a part faying in with the other parts of a great system, as a something made necessary to the universal ordering of our condition and character, and having both a necessitated beginning and continuance in our very nature, and acting upon it everywhere, and not as a mere arbitrary institution set up by man himself, out of convenience and choice, to be taken down, remodelled, and put up again, at his good pleasure, — then will it have to us an origin like that from which we ourselves sprang, and a bearing as lasting as our own existence; then will it become sacred in our eyes, a somewhat set over us,— our rule, our head. Authority will be seen written over its portal; and we shall take our shoes from off our feet as we enter in through its everlasting doors. Those, also, who wait at its altars, will, as its ministers, be held in respect, and, as announcers of its decrees, be listened to: they will, so to speak, stand out before the people as Law in visible presence. For it is not the man, in his short-lived, individual character, and with all the individual's infirmities, that we defer to, but the person abstracted from these, and representative of permanent Law. And subtile as this distinction may sound to the understanding, it is simple to our sentiment, and acts at one time or another upon all.

With this character of Permanency and Majesty before our eyes, submission to Law, and to those who represent it, will not beget servility, but rather that "proud humility" of which Burke speaks; for submission is servility, or right respect, as that to which we yield it is mean or venerable. And if we venerate the permanent and the majestic, even through such imperfect symbols, something of the permanent and majestic will penetrate our own souls.

To produce this sense of authority, permanency, and majesty, to give us a feeling of something which, though meant for us, is above us, it must not be a mere abstract principle, having form to us only as we ourselves give it form by administering it ourselves, or, at our own will, setting up from time to time those who shall administer it for us; but it must have self-life; and, in some parts of it, must be seen those who shall seem to have come out from its invisible self: it must have, as it were, a creating power, producing offspring from itself, to take care that it be respected and obeyed, — men who shall be impersonations of Law, having their birth and power, not from us, but from Law, — men who, though dying individually, shall, as Orders, through an ordained succession, possess life as permanent as Law itself. These hereditary Orders, call them by what name we will, present something definite to the mind, and help us to realize our Idèa of Law; while that power which we call Law, unseen by us in itself, yet acting upon our spirits, throws around these orders of men a mysterious authority, which our natures must for ever witness to, talk of it as we may, and even hate it as we may. That the mind does recognize such an influence is shown in the involuntary respect felt for an individual, when standing in this relation to Law, and the diminishing of this respect, when considered apart from this relation and regarded only in his character of a fellow-man. Let any one be honest with himself, and he will acknowledge this difference. He may call it the remnant of an old superstition, which the mind has not yet quite shaken off. France called it so, and overturned her throne and drove her nobles from the land. But human nature soon felt the want of something, she knew not what. She tried to smooth down the surface of society to a level, but there were elements beneath, more restless than the centre fires, perpetually heaving it up into mountains and hills; and the earth tossed like the sea. Man, in his pride, had been trying after equality, that which should leave nothing higher than himself; he would fain form his own Law and appoint those who should administer it for him. Poor, finite, dependent creature! That which should have governed him was of his own making, and might at any moment be by him unmade; and, therefore, he could not reverence it. Conscious of his insignificance, yet with nothing visible around him greater than himself, nothing to look up to, and looking up to, from it to gather strength, no wonder that the unquieted craving of his soul made him throw himself headlong and set the oppressor's foot upon his neck. He thought to destroy the principle of obedience in his heart, and he became a slave, — he rose up against that eternal law which God had ordained to regulate his being, and which, doubtless, is now visibly carried out through the ranks of heaven, and will ever be a living Law, — a Law without which on earth, man, who is linked in with eternity, can never be well with himself, nor with his fellow-men.

Instead, therefore, of vainly striving against a principle inherent in our natures and in the order of things, instead of blinding our minds by a mere name, — calling it superstition, — it would be better to look calmly into ourselves a little, and to see whether, in these outward, distinctive forms and orders, there be not a kindly adaptation to our inward needs, — whether, were we in our true state, we should not feel that there was something in us congenial with them, something to elevate thought and warm and make quick the affections. Law! What is it but an infinite abstraction, till it bodies itself forth in orders of men? Then it is as if the infinite, after which the mind had vainly stretched itself, gathered itself in, presenting some point at which we might come in contact with it, something where we might begin, something to which we might return. — We have been looking over the day-sky; and all throughout its clear expanse the eye has found no resting-place. Presently, from out it, a feathery little cloud puts forth; it enlarges, unrolling itself, fold upon fold; and there it lies, steady as the land, a mighty pile of dazzling splendour! Now, the eye is fixed, the soul filled, and our thoughts go up to it, like incense, to mingle with its glory. Yet, a little before, this cloud had been an infinitely rare, invisible vapour; our eyes saw nothing, our souls felt nothing. So Law, pervading, as it does, the universe of God, comes not upon us in its complete power till it takes hold upon our senses, and sits robed on its seat in human form. But suppose that, by some chemical process, we ourselves had gathered that cloud together and set it in the sky, would there have awaked in us an humble adoration as we gazed? As its piled heights flashed down splendour upon us, would not the spirit of self-complacency, rather, have moved in us? Then, it had been our cloud! — Alas! alas! there has been more than one mad Dennis, who has cried, That's *my* thunder! — This land of liberty, this land of "all sovereigns," is filled with the cry! — "Nothing but thunder!"

So, where all the representatives of Law are of our own election, they keep not our reverence; and through our want of this, Law itself becomes a mere thing of convenience, a somewhat upon which to make experiments, a caterer to the self-conceit of man, and thus Obedience, in time, dies, and Order, which holds all in place, is broken up. But if we learn to look upon these ministers as creations of the Law, and not as from ourselves, — as servants of the Law, and not as servants of the people, — a sanctity is thrown around them as its ministers, and Law itself is the more revered; and the effect of all this is a more willing Obedience, a feeling of fitness in gradations, a kindly reationship in Orders, a natural connection from the head to the foot.

Let this sense of patient and wise subjection to authority, this spirit of right Obedience, once possess a man, and its influence may be easily traced through his internal state, and through his character as it appears in its outward relations. It was Pride that rebelled against God; it is Humility that restores man to Obedience; and as the same spirit that prepares a man for heaven fits him for his duties and relations here, so humility, shown forth through obedience, brings out his good affections, and imparts a beauty and sentiment, and a wise calmness, to every station and relation of his life.

Gradations in society formed by Law and made permanent by it, and not — as where all is thrown open to every man — shifting and chance distinctions, rising and sinking like the waves, impress the mind with the sense of all-pervading, all-arranging, authoritative Law. Through Orders, its invisible spirit is made manifest everywhere in the connections of life; each one stands in his place, and there fulfils his duty in obedience to the command of the awful Power; man lives and acts under a wholesome reverence, whose cause and mode of working upon himself he may not comprehend, while yet it spiritualizes him and acts in him for good. The consciousness is thus kept up in him, that he is living under a power which he cannot overmaster, or change at will, and that he stands in certain relations not to be broken through for his mere pleasure and ease; and this makes him better comprehend the finite nature and the dependence of created man.

There being something of permanency and distinctness in his condition, the mind is unconsciously modified by it, and, in turn, acquires steadiness, and distinctness, and an apprehension of relations. Habit begets contentedness; and contentedness and a ready apprehension of such things as are immediately around him, though they be few and simple, impart a wise discernment to the general character, and the man is not easily to be deceived. The affections, also, are strengthened; for, where habituated to it, we come to love even that which, in itself considered, is indifferent, and to be unconscious of that which would otherwise give pain. Thus attachments grow around the occupations, the cares, the pleasures, and the intercourses of daily life; and where quiet attachments grow, there will sentiment, to refine the character, spring up.

I care not how humble this station may be, the fact that it is an inherited one endears it to a man. His father and his father's father lived here before him; the tools of trade and husbandry which he uses, they had handled; his homeliest labours are sanctified to him, and refining affections mingle with his daily toil. I am aware that this is an age in which such a condition of mind and heart is little set by, that sharp, and alert, and pushing spirits look upon such a meek and contented soul with something like contempt, and that taking delight in such views of human nature is set down for romance.

Did it never occur to those who speak thus floutingly, that the conditions and characters in life to which the romantic mind turns oftenest must, from this very fact, have something in them peculiarly connected with and congenial to the finer parts of our nature? That which we call romance, although it may be an excess in us, stands in close relation to the highest attributes of man. There must be something well in that to which we unconsciously go in our moments of quickened imagination and softened sentiment; and, on the other hand, something radically defective in that from which, in such moments, we as instinctively turn away. There is a beauty and a wisdom in a contented spirit, of which the world knows little now.

These clear distinctions of ranks have the further effect of producing in each man a certain pride in his particular Order; not a hard, but a softened pride, softened by the filial affections and gentle remembrances of which I have spoken, and by a desire of doing well, not only for the sake of his individual character, but for that, too, of the class to which he belongs.

Further, each one is in the way of having a just understanding of the Rights of his Class; for, the line being distinctly marked, it is plain when he himself oversteps it, or when another treads upon it. Now, selfish as we are, a discernment of our own rights helps us to a clearer apprehension of the rights of others. Indeed, our very selfishness puts us in more need of the former, that we may not misjudge the latter; for where we know our own bounds, conscience may keep us within them; but where they are not at all, or but indistinctly, marked out, selfishness will ever be disposing us to push beyond our fair limits.

A sense of Security, while within our Order, disposes us to allow, to those below or above us, whatever they are entitled to according to their several places. Hence the ease, the kind courtesy, (where rank is not questioned,) with which he of the nobler treats him of the humbler order, and hence the respectful return.

My Christian friend, you to whom wealth and a cultivated mind have given advantages over that poor, aged Christian woman, who can do little more than spell out her Bible, did there not stir in you, while you stood talking with her, a feeling for her humble condition, — a protecting benevolence? And as you heard her patient, meek spirit utter its thankfulness for all God's goodness to her, did it not come like gentle and unconscious rebuke from her to you? Did you not reverence her in her lowly earthly condition? Did you not reverence her all the more for it? Did you not go away more humble, more revering, than you would have gone from one ranking with yourself? And do you not believe that she took more heart-comfort in pouring out her soul to you, than she could have taken in so doing to one in the same condition of life with herself? Did not the earthly relation of rank, which she bore to you, run on in grateful sympathy with that humility in her which came from and related back to an infinitely high Power? Were you not both the better for the difference in your conditions? I know how you will answer me. And I know, also, what reply you would make, should I question you respecting any honourable and respectable quality in a fellow-creature standing in like difference of rank to yourself.

And, after all, much of the opposition to these differences in fixed social conditions grows out of an exaggerated and too exclusively outward view of them, and, with all the boasting about the dignity of human nature, out of a want of the true apprehension and feeling of what that dignity consists in. Your thorough equalizers are, of all people, the most apt to estimate a man according to his outer rather than his inner state, by his accidents rather than substance, by the circumstantial rather than the essential; — of the simple individual man, independent of his external condition and connections, they know and think little. And even when considering the man more apart from these, they subvert the order of his constitution, by making the instrument the moving power, setting the intellectual faculties above the moral nature, and thus leading to proud views of man, and thence to external distinctions, till the sense of the simple dignity of the humblest moral creature perishes within them. It is pride that looks on the aged beggar as an object of compassion only; it cannot realize how good it is to be humble before him to whom one gives an alms, or feel the words of Fuzeli, "The Patriarch of Poverty."

We may be assured, that where these distinctions are regarded from custom and old association, and reverenced as marked out by Law, existing rather as a sentiment in the community than as an arbitrary rule, (and here old Law is transformed into a sentiment,) pride on the one side, and a base feeling on the other, need not grow up; for the tone of sentiment which is awakened has in it no touch of these. Thus, strange as it may sound to some, there is a feeling of respect called out in him of the superior rank towards the individual respectable in his rank below, as well as in the lower towards him in the rank above. And this feeling runs along the electric chain which connects the lowest peasant with the solitary monarch upon his throne. And what a blessing it is to him, thus lifted up over his fellows, and with none above him but God and the Spirit of Law, to be held in sympathy with men by this feeling of reverence for his kind,—

> "Reverence,
> That angel of the world, doth make distinction
> Of place 'twixt high and low."

It is easily seen how this diversity of condition necessarily multiplies and diversifies the relations betwixt men, and how, running through these relations, the various passions and affections are brought into play, and the character, in its varied and more minute and delicate parts, drawn out, and how opportunity is given for the development of the entire inner man.

Law, in this form, is no longer a mere outer political rule, guiding public affairs only, and protecting men against wrong. It blends itself in kindly, congenial working with the finest feelings in man's individual being, his private relations, his solitary, cherished thoughts, and with his social joys and employments; and it falls into the stream of his religious influences also, adding to them, producing congruity, and giving continuity, through this congruity, to the healthful action upon his soul.

That has been called the best form of Law which leaves man the most to himself, which allows him to forget, save where he openly and purposely violates it, that he is under Law.

If by this were meant, that the less of Law there is in the form of arbitrary, teasing enactments, or dark oppression, the better, it may not be questioned. And yet, even where no immediate and outbreaking licentiousness is the consequence, there may be too little, as well as too much of Law, for man's well-being. For he needs frequent reminding of his limited nature, by the hindrances of set boundaries, or, in his forgetfulness, self-will would, first or last, carry him over all bounds. It is well for him that Law should now and then say to him, Thou shalt not do this! Thou shalt not do that! And if he ask, Why? — that she give no other reply than, Thou shalt not do it! But especially is Law well, where its all-pervading spirit reaches man immediately through his calling in life, and through the established distinctions of society, and thus brings him under its steady, diffusive, and multiplied influences, softened by the medium through which it passes, becoming emotion to the heart and reverence to the mind. Made one with his religion, his household, his toils, it imparts a unity, steadiness, and spirit of respect to his character, which must be for his common good, in his private relations, and in those more abroad.

Established Orders lead, also, to a more social disposition among men, and from the very circumstance, too, of the well-defined limits by which each is set off.

Here, all within their particular Order are so far, not theoretically and in name merely, but in very deed, on an equality, — an equality, too, not exacted, but unconsciously and cordially granted. Being of the same Order makes them a brotherhood; and the fact, that they stand in a nearer connection with one another than with those of any other class, gives them to feel nearer and freer with each other individually; there is more unbending, more free-heartedness, more open joy of countenance and voice, more ease in act. They have bonds of union in their peculiar employments, ties in their peculiar amusements, and characteristic thoughts, habits, and feelings of intercommunion, as insignia of their caste, which hold them together as one man, and constitute, as it were, a point in which the domestic and the public state may be said to meet and blend, but which partakes, mostly, of the easy and affectionate character of the former, and permeates the latter with its kindlier influences.

Now, with all the differences of characteristics which the humbleness or dignity of the several Orders must impart to them, this same principle of intimacy between the individuals who constitute an order is found to run through each class, from the highest to the lowest of them. And thus we see the great community divided up into small communities, each happy in itself, and the happier because it is by itself. For it will for ever hold true, however cosmopolitan we may grow, that we shall be happier and easier within our peculiar circle than with the world at large, and that, however much we may try to equalize the condition of individuals, ease and good-fellowship will never find their home in the great, general state, and that, as the lesser societies are merged in it, individuality will be merged in it, too, and man will lose his naturalness and internal freedom. It has been said already, that this principle of Orders does not cut off kindly interchange between individuals of different Orders, though the intercourse is modified by the relations in which ranks stand to each other. And I would appeal to those who remember the earlier state of our domestic relations, when the old Scripture terms of "master" and "servant" were in use. I do not fear contradiction when I say, that there was more of mutual good-will then, than now; more of trust on the one side, and fidelity on the other; more of protection and kind care, and more of gratitude and affectionate respect in return; and, because each understood well his place, actually more of a certain freedom, tempered by gentleness and by deference. From the very fact that the distinction of classes was more marked, the bond between the individuals constituting these two was all the closer. As a general truth, I verily believe, that, with the exception of near blood-relationship, and here and there peculiar friendships, the attachment of master and servant was closer and more enduring than that of almost any other connection in life. The young of this day, under a change of fortune, will hardly live to see the eye of an old faithful servant fill at their fall; nor will the old domestic be longer housed and warmed by the fireside of his master's child, or be followed by him to his grave: The blessed sun of those good days has gone down, it may be, for ever; and it is very cold!

> "What! my young master?—O, my gentle master,
> O, my sweet master, O, you memory
> Of old Sir Rowland!"
>
> "Let me go with you;
> I'll do the service of a younger man
> In all your business and necessities."

As the characteristics of each well-defined class reached to manners, and even to forms of speech and dress, they gave an enlivening diversity to the surface of society; and a perpetual change was going on under the eye of the observer, as, distinguished by the peculiarity of its class, object after object passed by. This kept the mind alive; the imagination was set in motion, the fancy roused up to play, and the associating principles of our natures put in action.

More than this, that equality before spoken of, which every one felt within his own class, leading, as before said, to freedom in the expression of thought and feeling, the character was acted out, and man became a subject of easier observation and more thorough acquaintance to his fellow-man: Men might be said, in the main, to have known each other better. Human nature being thus brought under Law as operating upon it through the diversifying influences of many classes, and being developed in all possible varieties at one time and among one people, moral and mental affinities took life, and led to numberless combinations, and upon these analyses more subtile than chemistry could work were carried on by the observant mind. Think of these objects as in themselves living and conscious, and acting and reacting upon each other in ceaseless and ever-increasing combinations and changes, and what a study have you of man! Is there not something here favourable to the bringing out of the various attributes of our being? And is there not a beauty to the mind, in beholding these quick and varied transitions — so multiplied as at first to seem mere confusion — all brought about by and carried through the harmonizing Orders of a great general Law?

I have sometimes thought it would be interesting to examine the changes in the states of society, in respect to their influences upon the poetic mind, and to point out in what way is to be traced to those changes the difference between such a mind in our present and in our earlier literature; how poets of this day, men of as high powers and of as sympathetic natures as their ancestors, have lost that dramatic spirit and form, and above all, that simple and delightful expression of a common humanity, which marked our poets of earlier times. This loss is not from the native poverty of the poetic mind of this age, but from the comparative meagreness of society, and a tendency to sameness in forms and manners, and in apparent, if not real, character. There is less vividness of spirit; and the poet, feeling the want of sympathy with what is dearest to him, is driven in upon himself, and, under a sense of solitariness, seeks a soothing yet sad fellowship with the fields and woods and water-courses alone.

This will not be thought by many a very serious objection to any form of Law; nor would it be by me, were my views of poetry the same with theirs. But that which to my mind is poetry, is a manifestation of the dearest faculties and affections of man, in their greatest strength, beauty, and variety: There is nothing more serious than poetry. Many content themselves with admiring its more delicate branches, its leaves and blossoms, not heeding that this fair array is put forth through roots which run down deep into the soil of our humanity, and are watered by its nether springs. If this be so, is not that state of society which is least congenial with poetry most unfavourable to human nature itself?

Nor is Law, acting upon us through established Orders, unfavourable to well-regulated liberty. Indeed, as these Orders serve as checks upon each other, that most reckless form of despotism, sudden and passionate Change, is brought to a stand. There are so many interests to be consulted, so many minor rights to be respected, so many different prejudices to be regarded, that change, to make its way at all, must work along slowly and deviously through these; and as some streams take the tinge of the soil, so change, thus moving forward, takes a hue from the very things it is meant to affect, while, by an almost imperceptible alteration, society is preparing for this change, and change conforming itself, in a degree, to the nature of the society; and thus strangeness and an unsuitableness of parts are avoided, and an agreeable and healthy homogeneousness is the result. Besides, Orders serving thus as checks, and giving to each member that familiar knowledge of his own and of another's rights before alluded to, it is only when that mad restlessness, which sets at naught all Law, gets possession of men, that such a society is in danger from a reckless, united minority, or from an unconscionable, irresponsible, domineering majority, and thence from the despotism of One. Further, were the respect shown to the upper ranks paid nakedly to the individuals in them, it might well lead to a blind submission, and a servile endurance of oppression; but blended with and growing out of the relation in which these individuals stand to a general Law, that reverential sense which Law excites elevates, not degrades men, and while it teaches decorum, educates the character, through a mysterious working, to take care that those whose rank stands on Law do not violate that Law: Through a sacred feeling for Law, and a sober watchfulness over its sanctity, they guard it well.

Having spoken of some of the beneficial tendencies of Orders established on Law, — of tendencies, for our fallen natures admit only of approaches to what is best, — let us now glance at the tendency of an opposite principle, — Equality.

If, through the infinitely diversified forms and uses of God's material and animal universe, we see a subordination to some one great purpose; if in that, all be held together by a principle of association by means of which unity is preserved; we can hardly suppose, that, in the ordering of his moral and intellectual kingdom, this principle would be neglected, — that, in this last and higher kingdom, Law — that mighty Power — would be introduced into the midst of these associations, pervading all other portions of God's universe, not to act in harmony with them in their influences upon man, but to be an exception to them, or, at best, not to be necessarily interdependent with them, but leaving us free to start with a sweeping, disuniting principle, such, for instance, as absolute Independence, Liberty, and Equality, among men.

This hardly seems to be a philosophical course; for it not only takes too much for granted, but also sets out the wrong way. Would it not have been more philosophical to have assumed, that Law should bear relationship to those other relations of man, and, from the study of these and of man, to have learned something of what the character of Law should be? Is it not by a knowledge of these and of man, of his affections, wants, powers, that we are to determine what form of Law is best adapted to him? Indeed, is there any other question than that of adaptation? — Is there any other Right?

In considering the influence of the Law of Orders upon man, its opposite, Equality, has necessarily been directly or indirectly touched upon. Equality in relation to Law, and, as a consequence, the right to appoint all ministers of Law, and these resorted to only for convenience' sake, seems hardly in agreement with the other relations of man. In respect to God, the finite and created stands in the relations of dependence and obedience, — dependence and obedience, not resting upon and paid to an abstract principle, but a Being, one from whom emanates Law and Control. This principle of personality is an all-essential one in its action on the nature of man; and every attempt to act, as some would do, upon a mere Principle of Right, irrespective of a Superiour as the living Person in whom that right centres, shows how feeble is the power of any principle which is not in some way impersonated to the mind. Hence, when, through sin, man lost his lively sense of the personality of his Creator, and it was said of him that he was without God in the world, to show how inexpressible is the craving for an Object to look up to, he fell down before images of his own making, of wood and stone.— And may it not be reverently asked, whether God, who in one work answers many ends, was not, among his high mysterious ways and purposes, manifested in the flesh to meet this desire in the heart of man?

Upon the same principle, Law, as has been said, in order to be long reverenced, must be bodied forth in its ministers, and that, too, not in creatures all made and unmade at our good pleasure. If not embodied, our notions of it become vague; if presented in forms of our own setting up alone, Obedience dies. Here, then, is a contradiction between our relations to this form of Equality in Law, and our relations to God. Look into some of our other relations. In that of Father and Child we find power and authority on one side, dependence and obedience on the other. We might go into others, and show how men are compelled to sell their boasted birthright of Equality, and be, their lives long, subject to one fellow-being or another, — a necessity not growing out of the particular wants of certain individuals, and bearing alone upon those wants, but pressing upon men everywhere, to carry forward the uniform and general purposes of life, and to attain great, general ends: — To command and to obey meet us at every turn.

Nor is this general necessity the growth of arbitrary institutions. Bring mankind to a level. How like would prove their condition to "the lightning, which doth cease to be, ere one can say, It lightens!" — circumstances under the whole surface forcing up some, and sinking others, in every quarter! Why, you might as well tramp the tossing sea into a plain, as keep mankind thus. Look through the countless orders in the animal creation, — everywhere superiour and inferiour, over the bröad earth!—The tall tree and the humble flower, the river and the brook, the mountain and the little hill, littleness and greatness, weakness and strength, — inequality everywhere pressed in upon our senses. Do not make light of these last instances, nor hold it philosophical to bring in a separation between influences which act upon the finer sentiment and tastes, or any of the attributes of man. For whether these come to him through the senses, or in whatever way, they centre in one being and tend to one end, — an harmonious character, association, and unity through variety, constitute the life of man. As this principle of harmony begins from God, and runs down through all the relations of public and private Law, even into that Law of the material world which determines the shape and height of the common weed, let us ask ourselves what must be the effect of a great leading principle in Law, which jars upon this harmony? Why, it brings discord into the soul of every individual being. Whither shall he turn, that, by some analogy, he may learn his true relation to Law?—He looks up to the heavens; the great, all-dispensing sun, the grateful, receiving moon, tell him, it is not there!—over the earth; it is not there! He is left standing, a lonely spirit on his lonely plain: Here are entire freedom and equal rights! Heaven shows him the inequality between him and it, and bids him obey; and earth answers to the voice of Heaven; Law, his Law alone, has no according voice!

To satisfy ourselves that this principle of Equality is only an arbitrary assumption, a factitious right, we must examine its tendency upon him who assumes it. As it stands apart from all else in man's condition, — an abstract right realized in no other of his relations, — while acting upon it, he must be a different being; all the teachings of his state, from his birth upward, not only failing to instruct him here, but his wonted modes of thinking, feeling, acting, running counter to it. Wherever these come into his reasonings or feelings in respect to Law, (and come in they will perpetually,) they confuse and perplex him, and he is thrown into a condition to feel, and think, and act inconsistently. Do what he may to reconcile them, his theory, and his experiences with their results, are ever standing in contradiction to each other. How shall he relieve himself from this internal self-conflict? It is a most uncomfortable condition; and had he the means of judging, he would, while in this state, use such means amiss. Shall he modify his darling theory a little by his other individual relations? Alas! there is a God above him, not accountable to him, — a God who has laid the line to the plummet, and will do with his creature as he falls on the one side or the other of it, — a God who took not him into his counsels when he gave Law to the universe, and who bids him obey it. Hedged in by overruling circumstances, which he was born to, and which have grown and strengthened around him as he has lived on, he finds it difficult to modify his theory of Law by any of these. Will he let go his hold, and allow Law to flow on with the mighty current of things? No! Pride swells self-importance, and the spirit of self clings to it. Turning from them, yet followed hard by them, he exaggerates his darling Right, that he may rid himself of their pressure upon him. He must not only magnify this right in theory, he must realize it as a fact, and, to this end, must use it.

To rid himself of that spirit of reverence, which supposes in the Law and its ministers something above him, and not to be inconsiderately touched by him, he speaks of Law as made for him, and not of himself as made for Law: He is neither born under the Law, nor brought into subjection to it.

His notion of Law having no relationship to other things habitual with him, and not being regulated by long existing checks and counter-checks, or bounded by settled demarcations, but lying loosely and confusedly in a mind jealous of its privileges and fond of power, he comes to esteem wholesome restraint to be lordly usurpation, and authoritative Law, bondage.

And, for the like reason, when in power, the exercise of uncontrolled will is but the use of the natural rights of a freeman with him, and opposition to it the rebellion of the few against the will of the many; for when of the many in feeling, the individual is the many. — Think of the all-pervading influence of that sin by which fell the angels, and in the strength of which man yet stands out against his Maker, and then think of the tremendous power of these confused forces!

In the proportion that this principle is strong, all antagonist principles are weak. Law, when not a power above us and moving on us, but subject to us and to be moved by us, becomes mere force in our hands. Besides, where power is not exercised through established ranks with settled duties and rights, but through a mere majority, accidental both in its birth and duration, made up of incoherent masses of men of all conditions, discordant in manners, thoughts, and feelings, and scarcely intelligible to each other, and with but one purpose in common, that purpose becomes a bond of union of enormous strength, even because it is only One.

Here, and here alone, are these men in sympathy, —

in the exercise of power without any of those lesser sympathies, which, when playing back and forth among men who have many ties of acquaintance, serve as alleviating influences to the intensity of a single passion and aim. And through this it is that a majority, under this *equality* form of Law, is so blind, so arrogant, so impatient of check, so unsparing and appalling in its character, its very holding together depending upon the intensity of the excitement of its single aim. This is the vital principle of the body; and if this is not kept up hot and quick, the extremities grow cold, and there being no other combining influence, the body decomposes and dies: It is felt that without strong excitement there is no longer life. In this exercise of power they have little to bound them beside their own wills. No established customs sanctified by time and associations awaken a kindly relucting in their hearts; no varieties of numerous orders, high and low, lie across their way: It is one level, broad, trampled road.

When the spasm is over, they have no old places to go home to, no hereditary private occupations and privileges, naturally, and with a relief of heart, to fall back upon and be at rest in. No! while there is any thing above them in heaven or earth, there is no equality for them; they must be stirring, and forming into parties, after freemen's rights, that is, Equality, and that is — Power.

To increase this restlessness, Change is a grand object with them, because permanency in Law is, in itself, control. Whatever has stood for a length of time is not only in their way, but is an offence to their pride, as something not yet subjected to their power, nor bearing marks of their authority: To be older than they, is usurpation, insult, and wrong. And thus we find, that while the love of power strengthens as obstacles lessen, so the principle of change comes in to finish the work and sweep all away.

> " Now he pulls down
> What old desert hath builded."

The final tendency of this condition of things, and of all such as resemble it, is to enthrone a Despot. No one is so likely to become the servile worshipper of an usurper as a thorough-going liberty and equality man. Law itself being in his eyes, at the best, but an instrument in his hands, for convenience, for the carrying on of mere public purposes, which look mainly to public physical advancement, it cannot be said to possess sanctity with him, or even respect; for he values it no further than he perceives its immediate *cui bono*, its earthly end. His treatment of it, then, will be directed by his narrow principle of Utility alone. But where man acts from a secondary, rather than from the highest principle, is not his tendency necessarily downward ? Where, then, we make that debasing system of philosophy, (if philosophy it may be called,) Utility, our principle of action, rather than that ennobling ultimate principle of our nature, Duty, — of which Law is the glorious announcer, and through which it is manifested, — we gradually lose the perception of true utility itself, and begin to limit its extent, till, by and by, we look no further than the present, and our operations are finally contracted within the circle of self. Law, having thus lost its venerable spiritual form to us, and being no longer an object of the mind's worship, that feeling of want of an object above us, which can never become wholly extinct in us, leads us at length to supply the place of the worship of Law, and of reverence for its legitimate priesthood, by setting up some idol fellow-being, independent of old Law, and standing upon power alone; — and before him we bow down, and haste to do his pleasure: The effect upon the mind is just that of atheism, whose course is to idolatry. — Your loud-talking liberals were, to a man, the debased worshippers of that fearful despôt, Bonaparte, who, but for England, would have set his foot on all Europe, and kept it there; and they gloried in their shame. And they gloried, because he was the impersonation of their great principle, Self-Will, — the antagonist of old authority, — usurper, as well as tyrant. It is at the Law-descended abuser of authority that such men rail, and more, too, from their hate of that Law which furnished the opportunity, than at the acts stretched beyond its sanctions, — it is, in heart, the tyrant's lawful origin that stirs their anger and raises their cry.

Each principle of the mind has its opposite; reverence of a true superiour produces kindness towards an inferiour, and the spirit of right obedience, respect for the claims of those below. — So those who are impatient under settled and old authority are the most capricious masters, and the most unreasonable and overbearing in their demands. — One may have often noted that a complete equality-man in public is apt to be the most absolute of men at home. Where any right principle is wanting in us, there will be found its contrary; where there is not reverence, there will be servility, tyranny. Who is that more unsparing despot than the leading despot himself? — Always, always, that despot's willing slave.

We may infer the effect of this form of Law upon man in his inward and private character, and upon those relations which lie out of what is more strictly termed private life; and the ground has all along been gone upon of the mutual influences of the private upon the public, and the public upon the private relations; — for let but one string be struck, and the vibrations run through the universe of God. And if public Law and the private condition do not assimilate, they cannot hold on several and distinct courses and be at peace: there must be strife between them. For acting, as they do, upon one object, man, if there be not harmony in their actions and purposes, the contentious question must be tried, — To which of them shall the man belong? And it is curious to see how this question is sometimes resolved, and how some, who begin with setting up the Rights of Man and arraying self-will against established Law, come round to making the individual but an instrument of the political mass, absorbing his will into what is called the Will of the People, and leaving him, as his proper own, neither wife nor children, houses nor lands; so that while he is absolute as a mere portion of this mass, in his individual capacity he is left without a right. Such a contradiction, monster, slave, must he be who starts, not with the idea of Obedience, but that of Self-Will; — a suicidal principle, ever destroying itself as fast as it takes life.

That notion of Liberty which has passed into the saying, that "The best form of Law is that which leaves man most to himself," has already been questioned; and something has been said of the healthful influences of the opposite principle upon the social character, in allowing the majestic power of Law to impress upon man a sense of subordination, and, by the various forms and Orders through which it may present itself, awakening a consciousness of restraint, and a need of self-denial, and a curbing of the will. Deprive the Law of this majesty and pervading presence, and the man soon grows negligent of the rights and feelings of his fellow-men, and regardless of those little proprieties, which, though too delicate to define, constitute the beauty of social life, and return again into the bosom of him who showed them forth. Without the spirit of subordination there *is* no liberty; without the restraint of Order, no freedom; without this awful Presence of Law, man is every body's slave, and, far worse, a slave unto himself.

I have spoken of the effect of the doctrine of Equality upon man's religious relations, and the tendency which the acknowledging of no superiour in his political connections has to produce that pride and that self-dependence which gradually dispose a finite and dependent creature to forget his true condition, and to give over his faith in that which reminds him of it. It has been usual to talk of the infidelity of the French Revolution, as accidental to it, or as simply an antagonistic principle owing its birth to the corrupt state of the Gallican Church. That there was corruption, and that it added to the power of this principle, need not be denied. Still, the Revolution was infidel in its very essence. The broad, unqualified principle of Equality contains in itself the seeds of infidelity, and they germinate, put forth, and flower, with it. Its tendency may be seen in even that part of the religious community which holds it at this day, — in hot-headed action, in a disregard of consequences, through a self-willed, impatient resoluteness to reach a certain end, and in the over-balance of the active in comparison with the meditative powers; in more of zeal than of apparent unction, in a certain hardness and confidence of manner, and a want of a courteous regard of others. And may not the popularity of those utilitarian views in religion, which measure our love of God by just what it may be worth to us, — a *quid pro quo*, bargain-system betwixt man and his Maker, — be in some degree one of the consequences of this same principle? May it not also be from the same source, that there is so strong a disposition to weaken the doctrine of dependence on God, and to talk of God as existing for man, rather than man for Him, — in the same way that man looks upon Law as made for his use, and not rather for his obedience, as made under the Law? This view of Law, when carried out, tends to enfeeble the apprehension of the divine Law, of its uncompromising strictness, of the awful sin and irreverence in its breach, of its direful penalties, and of the enlarged wisdom of that Justice which puts those penalties in force.

As this principle, when applied to our social state, places all on a level, and as, on the contrary, the course of things is to inequality, man, instead of doing what is best in his condition, is discontented in it, and restless after something lying beyond it. Moderation in his desires and aims being annihilated, his scrupulousness about means to ends is endangered. His eagerness after the unattained is increased, and the ties of customs, habits, local associations, and the countless little attachments so congenial with what is thoughtful, gentle, affectionate, social, cheerful, in his nature, die out. In short, the sentiment and poetry of his being — the highest state of being — are suffocated in the dust and sweat of the eager and selfish race of life.

Much of this may be seen in the change that our society has undergone within one life of man. We have become active, at the expense of meditation, wealthy, at the cost of that simplicity so needed for home comfort, and are all, as it were, grown strangers to our several conditions, for we are perpetually changing them; so that they are ever new to us, and we to them. This lessens ease of heart and naturalness of manners; for the heart craves an old, wonted home in which to be at rest; and naturalness of outward port comes of being habituated to our condition.

Men are less social, too, than of yore. For those habitudes, and sympathies, and unobserved assimilations, which grow out of having so much in common with a particular class of our fellow-men, are what put us at ease, and make us social. Even the old fashion of distinguishing garbs for the several classes once helped to give life to the social character. This and like distinctions are now done away; there must be no visible marks; all are now jumbled together, without affinities, into one huge, unsocial mass, and called — the people. Nor are men unsocial from this want alone of assimilating qualities within each class. As no man is willing to let Law determine his place, he has not, of mere right, any certain stand which nobody thinks of disputing with him. The want of this makes each one jealous of his neighbour, and quick to take casual inattention for intended disrespect. Another, esteeming himself, individually, a little higher than his left-hand man, and there being no Law by which this is settled, magnifies his state, and guards it with amusingly anxious minuteness, or with cold reserve. There can be no courteous notice of the man next below him, lest he assume upon it; and no pleasant return on the part of the other, lest he be thought impertinent. — We may rely upon it, that this Law of Equality is, in the long run, more anti-social in its effects than the law of the Turk. It not only runs through our out-of-door relations, producing distance and severance there between individuals, but it enters our houses too, and estranges master from servant, and mistress from maid. Indeed, the very terms are thrown back upon us with disdain. And it is a truly curious fact, that the only men among us humble enough to take upon themselves the name of servants are those who are set on high, to make and execute the laws by which the multitude are governed. And of so great meekness are these, and so ever ready to make up for the lack of the quality in others, that to nothing are they more given than to styling themselves the "servants of the people." This, to be sure, is setting an excellent example of humility! and there would be nothing objectionable in the phrase, were it not for the fallacy and hypocrisy involved in it, and for its encouraging an opposite and arrogant spirit in those it cajoles and flatters.

What effect has this form of Law upon the young? As they hear so much of Liberty and Equality, they must needs stand upon the same plane with their elders. Having little reverence for the majesty of Law and for its ministers, it is the natural course of the mind, that they should lose it for age also, as it is no easy matter to lack reverence for any one thing in itself venerable, without gradually coming to want it towards whatever is worthy of being revered: Where a principle is weakened in its action upon one object, it is hard to retain its strength where bearing upon others of a like nature. Hence a false state in our relations to each other. And as the false tends to excess, equality alone does not long content the young; they soon slight the old, and speak of their want of light and enlargement of mind; and when inclined to especial civility, assume a patronizing air, to put them at ease. A like influence is had upon the filial relation. But it is enough to show the operation of the principle in one instance; — all may apply it to other cases, for themselves.

We find this principle, again, in our schemes of Education. Every body must be educated like every body. And why not? For if, in this condition of chance circumstances, one be down to-day, he is looking, through this *equality* system, to be at the top to-morrow. And as there are no obstacles from Orders by Law to retard this, and each expects to rise to the top as naturally as cork in water, though the course of events are against it, the thousand are educated for that which possibly may be the good luck of the one. But as, do what we may, circumstances and situation, as well as books, will have a hand in educating us, the unhappy scholar is in the condition of one who is under the charge of a score of teachers with a score of discordant systems. Hence follows a discordant character in the person taught. Embroidery, the piano-forte, bad French, and — for what is called composition — worse English, do not exactly sort with the multifarious drudgeries of humble life. This would be a small matter, did it not bring along with it dissatisfaction at our condition, and an aim, not so much to be respectable in that, as to pass for belonging to a better, — did it not fill the head with vain fancies, and destroy simplicity of character, by tempting us to ape that which we are not: Accomplishments is the word, and a smattering on many subjects the thing; and the result of all, little of real knowledge, and less of true wisdom. With all our show of academies, and all the hodge-podge of lyceums, our fathers and mothers, in the same walks of life, possessed more rightly balanced and quite as wise and discerning minds as we; for pretence to that which is not really ours unfits us for the use of that which is. In their little, yet careful reading, in their limited objects of knowledge, yet thoroughness in what they knew, there was a harmony with their condition, the result of which was congruity of character, good sense, and a consequently prepared mind for any change of circumstances.

One might go on through the multitude of conditions in life, and show how Law, having helped to produce this in the private relations, is acted back upon by these relations; but enough has been said to make the principle understood.

If the view here taken be, in the main, just, it will continue to be so. The principle must remain a fundamental one, though there may be modified applications of it, in particulars, to the changes that society may undergo. If Law is ordained to have an influence upon the passions, sentiment, and affections, let it be remembered, that these are the prime constituents of man's nature, and must exist along with it; and that all endeavours to annihilate them, or to bring them into subjection to the understanding, by first of all pouring knowledge into the mind, is beginning at the wrong end, and attempting to subject the moving powers of the soul to that which is moved by them. While, for instance, there is pride in the heart, it is in vain to attempt subduing it by adding to our knowledge; for here "knowledge puffeth up." While there is malignity, craft, envy, the more knowledge, the more with and upon which these may act. The selfish principle may change its mode of operation, through its increased knowledge of means; but it is still the master-mover, and will continue to be so, till the moral evil is first subdued, and the head be taught wisdom through the heart. It may be, that God is permitting the popular system of education to be tried out, only to convince man how worse than in vain is the endeavour to bring society into order by any other way than by first bringing the heart into an ordered harmony with Himself. The first breach of God's Law was not a mistake of the head, it was a sin of the heart; and thus discord was brought in; and that man may come once more into harmony with himself and with his fellow-man, he must again come under obedience of heart to his God: As ignorance was not the cause of sin, so knowledge will not cure it. And, in very deed, there cannot be a just perception of a moral truth, save through a first quickened moral affection. If this be so, that form of Law which is best fitted to awaken and keep alive these principles in man will be just as necessary in ages to come as it is now; man will ever need those influences which shall shed through the soul the spirit of Obedience, Humility, and Content.

"But," say some good people, "Religion is to be a substitute, and is to come in and do all which Law, through Authority and Orders, may have done." Right Law will always act upon the same principles in man that religion acts upon, — they are co-workers; and from all we have yet seen of the Christian world, it will be in no state to do without this connection. True, when Christianity shall have had a more thorough and enlightening influence upon man, (being felt by him through all the relations of life,) Law may not bear to him so severe an aspect as now. But it will be the change wrought in himself, and not in Law, that will make its face more gentle to him; it will be because the spirit of Submission has spread throughout his soul, and Obedience is easy unto him, and his lot in life pleasant unto him, whatsoever it be. Had Christians more enlightened views and a juster feeling of what will be their relations and duties in eternity, they would not be striving after such Utopias here.

It is not the end of Religion to put all men upon a footing. There is good reason to believe that there will be quite as great a variety of duties to perform, of obligations to regard, of ranks and orders to be respected, each by each, in heaven, as now there are here. Can it be supposed that many of the faculties and affections of man are to be annihilated or for ever to lie dormant within him? Are there to be no occasions between spirits for the exercise of humility, gratitude, kindness, condescension, content? No opportunities for considerateness and gentleness in commands? for cheerfulness and faithfulness in performing them? Are there not to be the helper and the helped, the weaker and the stronger, the more and the less wise? Is not heaven to be a social state? And if so, is it to be stripped of the best exercises of the virtues of that state? As man stands related to two worlds, and he and this world are made up of correspondences to each other, may we not conclude that this world also, in its perfect idea, must correspond in its ordering with heaven, and that man, in his true condition, and conforming to Law and Orders here, is only assimilating to the ordered state of that world beyond? — that, as in the course of being he must act in and be acted upon by both, and both meet in him as a common term, so each, marred even as this world is, must, in its essential structure and constituted order, bear resemblance to each? Law, then, is meant as a helper in preparing us for that state. And

Christians will yet learn that it is not the purpose of religion to lay level these distinctions in the form of Law, but to prepare the heart to respect them; to fit it for contentment in its lot, faithfulness in its duties, and, through the right use of these its earthly relations, to be helped in being made meet for those above, — to dwell for ever in peace, amidst thrones, dominions, principalities, and powers. The great change that man is to undergo, in entering upon his labours and joys above, will not be in the paralyzing of any of his intellectual and moral powers and affections, or in laying aside their conditions and uses, but in the sanctification of them all. If we would but realize this a little more, how much better should we, even now, realize eternity, and how far better should we harmonize with our duties and relations here!

In these few and desultory thoughts upon the question, What Form of Law is best suited to the Individual and Social character of Man? the two Forms have been considered chiefly in their tendencies; for nowhere can be found either men or Law, as they actually exist, doing more than making approaches towards what has been here supposed. Nor will it ever be otherwise here. What are the true limits under either form, — how far the principle of Obedience, and of learning in whatsoever state we are therewith to be content, should be carried, — or, on the other hand, how much of Liberty and an approach to Equality are necessary in order to manliness of character, well-grounded hope of prosperous, crowning endeavour, and to energy and activity of life, — no man can precisely measure.

If I have shown a preference for the former rather than for the latter state, I have done no more than to declare my honest and serious convictions. And let it be remembered, that on the side of these convictions lay the prophetic fears of our Fathers for the safety of our land, to guard which the wisest of them surrounded us by as strong a Form of Law as the people would consent to adopt, or, when adopted, would bear.

Though it has been my purpose to treat this subject simply as an abstract principle, I cannot leave it without a word of application to ourselves.

The spirit of the age, as it is termed, which is now at work in the mother country, to the harm, it is to be feared, of much that has constituted the peculiarity and the excellence of the English individual and national character, is rife here, and rife, too, without those needful checks and influences which are as yet spared to her. Need I speak of those reckless combinations of men, called mobs, which are breaking out over our land? They are but the momentary eruptions of fires burning at the centre of our System itself. The principle may be found running through all classes of our society, from the lowest up to the highest. And although, at this moment, a wholesome fear may be operating upon the upper classes, is it not a fear for the security of property, rather than an alarm which springs from a discerning of the poisonous growth which is rooted in our soil? Yet, does not our condition show the truth of what I have endeavoured to make plain? Is there any need of going over the ground again, and of tracing up to the form of Law which is peculiar to us, that all-pervading, all-absorbing love of gain, which is our besetting sin; that tyranny of opinion, which leaves to no man the freedom of his own thoughts; that prying spirit, which *mouses him out* in his most secret retirements; and that meddling disposition, which puts shackles upon the freedom of his words and acts? Are not these things so? Let any man walk our streets. How sharp, and eager, and careful, are the faces he looks into! Let him lend an ear to what is said as he passes along; and will he not, when he goes home, and shuts his door after him, cry in weariness of spirit, with him of old, "*Their* talk is of bullocks"? Let us lay aside awhile our sensitive national vanity, and ask the liberal and intelligent who visit us from all lands as to the reality of these things. In our Form of Liberty, then, is there not a subtile and pervading spirit of bondage weighing upon the freedom of the soul of man?

Another evil is threatening us; the hatred the poor bear towards the rich;—no, not so much the very poor, perhaps, as those who are well housed, and well clothed, and well fed, and who make their daily gains, and to whom the highway to wealth is as open as to those who have gone on before: These are they who are laying hold on their brother's heel, and would fain get from him his inheritance. And it is curious to remark how, in the portion of God's heritage in which the principle of Liberty and Equality has been attempted to be most thoroughly carried out,—in New England,—this spirit is now most restless and alive. And why is it so, but from the very absence of checks and balances, and settled orders, and distinctive habits and associations, and the want of an agreement between the ordinary courses of Providence and our outward, public Form of Law? The theory of perfect Liberty and Equality, when aimed at in act, ends in nothing more or less than despotism in its worst form,—the despotism of the mad many over the considerate few. Money-loving as we are said to be, this restlessness does not come from our desire for wealth alone, but from our impatience at inequality of condition too. Property happens to be its object, because property is tangible, and addresses itself to the senses, and because, too, it is not a peculiar and individual characteristic of any one in particular, but intrinsically accidental, and in its nature within every one's reach: the very fact that it does not lie without the compass of any one seems to make the possessor of it the object of envy to all. If this spirit went only to take wealth from the hands of its present possessors, it would be an evil comparatively light. But with the cry of Liberty and Equality, it goes to deprive each individual of the free exercise of his moral endowments and intellectual powers, — of his self-denial, his prudence, his sagacity, his enterprise, his industry, and his strength of will; for it takes away the motive to their exercise, and thus destroys their life in robbing him of their rewards. What oppression is here! The impossibility of realizing the notion of Equality can, perhaps, in no instance be more distinctly seen. It is in contradiction to the exercise of every moral and intellectual attribute, and shows us that there is no Liberty without settled limits and restraints, and without inequalities in the social system, no security to rights.

Although some may think that too little of the good and too much of the ill in that Form of Law which our Constitution most resembles have been dwelt upon, few will think that the true character and causes of those ills have been mistaken, or will doubt their lying deep in the workings of our natures, or that they needs must be guarded against by a watchfulness over every movement of pride, and by a strengthening of every principle of obedience and humility in man.

But in considering the tendency of an erroneous principle, even the forethoughtful are too apt, perhaps, to overlook the fact, that seldom is it left to carry out its work to its feared results, but that, from the very sufferings it is generating, there often springs up a counteracting force, which qualifies or neutralizes the otherwise unmixed evil in which it would end. Hence, the forebodings of political prophets are wont to be made light of; and even those of Burke have been treated thus, because, indeed, it turned out that the Revolution of his day in France failed of at least one attribute of hell,—that of duration. With us, too, there is a fashion of speaking of every obstruction to the overflowing of an evil, as a mound raised against it by that virtue and forecast in ourselves which will continue to serve us in each extreme need; instead of our seeing that the shifting or stoppage of its current may come from the jostling and jamming together of what have been swept along in its course. It is a superficial view of things which leads us to give in to the faith, that because a present difficulty is mitigated or turned aside, though the principle in which it originated retains life, still all will be well. It awakens misgivings in one, to find even the great men now struggling for our preservation adding strength to this confidence, and, to stave off an immediate and pressing evil by winning the people to their side, imbuing them with a rash assurance of final and permanent success, by haranguing them about their broad territory, their diffused wealth, their interwoven interests and implicated commercial ties, as if these were their gods, and would ever hold in peace eager, restless, and inflated men,—or, worse than this, declaiming to them about their light, their knowledge, their virtue, and their power;—thus fitting them to renew past perils, or to bring down upon themselves worse than these, — worse to them, made presumptuous through present escapes. Let the voice of our wise Witherspoon warn us, — "I look upon ostentation and confidence to be a sort of outrage upon Providence; and when it becomes general, and infuses itself into the spirit of the people, it is a forerunner of destruction."

We must beware, then, of that popular, but most dangerous creed, that a free country will work off its evils. No country is free, that is not moral; and no country moral, that bows not itself in lowliness of spirit to its God, and moves not on in patient Obedience, through the many wise arrangements of His Will.

REVIEWS.

ALLSTON'S SYLPHS OF THE SEASONS.*

It will, perhaps, appear to our readers a late hour in the day for us to take up this volume. But we should be sorry to have it said of us, a few years hence, when these poems shall be more generally read and understood, that we were so wanting in good taste as to pass them by without notice, and that, while we were joining in the common lamentation over the lack of American poetic genius, we were too dull to discern the almost single exception from the cause of our mortification and grief. Though we are not of those who wear home-spun, however coarse, because it is patriotic so to do, yet we trust that we have the common-sense to look at the quality of our garb without caring much whence it came. We think that some good thing may come out from us; and with that confidence with which all reviewers are, or should be, blessed, we are content to venture an opinion upon the works of our own country, without waiting till they have forced their way into notice through the cold indifference of a foreign land.

English in our origin, and owing to that origin most

* From the North American Review for 1817.

The Sylphs of the Seasons, with other Poems. By W. Allston. First American, from the London Edition. Boston: Cummings & Hilliard.

that we have cause to be proud of in our natures; speaking the language of England, and looking upon her literature as our own; boasting of her works of genius in the entire forgetfulness that they were not produced here, and defending them with the same earnestness of partiality as if our own reputation were at stake; — we seem to have been unmindful that it was possible for us to have a literary reputation, and writers of our own to read and admire. We look to England for most of our modern learning and entertainment; our systems of metaphysics and morals are drawn chiefly from her; and for poetry, the common reading of all countries, we naturally, and as of right, enter into the assembly of her bards. This continued dependence upon England has not only turned us away from the observation of what is well done here, but has begotten a distrust of our own judgement and taste. We hesitate at pronouncing an opinion on what has not received judgement there; and dare not confess where we have been offended or pleased, lest her tribunals of criticism should, by and by, come down upon us and tell us we were wrong.

Further than this neglect of our own productions, and timidity of opinion upon their merits, the rank of our authors in society is humbling to minds rightly proud of their powers, and quick and sensitive from culture and native feeling. One generation goes on after another, as if we were here for no other purpose than to do business, as the phrase is. The spirit of gain has taught us to hold other pursuits as mere amusements, and to associate something unmanly and trivial with the character of their followers. If a work of taste comes out, it is made a cause of lament that so much talent should be thus thrown away; and the bright and ever-during glory in which it is, in mercy, hiding our dull commonness, is neither seen nor felt. We hold every thing lightly, which is not perceived to go immediately to some practical good, — to lessen labour, increase wealth, or add to some homely comfort. It must have an active, business-like air, or it is dreaded as a dangerous symptom of the decay of industry amongst us. To be sure, we read English poetry; but for the same reason that we take a drive out of town, because we are tired down by business, and must amuse ourselves a little, to be refreshed and strengthened for work to-morrow. And, besides, the English, we say, can afford to furnish us with poetry. They are an old, wealthy people, and have a good deal of waste material on hand. And so it comes about, naturally enough, that poets are set down as a sort of intellectual idlers, and sober citizens speak of them with a shake of the head, as they would talk of some clever idler about town, who might have been a useful member of society, but, as to any serious purpose, is now lost to the world.

Little, indeed, do such men see, that the out-of-door industry, which leads to wealth and importance, owes much to the poet for its thriving existence; that the poetry of a people elevates their character, and makes them proud of themselves; quickens the growth of the nicer feelings, and tones the higher virtues; that it causes blessings to shoot up round our homes; smooths down the petty roughnesses of domestic life, and softens and lays open the heart to the better affections; that it calls the mind off from the pursuits of the tainted and wearing pleasures of the world, and teaches it to find its amusements in the exercise of its highest and purest powers; that it makes the intellect vivacious, and gives an interest and stir to the society of the wise; shames us from our follies and crimes, turns us to the love and study of what is good, gives health to the moral system, and brings about what must always go along with the virtue of society, the beauty of order and security. Little, too, do they know of the poet's incessant toil. His eyes and thoughts are ever busy amidst the forms of things. He looks into the intricate machinery of the heart and mind of man, and sees its workings, and tells us to what end it moves. He goes forth with the sun over the earth, and looks upon its vastness and sublimity with him, and searches out with him every lesser thing. His studies end not with the day; but when the splendour of the west has died away, and a sleepy and dusky twilight throws a shadowy veil over all things, and he feels that the spirit which lifted him up and expanded his frame, as he looked forward on the bright glories of the setting sun, has sunk slowly and silently down with them, and that the contemplative light about him has entered into his heart, and the gladness of the day left him, he turns and watches the lighting up of the religious stars, by which he studies in soberer and more intent thought the things that God has made.

The present age abounds in poets, and of a kind to show that a better taste is reviving, and natural feelings coming into free play again, and it is grateful to consider, that close descriptions of mind and heart, which grow up and intertangle with them, are relished and understood. For to love nature, and to have an eye that sees her truly, shows that there is a moral tone in chord with her sounding at the heart, and some pure spots in the mind, on which her images play like young leaves on calm and clear waters. It is well for the mind, that the gates are burst open, and the walls levelled with the ground, and that we are let out, from exactly-cut hedges, artificial mounds, and straight canals nicely sloped and sodded to the very brink, to the free and careless sweep of hills, and winding run of the stream, to which God seems to have given instinct enough to work its way through a strange country to its home in the sea. It is pleasant to be set at large once more among varied and irregular creations, and the abundant and wide wealth of the earth; for there we find enough, and even more than the mind can fold in; so that we are ever eager to learn, and associations are crowding upon us and shifting, to give growth to our sentiment, and breadth and thought to our minds. Nature is suggestive, and makes him that studies her work with her. She is always active; and out of the very decay of things comes life. When the mind is in this way left to its own pursuits, it gains vigour and quickness, and truth of observation, from its independence; and the factitious and false, which had crusted it over in the confused and hot stir of pent society, loosen, and break up, and fall off, and it opens to fair impressions, and has a clear and calm expanse, like the heavens over our heads.

But poetry has not only been set free from its narrow views of material nature, so as to give us a feeling of kindred with the very pebbles on the shore; but it has thrown aside, too, the distinctions of society, and treats of us all in common, as creatures of like passions, sensible to like impressions, and capable of like thoughts; it makes us heart-sick with grief at the low-breathed sorrows of Wordsworth's weaver's wife, or the humble Ellen Orford of Crabbe, and to shudder at the intenseness of the evil passions in Peter Grimes. With an enlarged philosophy, it teaches us that there is nothing vulgar but vice, and that there is scarce an object through the whole of existence that is not in some way poetical to a truly poetic mind. We have thrown out these few thoughts, because we think them essential to a right understanding of what poetry is; and feel anxious for the knowledge of the truth on all subjects, as it not only leads us to a right understanding of the particular object of our contemplations, but makes us better acquainted with something else; for there is nothing lonely in nature, but each thing is connected with many others, by more ties than those which hold a tree in the ground. We hope soon to have an opportunity of entering more fully into this subject.

But enough of this; and now to our author. He must excuse us; for reviewers, like the ladies, must follow the fashion, and a review, now-a-days, without a dissertation at its head, would look about as singular as would a slender maid of sixteen, in close-wrapped muslin, and simple, smoothly parted hair, amidst expanded hoops and storied head-dresses, on a St. James's court-day.

As, in this country, every body knows every body, and what every body has done, is doing, and intends to do, it is hardly necessary to state that most of the volume before us was written during Mr. Allston's short residence in Boston, a few years since, and was read in manuscript by a goodly number, and talked about and admired. But, unfortunately, the book was published in a country in which our author was a stranger, and which has never been in haste to search out our merits, or give them deserved praise, and so the work passed unnoticed. And we, here, seemed to have come to the resolution to forget our former praises, and not risk our reputation by the declaration of an opinion upon the merits of a production which came upon us in all the formality of print.*

This volume is made up of several poems, the longest of which contains between six and seven hundred lines. It was written, we believe, in what were Mr. Allston's moments of rest from his professional pursuits, at odd times, and with great rapidity. We would not set up for the author the old and impudent apology of "leisure hours", nor urge the quickness with which it was written, as an excuse for negligence in the finish. Indeed, we do not think that it discovers such negligence, but hold it as one among many instances of powerful and tasteful minds working surest and to most effect the more rapidly they move. The imagination and feelings are then excited, and there is at the same time a truth of touch which makes them turn off from what is out of form or place.

If we rightly remember, Warton has expressed doubts of Pope's right to the rank of a poet, because he never produced a work of somewhat the respectable size or form of an epic. Had he done so, it is probable that the world would not long have remained in doubt, but that he would have been set down by the greater part, as he now is by a sacred few, for a man full of strong common-sense, of infinite wit, and of a fancy sprightly, indeed, but more conceited and ingenious than strictly poetical. As we think there are better reasons, which we should be happy to state were there time, than Warton's for denying to Pope what is peculiarly and in its highest sense poetry, and should not have doubted as to Campbell's poetic genius had he lived to

* We should except a well-written notice of these poems in the Analectic Magazine.

write no more than the "Battle of the Baltic," we may be allowed to speak of what is before us as poetry, notwithstanding the shortness of its pieces.

The first poem, and that on "Eccentricity," are sketchy, and would have been improved by filling up. The others are, perhaps, as complete as the nature of their several subjects, and the sprightly narrative manner in which they are treated, would admit of. Without intending to take from their merit, we should rank them with the lighter kind of poetry. They have not the continual shifting and bustling scenes and breathless speed of Scott; nor does Mr. Allston, like Byron, stir the fiery passions within you, or carry you down into the dark and mysterious depths of the soul, moving you to and fro in their wild and fearful workings. He is not majestic and epic; nor does he make you serious, like Wordsworth, or show you a stained world, and dejected virtue, throwing a hue of thoughtfulness over brightest joys. His mind seems to have in it the glad, but gentle brightness of a star, as you look up to it, sending pure influences into your heart, and making it kind and cheerful. He paints with a particularity and truth, which show that he has looked upon nature with his own eyes, and not through those of other men. He has not only an eye for nature, but a heart too, and his imagination gives them a common language, and they talk together. As we said of the poetry of the present day, so with him, every thing has soul and sense. Never has he turned toward a morning or evening sky, but

> "The clouds were touched,
> And in their silent faces did he read
> Unutterable love."

His scenes, for the most part, are of the beautiful

kind, and lie quietly in gentle sunlight, though the clouds are sometimes seen mustering up and passing with their giant shadows, like dark spirits, over them. His imagination is cheering and youthful, and each thing has fanciful qualities and uses for him, and an imaginary as well as a real birth. His mind is creative, and, without being fantastical or extravagant, gives as many characters to objects about him as a child to his playthings. He views his scenes with a curious and exquisite eye, instilling some delicate beauty into the most common thing that springs up in them, imparting to it a gay and fairy spirit, and throwing over the whole a pure, floating glow. He searches into what is excellent and fair in creation, and, even in his satires, plays with the follies of mankind with an undisturbed gentleness of heart, and turns away from their vices, and shuts out their loathsomeness from his mind. He seems to look upon the world in the spirit in which it was made, — the spirit of love; and, though marred, to see the beauty in which it was ordained, and feel its purity through all its defilements. We cannot read any part of this book, without being ashamed of the angry and bitter passions which are so often rising up within us, nor without wishing that our own minds were as void of pride, suspicion, and hate as is all we there find, and that as clear and happy an innocence were shed over our own hearts as shines out there.

Though we have not allowed to Mr. Allston a mastery over the more intense passions, yet he seems filled with the milder feelings, and to have nothing pass through the imagination untouched by them. All that the world contains is, with him, a sentiment, and quickens the feelings and thoughts. Indeed, it seems to be peculiarly the character of his, and of most good modern poetry, to make all that surrounds us within doors, and in our daily affairs abroad, administer good to our hearts and minds, so that, if it does not make poets of us all, it will make us wider thinkers, as well as better men.

Besides this character, the poems before us sometimes run up into the wild, visionary, and magnificent; and the eye brightens and enlarges, and the spirits are lifted, as we look. All, however, partakes of the same joyous temperament; for if the scene, viewed alone, would be dark and awing, you find it in the midst of satire and humour, and the lights of these are observed playing and sparkling over it, — as in "The Paint King," and "The Two Painters." And this brings us on our way to other qualities in these poems, — the character of their satire and wit. It is usual to rank every production in verse under the head of poetry; so that poetry has come to be a matter of measure, as much as broadcloth; and, provided it be strong and smooth, the question is not asked, whether it is indeed what it passes for. As we have but one name, poetry, for all works in verse, and perhaps, were another found, the world would be for ever disputing by which each particular production should be called, it must be left to the better class of readers and the discussions of critics to give every man his rank at last. Through this indistinctness as to what constitutes poetry in its essential nature, works, from which no one would think of withholding the fullest praise as satires merely, — admitting their insight into human vices and follies, their humour, wit, closeness, and vigour of verse and thought, a certain quick fancy even, but still wanting profound sentiment and the great ideal quality of poetry, — come to be so indiscriminately praised, that it might be supposed Butler, and Swift, and Pope, and Churchill, were so many Shakspeares and Miltons, or, if differing in degree, not materially differing in poetic kind. But all good satire in verse is not necessarily high poetry too. Not that satire may not be poetry, truly and distinctively poetry, permeated by, and indeed often springing from, deep sentiment, vivid, varied, and ascending fancy, and expansive imagination. With this fancy, and with even something of this faculty of imagination, we think the satirical portion of the volume before us more or less imbued. We find it relieved by natural scenery both beautiful and grand, and the regions of the imagination travelled over to find objects for it. Rather, we should say, perhaps, the spirit of satire travels over these, — and, were it taken away, would leave behind a wild yet lovely prospect, such as the eyes of few satirists have looked upon. Yet, with all this, the satire is not made subordinate to the scenery through which it passes. There is nothing bitter or hard in it. But it appears so bright and playful, that the fairest prospects look gladder in it, and we see it flickering along the more gloomy, like a stream of moonlight, stretching a glittering and silvery line over the steely blackness of the waters, as they lie sleeping under the brown, solemn hills. It sports with the ridiculous in the good-natured manner of Gray, and avoiding, with perhaps something of a weak amiableness, the vices of the world, would correct our affectation and foibles, without wounding our spirit. There is a sensitiveness about the goodness of some men, that makes them recoil from the touch of crime, and unfits them for wrestling with the violence of the bad. But though strong men are wanted for the contest, yet the former have their uses; for they prevent our sternness turning to inhumanity and thus making our very excellences pander to our faults; and they tell us, with a timely caution to our pride, that indignation against vice is not alone virtue.

It is time for us to leave our remarks upon the general character of our author's work, and proceed to give some account of the several poems, together with extracts. The first, "The Sylphs of the Seasons," describes the scenery peculiar to each season of the year, and more particularly the different influences of each upon the mind. The poet represents himself as, tired by mental travel, betaking himself to rest, when the following vision arose: —

"Methought within a desert cave,
Cold, dark, and solemn as the grave,
I suddenly awoke.
It seemed of sable Night the cell,
Where, save when from the ceiling fell
An oozing drop, her silent spell
No sound had ever broke.

"There motionless I stood alone,
Like some strange monument of stone
Upon a barren wild;
Or like (so solid and profound
The darkness seemed that walled me round)
A man that 's buried under ground,
Where pyramids are piled."

He is soon carried by the magic of his dream — and dreams often outdo the magic of waking wonder-workers — from this cave, into a castle upon a mountain plain, below which a region is spread over with scenery of every season.

"And now I paced a bright saloon,
That seemed illumined by the moon,
So mellow was the light.
The walls with jetty darkness teemed,
While down them crystal columns streamed,
And each a mountain torrent seemed,
High-flashing through the night."

In the midst is a double throne, about which are grouped four damsels of Fairy race, representing the four Seasons. He is addressed by one of them, and informed that the throne is his, and that he is to rule "o'er all the varying year." But he is first to choose one of those before him as the partner of his throne, since, man being dissatisfied with their "varied toil," the plan is to be rectified by art. They then, in turn, beginning with Spring, sing to him their several charms of person and mind. We extract the following, though not peculiar to any season, as new and wild.

"Then, wrapped in night, the scudding bark,
(That seemed, self-poised amid the dark,
Through upper air to leap,)
Beheld, from thy most fearful height,
The rapid dolphin's azure light
Cleave, like a living meteor bright,
The darkness of the deep."

And the following, as showing the careful eye of the poet, searching amidst the beauties of nature, and bringing them out, new and fresh, and setting them distinctly before us.

"Or, brooding o'er some forest rill,
Fringed with the early daffodil,

And quivering maiden-hair,
When thou hast marked the dusky bed,
With leaves and water-rust o'erspread,
That seemed an amber light to shed
On all was shadowed there."

Spring then speaks of her cheerful influences upon the mind, in that tone of sentiment through which we have said nature is always seen by our author.

" 'T was I to these the magic gave,
That made thy heart, a willing slave,
To gentle nature bend ;
And taught thee how, with tree and flower,
And whispering gale, and dropping shower,
In converse sweet to pass the hour,
As with an early friend ;

" That 'mid the noon-tide sunny haze
Did in thy languid bosom raise
The raptures of the boy ;
When, waked as if to second birth,
Thy soul through every pore looked forth,
And gazed upon the beauteous earth
With myriad eyes of joy."

She ceases.

" And next the Sylph of Summer fair ;
The while her crisped, golden hair
Half veiled her sunny eyes."

She says to him, —

" And then, as grew thy languid mood,
To some embowering, silent wood
I led thy careless way ;

Where high from tree to tree in air
Thou saw'st the spider swing her snare,
So bright! — as if, entangled there,
The sun had left a ray;

"Or lured thee to some beetling steep
To mark the deep and quiet sleep
That wrapped the tarn below;
And mountain blue and forest green
Inverted on its plane serene,
Dim gleaming through the filmy sheen
That glazed the painted show;

"Perchance, to mark the fisher's skiff
Swift from beneath some shadowy cliff
Dart, like a gust of wind;
And, as she skimmed the sunny lake,
In many a playful wreath her wake
Far-trailing, like a silvery snake,
With sinuous length behind."

Then comes a description more large and elevating, and, as we have before observed, giving to the real an imaginary character and life. This fanciful view of things may be perceived nearly throughout the poem.

"Or if the moon's effulgent form
The passing clouds of sudden storm
In quick succession veil;
Vast serpents now, their shadows glide,
And, coursing now the mountain's side,
A band of giants huge, they stride
O'er hill, and wood, and dale."

She ends; —

"And now, in accents deep and low,
Like voice of fondly-cherished woe,
The Sylph of Autumn sad."

After summing up the wealth of that season, she tells him, —

"With these I may not urge my suit,
Of Summer's patient toil the fruit,
For mortal purpose given;
Nor may it fit my sober mood
To sing of sweetly murmuring flood,
Or dyes of many-coloured wood,
That mock the bow of heaven.

"But know, 't was mine the secret power
That waked thee at the midnight hour
In bleak November's reign;
'T was I the spell around thee cast,
When thou didst hear the hollow blast
In murmurs tell of pleasures past,
That ne'er would come again;

"And led thee, when the storm was o'er,
To hear the sullen ocean roar,
By dreadful calm oppressed;
Which still, though not a breeze was there,
Its mountain-billows heaved in air,
As if a living thing it were,
That strove in vain for rest."

Who, that has stood on the sea-shore at such a time, has not felt the struggle, working by sympathy, at his own heart, and an impatient longing to know something of the restless spirit moving in the depths of the sea?

Autumn speaks to us of the passing away of all things; and as she throws a sombre light over a decaying world, carries up our thoughts to one of unstained and lasting joys.

"And last the Sylph of Winter spake."

We extract the following: —

> "When thou, beneath the clear, blue sky,
> So calm no cloud was seen to fly,
> Hast gazed on snowy plain,
> Where nature slept so pure and sweet,
> She seemed a corse in winding-sheet,
> Whose happy soul had gone to meet
> The blest angelic train."

How purified does the world appear, as she then spreads it out to us, when not even the dim shadow of a naked tree stains the whiteness of the endless extent of snow, and the innocence of heaven seems here!

We will give one more picture of busy and creative fancy.

> "Or seen at dawn of eastern light
> The frosty toil of Fays by night
> On pane of casement clear,
> Where bright the mimic glaciers shine,
> And Alps, with many a mountain pine,
> And armed knights from Palestine
> In winding march appear."

The Sylphs cease, and the poet stands motionless and undecided.

> "When, lo! there poured a flood of light
> So fiercely on my aching sight,
> I fell beneath the vision bright,
> And with the pain awoke."

The next in course is the story of "The Two Painters." We trust that we shall not be charged with bestowing over-praise, when we say, that, in easy and familiar narrative style, it reminds us of the tales of Swift, Prior, and Gay. Here we find satire sparkling over poetic imagery, and blending with scenes wild and picturesque. It is written in ridicule of the attempt to reach perfection in one excellence in the art of painting, to the contempt and neglect of every other; and attributes this false and narrow endeavour to pride and sloth. It is set forth in the Shades of two lately departed painters, the one a *colourist*, the other a painter of *mind*.

"Once on a time in Charon's wherry,
Two painters met, on Styx's ferry."

The jealousy and enmity, but too common among brother artists, soon break out into noisy dispute. They are called to order by Charon, who tells them that they are to be brought to the court of Minos.

"'T is he will try
Your jealous cause, and prove at once,
That only dunce can hate a dunce.

"Thus checked, in sullen mood they sped,
Nor more on either side was said;
Nor aught the dismal silence broke,
Save only when the boatman's stroke
Deep-whizzing through the wave was heard,
And now and then a spectre-bird,
Low-cowering, with a hungry scream,
For spectre-fishes in the stream.

"Now midway passed, the creaking oar
Is heard upon the fronting shore;
Where, thronging round in many a band,
The curious ghosts beset the strand.

Now suddenly the boat they 'spy,
Like gull diminished in the sky;
And now, like cloud of dusky white,
Slow sailing o'er the deep of night,
The sheeted group within the bark
Is seen amid the billows dark.
Anon the keel with grating sound
They hear upon the pebbly ground,
And now, with kind, officious hand,
They help the ghostly crew to land."

We know of few passages which open such a scene as Mr. Allston has here placed before us; — the desolate cry of the spectre-birds, — the boat just visible, — the sheeted dead, in "dusky white," seated silent and motionless within it, — and all shadowy, and dimly seen through the gloom. The air breathes upon us as from another world, and we pause amidst the awful and unreal.

Upon landing, they are accosted by a patriot; — a rake, who asks, "What think they of a buck that's dead?" — philosophers, poets, and others, inquiring what characters they still hold among the living, and laying open the motives of their conduct when on earth.

The two painters are then called up for trial, and Da Vinci's shade is appointed by Minos to preside on the occasion. Each sets forth his own excellences with no little vanity, and speaks of the other with no less contempt. They at last request that their works may be brought, to determine their respective claims to superiority.

"Such fair demand, the judge replied,
Could not with justice be denied.
Good Merc'ry, hence! I fly, my Lord,
The courier said. And, at the word,

High-bounding, wings his airy flight
So swift, his form eludes the sight;
Nor aught is seen his course to mark,
Save when, athwart the region dark,
His brazen helm is spied afar,
Bright-trailing like a falling star.

" And now for minutes ten there stole
A silence deep o'er every soul, —
When, lo ! again before them stands
The courier's self, with empty hands.
Why, how is this ? exclaimed the twain ;
Where are the *pictures*, Sir ? Explain !
Good Sirs, replied the God of Post,
I scarce had reached the other coast,
When Charon told me, one he ferried
Informed him they were dead and buried ;
Then bade me hither haste and say,
Their ghosts were now upon the way.
In mute amaze the painters stood.
But soon upon the Stygian flood,
Behold ! the spectre-pictures float,
Like rafts, behind the towing boat ;
Now reached the shore, in close array,
Like armies drilled in Homer's day,
When marching on to meet the foe,
By bucklers hid from top to toe,
They move along the dusky fields,
A grisly troop of painted shields ;
And now, arrived, in order fair,
A gallery huge they hang in air.

" The ghostly crowd with gay surprise
Began to rub their stony eyes ;
Such pleasant lounge, they all averred,
None saw since he had been interred ;

And thus, like connoisseurs on earth,
Began to weigh the pictures' worth."

The pictures are described, and then criticized by the ghostly connoisseurs, and in a most humorous and diverting manner are their faults and blunders represented. The anachronism as to Socrates and Galen, and the awkward meeting of turban, mantle, and satin breeches, which had been strangers to each other all their lives, are amusingly given.

"And pray, inquired another spectre,
What Mufti 's that at pious lecture ?
That 's Socrates, condemned to die ;
He next, in sable, standing by,
Is Galen, come to save his friend,
If possible, from such an end ;
The other figures, grouped around,
His scholars, wrapped in woe profound.
And am I like to this portrayed ?
Exclaimed the Sage's smiling Shade.
Good Sir, I never knew before
That I a Turkish turban wore,
Or mantle hemmed with golden stitches,
Much less a pair of satin breeches ;
But as for him in sable clad,
Though wondrous kind, 't was rather mad
To visit one like me forlorn,
So long before himself was born."

We quote the following of Alexander. It is rather long for an extract, and, in some parts, may be offensive to weak appetites ; but it is done with a spirit and truth which will make it relished by healthier constitutions.

"And what 's the next ? inquired a third ;
A jolly blade, upon my word !

'T is Alexander, Philip's son,
Lamenting o'er his battles won;
That, now his mighty toils are o'er,
The world has naught to conquer more.
At which, forth stalking from the host,
Before them stood the Hero's ghost.
Was that, said he, my earthly form,
The genius of the battle-storm?
From top to toe the figure 's Dutch!
Alas, my friend, had I been such,
Had I that fat and meaty skull,
Those bloated cheeks, and eyes so dull,
That drivelling mouth, and bottle nose,
Those shambling legs, and gouty toes, —
Thus formed to snore throughout the day,
And eat and drink the night away, —
I ne'er had felt the feverish flame
That caused my bloody thirst for fame,
Nor madly claimed immortal birth,
Because the vilest brute on earth;
And O, I 'd not been doomed to hear,
Still whizzing in my blistered ear,
The curses deep, in damning peals,
That rose from 'neath my chariot-wheels,
When I along the embattled plain
With furious triumph crushed the slain;
I should not thus be doomed to see,
In every shape of agony,
The victims of my cruel wrath,
For ever dying, strew my path;
The grinding teeth, the lips awry,
The inflated nose, the starting eye,
The mangled bodies writhing round,
Like serpents, on the bloody ground;
I should not thus for ever seem
A charnel-house, and scent the stream

Of black, fermenting, putrid gore,
Rank oozing through each burning pore;
Behold, as on a dungeon wall,
The worms upon my body crawl,
The which, if I would brush away,
Around my clammy fingers play,
And twining fast with many a coil,
In loathsome sport, my labour foil."

We have only room for the sentence of the judge.

"Then know, ye vain and foolish pair!
Your doom is fixed a yoke to bear,
Like beasts on earth; and, thus in tether,
Five centuries to paint together.
If, thus by mutual labours joined,
Your jarring souls should be combined,
The faults of each the other mending,
The powers of both harmonious blending;
Great Jove, perhaps, in gracious vein,
May send your souls on earth again;
Yet there One only Painter be;
For thus the eternal Fates decree:
One Leg alone shall never run,
Nor two Half-Painters make but One."

We shall make but one or two extracts from the poem on Eccentricity. In the attempt to be striking, the characters are seldom overdrawn, but are such as will come up in the memory of any man who has been an observer of the ridiculous and affected in human nature. The amateur *in halters*, we believe, is taken from fact. We shall quote the first character that presents itself.

"Behold, loud-rattling like a thousand drums,
Eccentric Hal, the child of Nature, comes!

Of nature once,—but *now* he acts a part,
And Hal is now the full-grown boy of art.
In youth's pure spring his high, impetuous soul
Nor custom owned, nor fashion's vile control.
By Truth impelled where beckoning Nature led,
Through life he moved with firm, elastic tread;
But soon the world, with wonder-teeming eyes,
His manners mark, and goggle with surprise.
'He 's wondrous strange!' exclaims each gaping clod,
'A wondrous genius, for he 's wondrous odd!'
Where'er he goes, there goes before his—fame,
And courts and taverns echo round his name;
Till, fairly knocked by admiration down,
The petted monster cracks his wondrous crown.
No longer now to simple nature true,
He studies only to be oddly new;
Whate'er he does, whate'er he deigns to say,
Must all be said and done the oddest way;
Nay, e'en in dress eccentric as in thought,
His wardrobe seems by Lapland witches wrought,
Himself by goblins in a whirlwind dressed,
With rags of clouds from Hecla's stormy crest."

And again.

"Nor less renowned whom stars inveterate doom
To smiles eternal, or eternal gloom;
For what 's a *character* save one confined
To some unchanging sameness of the mind;
To some strange, fixed monotony of mien,
Or dress for ever brown, for ever green?

"A sample comes. Observe his sombre face,
Twin-born with Death, without his brother's grace!
No joy in mirth his soul perverted knows,
Whose only joy to tell of others' woes.
A fractured limb, a conflagrating fire,
A name or fortune lost, his tongue inspire.

From house to house where'er misfortunes press,
Like Fate, he roams, and revels in distress;
In every ear with dismal boding moans, —
A walking register of sighs and groans!"

The draught of the following character is after Pope's happiest manner, and sketched with much of his freedom and accuracy of touch.

"But who is he, that sweet, obliging youth?
He looks the picture of ingenuous truth.
O, that 's his antipode, of courteous race,
The man of bows and ever-smiling face.
Why Nature made him, or for what designed,
Never he knew, nor ever sought to find,
Till Cunning came, blest harbinger of ease!
And kindly whispered, "Thou wert born to please."
Roused by the news, behold him now expand,
Like beaten gold, and glitter o'er the land.
Well stored with nods and sly approving winks,
Now first with this and now with that he thinks;
Howe'er opposing, still assents to each,
And claps a dovetail to each booby's speech.
At random thus for all, for none, he lives,
Profusely lavish though he nothing gives;
The world he roves, as living but to show
A friendless man without a single foe;
From bad to good, to bad from good, to run,
And find a character by seeking none."

We must express the hope that Mr. Allston will write no more "didactic poems," as they are styled. To be sure, no man would part with those of Cowper, for instance; yet, for the most part, they are apt to act in way of restraint upon the invention, and to shut it up from plot, and varied incidents, and freshly created worlds. Certainly, an intellect like Mr. Allston's, delighting in the fanciful, sacrifices its best powers in this lecture-room of the Muses. They should be left for men of the character of Queen Anne's time, who were formed to shine in such works, and were little at home with thoughts and images belonging to minds of our author's cast. We do not object to the satire and character-drawing; but we should always be glad to see them enlivened by incidents, with something of dramatic activity, and placed in scenes as new and poetical as those in which we find "The Two Painters."

"The Paint-King" is a mock romantic tale. Unlike most other works of the kind, it is crowded with imagery, sometimes almost sublime, and then delicate and beautiful. "The Paint-King" carries off the "fair Ellen," for the purpose of grinding her into paint, with which to produce a true likeness of the beautiful queen of the Fairies, and thereby win her good graces. It is so worked together in the narrative, that we hardly know how to take out any part of it. We will, however, give the carrying off of Ellen.

"She turned and beheld on each shoulder a wing.
'Oh heaven!' cried she, 'who art thou?'
From the roof to the ground did his fierce answer ring,
As, frowning, he thundered, 'I am the PAINT-KING!
And mine, lovely maid, art thou now!'

"Then high from the ground did the grim monster lift
The loud-screaming maid like a blast;
And he sped through the air like a meteor swift,
While the clouds, wandering by him, did fearfully drift
To the right and the left as he passed.

"Now suddenly sloping his hurricane flight,
With an eddying whirl he descends;

The air all below him becomes black as night,
And the ground where he treads, as if moved with affright,
Like the surge of the Caspian bends.

" 'I am here!' said the Fiend, and he thundering knocked
At the gates of a mountainous cave;
The gates open flew, as by magic unlocked,
While the peaks of the mount, reeling to and fro, rocked,
Like an island of ice on the wave."

He is then represented sitting in his cave, which is thus described.

" On the skull of a Titan, that Heaven defied,
Sat the Fiend, like the grim Giant Gog,
While aloft to his mouth a huge pipe he applied,
Twice as big as the Eddystone Lighthouse, descried
As it looms through an easterly fog.

" And anon, as he puffed the vast volumes, were seen,
In horrid festoons on the wall,
Legs and arms, heads and bodies emerging between,
Like the drawing-room grim of the Scotch Sawney Beane,
By the Devil dressed out for a ball."

He tells her to what she is doomed, and then sets about his work like an old artist, and having nearly finished the picture, —

" Then, stamping his foot, did the monster exclaim,
'Now I brave, cruel Fairy, thy scorn!'
When lo! from a chasm wide yawning there came
A light, tiny chariot of rose-coloured flame,
By a team of ten glow-worms upborne.

" Enthroned in the midst on an emerald bright,
Fair Geraldine sat without peer;

Her robe was a gleam of the first blush of light,
And her mantle the fleece of a noon-cloud white,
And a beam of the moon was her spear."

After the Fairy has appeared before him and reminded him of his former failures, he proceeds in his work; but when about painting the pupils, he suddenly discovers that he had neglected grinding up the eyes of Ellen, and, looking round, sees them in the jaws of a mouse, which bounds off with them.

"'I am lost!' said the Fiend, and he fell like a stone;
Then rising the Fairy in ire,
With a touch of her finger she loosened her zone,
(While the limbs on the wall gave a terrible groan,)
And she swelled to a column of fire."

She smites him with her wand, hurls him down a chasm, and restores Ellen to life. The painting of the picture is described with the skill of an artist, and with great beauty.

This is followed by two short poems, the first, "To a Lady who lamented that she had never been in Love"; the other, to one "who spoke slightingly of Poets." There are the same unceasing activity of fancy and the same delicate sentiment in these, that we find in the preceding poems. But we must not quote any further.

The volume closes with about half a dozen sonnets, and three or four poems in the ballad style. Of the former we would mention particularly "The Falling Groups, in the Last Judgement," and "The Three Angels before the Tent of Abraham." The remaining poems are written with much simplicity and nature. But there are so many readers who are apt to mistake simplicity for childishness, that we will not disturb them here by bringing up the subject of ballad simplicity, but content ourselves with leaving Mr. Allston to the judgement of those who are conversant with such delicate matters.

We should have been more particular in our remarks upon the several extracts, had we not been so full in our observations upon the general character of this volume. Besides, it would have looked a little too officious, to be continually pointing out obvious beauties.

The volume before us is clearly original in its character. We do not find in it imitations of the style, or borrowing of the circumstances, situations, or images of other authors. Many of its subjects are new, and all are marked by the peculiar cast of our author's mind. To this very novelty may be, in a measure, attributed its want of popularity. We are surrounded by a multitude of critics here, who set down every thing new and peculiar, and not backed by authority, as in bad taste, and extravagant. Such critics are to poets what connoisseurs (a troublesome set of gentlemen, with whom, no doubt, our author is well acquainted) are to artists; who gaze upon pictures all their lives, without its once occurring to their minds, that, to be a judge of paintings, one should study nature, from which they are taken. So with our critics: if a work comes out unlike what has been seen before, they have no mode of determining its merits; for their models are no longer guides. Never having learned that combinations from nature are endless, and that they may be given in as many and various views as the hills that break her surface, they seem to be governed by the notion, that their few models had taken from her all that was worthy our notice, and that what is left should be thrown aside as worthless; just as if all that is good or beautiful in creation were to be grasped by a few feeble mortals, and not rather to remain the study of the beings placed in the midst of it, to the end of time. Surely all is the well-ordered and consistent design of One Being, who, as He has given infinite breadth and variety to the mind, so has He spread before it a scene as wide and changing; and to set up rules discordant with this plan is bad philosophy, (we might almost say, false religion,) and paltry taste, narrowing our observation, and weakening the constantly renewing vigour of the intellectual powers.

Mr. Allston's verse is easy, and reads as if it were produced with unusual facility; and his language, too, is good. Yet we think that both would have been richer, had he made the old master-poets more his study in early life. But while the poets of the present times have done well in freeing themselves of much that was introduced at the Restoration, we hardly look for the return of that affluent, poetic diction, that rich and varied tone and deep harmony, which, with its individual varieties, marked the works of Spenser, Shakspeare, and Milton.

As we are of the number of those who saw most of these poems in manuscript, we may be allowed to express our regret at the alterations made in the publishing. So far as we recollect, though few, they are for the worse. The "gushing fount of day," in the description of the cave in the "Seasons," certainly is not an improvement upon "sunny thread." And in that beautiful image,

"Yon bird that trims his purple [sunny] wings,
As on the bending bow he swings,"

purple is but a poor substitute for the original epithet. Again, in "The Paint-King," the change to "Ovidian art" is coldly classical and out of keeping amidst the warm, natural English character of the volume. And so of the rest. We were sorry at not finding in "Eccentricity" one or two passages, which we thought amongst its most beautiful when we read the manuscript. But this between ourselves and the author, — who must not be offended at our laying down his book, and taking up his loose papers, but put our overstepping the province of reviewers to the interest which we take, not only in his book, but in him also, deepened by the reflection that he is now a stranger in a foreign land. We will venture the conjecture, that the alterations were made at the suggestion of some fond friend, of good intentions, perhaps, but not of so good judgement.

Now that we have gone through with our notice of the few faults of this volume, we would advise our readers to make themselves acquainted with it. They will find it worthy their pride, in the general poverty of literature in our country. It remains for us to thank our author for what he has done for our good name, and to hope from him still more. May he find the strangers by whom he is surrounded as fair, and void of prejudices, as is his own mind, and may his solitary labours be cheered by that fame which he so well deserves.

EDGEWORTHS' READINGS ON POETRY.*

THE character of different periods of society varies almost as much as the seasons, and perhaps to similar uses. It has its times of darkness and storms, when the violent passions are abroad, and the milder affections are beaten down and lie broken and perishing. But the seeds of good feelings do not decay, nor do the fast and strong roots of principle turn to rottenness. The gloom passes off, and the attachments of the heart shoot up in young and healthful hopefulness, and the sterner virtues, that had stood out in the stir and violence, alone and naked, are once more seen clothed in honour. In time, all changes again; the tender die, and the honours of the strong fade and fall off, and all is left bare, and calm, and cold. Men undergo such changes in passing through the different stages of society, that the last of the same nation become the opposite of the first. Where they were once daring and hardy, we now find them cautious and enervated; and where were those who sprang up in the warmth of the feelings, and grew vigorous in the strife and shake of the

---

* From the North American Review for 1818.
Readings on Poetry. By RICHARD LOVELL EDGEWORTH and MARIA EDGEWORTH. Boston: Wells & Lilly. 1816.

passions, there we now see men slow to be moved, and quick to calculate, reasoners in their love, and prudent in their hate.

These alterations are not only seen abroad in the world, but run also into the pursuits of our minds. Besides holding an influence over our daily conduct, our studies and retired reflections are guided by them; and these, again, send us forth among men, tempered and cast anew.

Thus mutually operating, in an age of simple and natural manners, there was an absence of artificiality in most of its literature. You seemed to be looking into the very minds of its authors, and even in their conceits there was an air of good-nature and honest playfulness, which put you at ease, and begat a kind of companionable acquaintance. You never stood upon ceremony; nor was an author's book a court-dress for his thoughts and feelings. So nigh did he come to plain truth in descriptions of outward things, that, instead of feeling you were looking at nature through another's eyes, you forgot you were not with him amidst the scenes he was describing, — you felt on your hand the coolness of the dark-green, polished leaves as you caught at them bending to the "breathing wind," and heard

> "Soft rumbling brookes, that gentle slumber drew."

With a change in literature went along a change of manners; and with the natural, and vigorous, and chivalrous, and marvellous in books, was laid by a marked and free conduct in life. Then came profession for sincerity, the heartlessness of wit for the feeling of genius, and an ingenious and curious finishing of forced thoughts, and an artificial ornamenting of dim images, for strong and simple reflections, and figures as distinct as those of nature, and attired in her beauties. Men at last grew tired of this excess of artifice, for every thing they saw or touched was tarnished with its paltry daubings till the senses ached at it; its mannered trickery became stale and common, and its faded tawdriness was, in the end, thrown into a corner, a fashionless cast-off.

To this has succeeded a time of dull tranquillity, a solemn parade of reason, holding boastful dominion over passions too feeble for rebellion, and laying restrictions upon the wanderings of earth-bound and sluggish imaginations. Instinctive actions are holden dangerous; we are made mere reasoning machines, unmoved by natural impulses; and instead of quickening the growth of the fancy and imagination along with that of the understanding, these are cut off as profitless shoots which would overtop and dwarf the judgement. In our new-gotten zeal for the useful, we overlook our mixed condition; not considering that every sinless quality of the heart, and every faculty of the mind, is bestowed on us for good, that the romantic may give a warmth and action to feelings dulled in the tame business of the world, and that reachings after qualities higher than our common natures may shed a pure exaltation of spirit over us, which will brighten and make glad the humblest actions and relations of our lives. — We are freshened and restored by the marvellous; and looking on finely touched beauties opens us to innocent cheerfulness and a tenderness of heart, which keep kindred movement with all about us. This gives an exhilarating variety to society, which makes us better pleased with each other, and happier in ourselves. Life, it is true, is crowded with homely duties; and far-reaching calculations, and untiring labour, must procure and hold its comforts. But, surely, this is not an age marked by the want of such virtues, nor are our sins those of over-wrought imagination, or of too softened sentiment. The armour of knights-errant may rust by the wall for all us; nor do we hear of such lovers as blessed the days of Mrs. Lucy Hutchinson, when one became enamoured of the mere description of a woman, and sighed out his life kissing her little footprint on Richmond Hill.

This state of things would not so much alarm the lovers of the natural, were it confined to "grown folks"; for nature has a self-restoring power, and would grow up and spread again with the generation that is coming on, and the mingling of unforced with cultivated beauties would come to be loved in things and characters. But we have foreseen and provided against this change. We have not only piled system upon system for our own defence, but our children, too, are training up for the contest. In their dwarfish and tender infancy they are clad in the heavy and hard panoply of the understanding, as if they were surrounded by outraging passions, wild and gloomy superstitions, murderous giants, and fiendish ogres. A severer contest and a meaner servitude threaten them, — cunning, watchful selfishness, petty envyings, and, even in their better deeds, an impertinent intermeddling with the rights of others, an ostentatious show of charities, and a self-consequence in doing good.

Amidst the multitude of mankind, it is the mean vices that are most numerous and have freest play, that enter too deeply into men, and are too thoroughly ingrained to be reasoned out. Opposite passions must be brought into the contest, — self-sacrificing love, ardent longings after far-off excellences, and all glimpses of forms and undefined creations that live and move in the beautiful and glorious spectacles of warmed imaginations. These need not bear down or harm the judgement; but in proud subjection may give it strength and widen its dominions. The mind that sometimes passes out from the commonness of life into ideal wonders will come back better fitted to understand the world, and with a deeper relish for the repose of reality.

But, by the present system, the strong passions of children are to be cut off, no high excitements are to be set in their way, the little creatures are scarcely allowed to feel, until they can explain why and how they are moved; and they are taught to analyze their passions, till these are wasted away in the process. We seem to forget that, after all our attempts, they must grow up the subjects of some kind of sensations, and that if we root out the great, we are only making way for the petty feelings; that the reason will be perverted by selfishness, if it is not sometimes lighted up by a chivalrous generosity, and that untaught indignation may often prove as sure a safeguard against vice as laboured reason. Their light emotions and excursive fancies are taught to pause, till all things in connection with them are vainly attempted to be explained and understood; their just kindling ardour is put out, lest it should throw a false glare over objects; and what was intended to strengthen and give eternal freshness to character is destroyed, lest it should warm into existence, along with all the good it might bring, some short-lived errours of early years.

We have become too officious in our helps to children; we leave not enough to the workings of nature and to impressions and tints too exquisite and delicate for any hands but hers; but, with a vain and vulgar ignorance, distort the character she was silently and slowly moulding into beauty, till it is formed to our narrow and false taste. Anxious lest the clearness of their reason should be dimmed, their minds are never left to work their own way through the obscure; but ever-burning lights are held up before them. They are not indulged in the conjectural, but all is anticipated and over-done. We do not enough consider, that, oftentimes, the very errours into which they fall, through a want of thorough knowledge of what they see or read, bring the invention into action, and thus give a life to the mind which will survive when those errours are removed and forgotten. Children may reason well, as far as their knowledge carries them along, and their reason may still preside over what their imagination supplies.

An over-anxiety to make of babies little matter-of-fact men, and unbreeched philosophers, will not add much to their sum of knowledge in after life, and nothing to that faculty which teaches them to consider and determine for themselves, and begets that independent wisdom without which their heaped-up knowledge is but an encumbrance. A child now "learns by heart" how a shoe is made, from the flaying of an ox for the leather to the punching the last hole, and can give the best of reasons for its being so made, when it had much better be chasing a rainbow. Such a system may make inquisitive, but not wide-ranging minds. It kills the poetry of our character without enlarging our philosophy, and will hardly make us worthier members of society, or give us the humble compensation of turning out better mechanics.

We do not mean by this that those faculties and acquisitions which rank as the merely useful should not be cultivated with care; but that they should be mingled with and partially concealed amidst the growth of higher powers. For it is not those alone that send a healing influence up through society; but the latter, too, shine out over the world, and in their splendour are warmth, and life, and joy. Poetry is no less necessary to society than is well-ordered industry; and feelings akin to it, in the lowest of our race, will lift up their thoughts and purify their hearts. Society should be like the earth about us, where the beautiful, the grand, the humble, the useful, lie spread out, and running into each other; where, indeed, for the most part, so beautiful is the useful, that we almost forget its uses in its beauty.

We have been led to these remarks, by associating whatever Miss Edgeworth writes, not only with her system of education, but with the little models formed on her system, and which may be seen in the families of her admirers. Children may be met with every day very knowing in the mechanic arts and the chemistry of cookery. The principles of boiling a tea-kettle, making tea, and making bread and butter, (which they should be eating contentedly in silence,) are very orderly detailed. We do not mean to throw upon our author all the errours of her disciples; but it will be gathered from what we have said, that we think she has serious errours of her own.

She appears to us to have considered society too narrowly; to have allowed too little to the differences of conditions; to have confined herself too closely to but a part of our faculties; and not to have attended enough to the varieties of individual character. We do not say that she has inculcated the doctrine, that all minds and dispositions should be reduced to one rule, but that she has not denied it with sufficient distinctness. She should have urged the language of her great master, Locke, — "Every one's natural genius should be carried as far as it could; but to attempt the putting another upon him will be but labour in vain; and what is so plastered on will at best sit but untowardly, and have always hanging to it the ungracefulness of constraint and affectation."

It is time that we said something upon the book before us. It is entitled "Readings on Poetry," not because the commentaries go to explain the poetical character of the text, except in a few places, and in those most lamely executed, but because they give the meaning of certain words which happen to be found in the poetical extracts. It is just the reverse of Johnson's quarto Dictionary, where words are defined, and the quotations follow as illustrations. Here you have an extract from Gray or Wharton, and then a long string of definitions, for the most part of very common words, in a truly unpoetical and lexicographical style. It would, no doubt, be quite as entertaining, and a little more instructive, to have been turned at once into the Doctor's large squares. We could then have learned the signification of most of the words of our language, besides having a wide and varied range of very pleasant reading of the best poetry of our tongue. We are quite sincere in this, and do advise all anxious parents, who are alarmed at the thought of their children reading books every word of which they may not fully comprehend, to begin with the first word in the dictionary, and so go through. The book then is in their hands, ready, in its proper place, to explain any word in the quotation of which the "little reader" knows not the meaning; and the parent may escape the most puzzling of all undertakings, that of defining.

Indeed, the book before us can be of but little use in the way intended, as the words explained are few in number, and, for the most part, the commonest in the language; while there are thousands passed over quite as important, and less familiar. Besides, by taking Dr. Johnson's quarto instead of the "Readings on Poetry," a child will avoid having its taste perverted by such wretched criticisms as now and then occur in the work before us, and, what is tending to the same evil, will escape the mistaken idea, that, because it has read at the bottom of a passage what is meant by "cleave," "disdain," "cheer," "victim," "contest," "apprentice," &c., &c., it has a more distinct notion of the *poetry* it has been over. It is true that this book goes a little further, and has wisely turned certain passages into prose, to deepen, we suppose, the poetical impression upon young minds. But, unluckily, they are, for the most part, passages which did not need clearing up, and are quite as intelligible in the original as in the renderings.

It is the destructive effect which the plan of our authors must have upon the very subject they are attempting to make clear and familiar to children, which has led us to notice their work. What they call elucidations of poetry have little more to do with that than with prose; and all which is ethereal and peculiar to poetry must be lost in the dull and clumsy endeavour to prevent a few misconceptions which time would do away, and to cram down knowledge which the even course of things would bring in.

To stop a child in the midst of its pleasing sensations, to give a long account of "quacks," may teach it something else; but will never give it, what, we take for granted, poetry is read for, some poetry of mind. If this work had taken for its examples merely plain sense prose, though we might even then have doubted the utility of its plan, we should have had a less abuse to complain of.

Miss Edgeworth, in her preface, (we presume it is hers, being almost the only well-written part of the book,) argues against what she calls "transcendental metaphysicians, who would have us believe that matters of taste and sentiment are not cognizable by the laws, or amenable to the tribunal, of reason." This doctrine, we believe, died with the Della Cruscans; and Miss Edgeworth carries on a warfare with beings of her own raising up. We have thought all the great powers of the mind to be united in poetry; and Coleridge, the most tasteful and acute of critics, has shown us that the deepest metaphysics are involved in the study of the imagination and the powers of words.

Miss Edgeworth has sometimes reasoned well enough, but, notwithstanding, has given a helping hand to the putting together of a foolish book. She seems not to have considered that a dictionary appended to a poem, and deformed versions of poetry into prose, do not constitute an analysis or reasoning upon works of taste and poetry, — that a true knowledge of poetic words is not to be obtained from Johnson or Entick, but is infused into us with untold associations, and grows up in us with our readings, and feelings, and reflections, — that to have images floating before us in clear visibility needs not a prismatical arrangement of rays, but that they look more beautiful in the natural sun of a poetical mind, and that if they do not always stand out as distinctly to the eye of a child as in broad day, but lurk a little dim and distant, they yet appear like the objects in Milton's moonlight, which, "shadowy, sets forth the forms of things."

Miss Edgeworth would have her children clear-minded, sound reasoners. But she seems to have forgotten that they must first have imagination, a poetical sense, and the unnumbered and defineless connections and feelings which make up that wonder of creation, that being of this and of other worlds, a poet, before they can understand his character or works. Perhaps there is not a more pitiable object, setting aside the vicious, than what is often called a common-sense man, descanting on the productions of the imagination.

It would be childish not to acknowledge to the full Miss Edgeworth's uncommon powers. But that her mind is highly and characteristically poetical may at least be doubted; nor will her fondness for the sensible, cool, and formally stately Akenside go far to do away our opinion.

This book is made up of extracts from Shakspeare, Milton, Pope, Parnell, Gray, and Wharton, which are treated in the manner we have already mentioned. It is quite impossible to judge from it of what age it was intended its readers should be. Words and passages are laboriously explained, which a child five years old could understand, while more difficult ones are passed over. Some of the notes, again, require the matured knowledge and judgement of twenty years to comprehend them. A child, we fear, will be more sadly puzzled with the commentary than with the text. It is a book for which every one, to use the words of the authors, "must be too young, or too old." If too young, let it be laid aside at present; if too old, let it be laid aside for ever.

It is time to proceed to extracts.

"'Him portioned maids, apprenticed orphans, blest,
The young who labour, and the old who rest.' — *Man of Ross.*

"An apprentice is so called, from French and Latin words that mean to learn. Boys are put out apprentices when they are strong enough to learn trades; they are usually bound to their masters for seven years, sometimes only for five, during which time the master is required to feed and clothe the boy, and teach him his trade; the boy and the master are mutually bound in writing to perform their respective parts of the contract. If either of them act wrong, it is in the power of a justice of the peace to oblige them to fulfil their contract.

"During the first years of the bargain the master suffers a loss in feeding and clothing the young boy; but towards the end of the seven or five years, the boy's work is not only sufficient to pay for his clothes and diet, but his work becomes profitable to his master. It is obvious, that the time which an apprentice ought to serve should be different in different trades."

We promise not to make another extract of such length. We have done it this once to give our readers some notion of what are "Readings on Poetry."

To say nothing more about the poetical effect of notes like this, the utter absurdity of the attempt is too obvious to require much remark. The boy who did not stay to consider whether he understood the lines he was repeating before he went over this note, will now strut in the full assurance that he knows all about them, and, the next time there are strangers by, will take care to explain them to his little sister. Yet the poor thing is nearly as deep in ignorance as before; for what is the signification of the word "portioned," and what, indeed, does the note mean? "What is meant, papa, by a boy's being bound to his master? they don't tie him to a big man for seven years, do they? And what is a justice of the peace? I have heard of such folks, but don't know what kind of people they are."

There is no absurdity in supposing a child puzzled by such doubts, who is ignorant of the word the meaning of which it is here attempted to explain, or of others which we shall presently find experimented upon. The folly is in confounding the child in our eagerness to hurry in knowledge, which would be acquired in due proportion with the growth of the mind's powers, and when he can understand distinctly what his green and tender faculties can now receive but vague impressions of. Children are quite inquisitive enough for their powers of comprehension; and if this disposition of childhood is not thwarted, or treated with indifference, it will lead them to all the information of which they can make use. Men have ceased to be pedants in books; we are now to have a growth of pedants in things.

After the learned law-note just cited, it will be well to mention a few of the words, which are defined for the same children for which that was written: "Engrossed," "swain," "solace," "contest," "antique," "glade," "expanse," "cleave," "disdain," "vitals," "mortar," "ethereal," "lacked," "prize," "scared."

"'Is any sick? The Man of Ross relieves,
Attends, prescribes, the med'cine makes, and gives.'

"This requires no explanation."

Notwithstanding this note, we very well remember a good couple, who could both read and write, and yet were mainly puzzled with the word "prescribes." "The Doctor," said the man, "subscribed for me." "No," said the wife, "you should say perscribed, not subscribed."

In another place, however, we find our authors alarmed lest the "little reader" should have his mind irretrievably injured by misunderstanding the following words:—

"'Ruin seize thee.'—These are simple words, but I find that they require explanation. . . . . . Ruin means destruction,—I wish that ruin may seize thee."

But we despair for the poor child's intellect; for what does destruction mean, papa?

"'Go, seek it there, where to be born and die,
Of rich and poor, make all the history.'

"That is to say, go and seek it in the parish registry. There is, or, by law, there ought to be, kept in every parish, a book called the parish registry, in which an account should be kept of every birth, christening," &c., &c.

But we have promised to make no long extracts of such a nature.

These learned essays on common or statute law, for children, are too absurd to be treated seriously. Yet it is a subject rather of pain than of mirth, to see a mind like Miss Edgeworth's so warped by system.

Could Mr. and Miss Edgeworth suppose that the epithet "watery" was given by Gray, because, like all other low lands along a river, these glades were, perhaps, overflowed once or twice in a year? Why did they not look out through these narrow and shadowy openings between the trees, into the world of sun, and see the Thames, with its bright, silvery stream, winding along the deep green, and sending little glad and quivering sparkles of light into the solemn gloom of the woods?

"'Chase the rolling circle's speed.'

"These are all poetical expressions."

In how much better taste it would have been to have said that it was an affected periphrasis, and arose from a characteristic fault in Gray, — a fastidiousness which would not allow him to express a common thing in the usual way.

"'To bitter scorn a sacrifice,
And grinning Infamy.'

"Here infamy also is made a person, and is supposed to mock the wretch who is rendered infamous; this personification is, perhaps, too bold."

Besides the morsel of choice criticism which this contains, we have a specimen of the intermeddling manner of making useless explanations which runs through the whole of this work.

"'Thought would destroy their paradise.'

"Paradise is the name in Scripture for the garden of Eden, where Adam and Eve were placed by Providence," &c.

We have observed, with mingled surprise and pleasure, the mention of the Bible, more than once, in this work; though we are sorry that Miss Edgeworth should be under the necessity of drawing the conclusion, that the information intended to be contained in this note would be required by children educated upon her system, and who were old enough to study the works of Gray and Wharton.

Parnell, in his Hesiod, has these lines: —

"He gave her words, where oily flattery lays
The pleasing colours of the art of praise."

On which our authors make this remark: —

"Oily from the smoothness and softness of flattery; the epithet oily is also proper, as it is connected with the idea of laying colours, which are mentioned in the next line; colours are usually mixed with oil."

Instead of giving this information, if it were necessary to say any thing upon the passage, it would be better to tell the child at once, that it is one of those commonplace passages, which, without presenting any distinct image, partake just enough of the figurative to dim the plain meaning; and that, if Parnell had in mind the painter's oil, he was guilty of ingenuity amounting to conceit. An illustration may be too minutely close as well as too indefinitely general. To a poetic simile — which such figures are essentially — may be applied the old maxim, "No simile runs on all fours."

Our authors are perpetually forgetting how very ignorant their "little readers" are supposed to be; as an instance of which, we cite their talking to them of "Pandora, not sophisticated with perfumes."

Adam's Morning Hymn is next entered upon, with prose versions, and notes critical, and notes explanatory, to which are tacked a little astronomy and a little mineralogy, for little boys and little girls.

> "'Speak ye, who best can tell, ye sons of light,
> Angels.'
>
> "Why Milton calls angels sons of light is not clear."

We had thought there was a glory in the epithet that would make it visible to the blindest minds. As it is, we would suggest, that, by consulting the Word of God, it possibly might be made "clear."

> "'Fairest of stars, last in the train of night,
> If better thou belong not to the dawn.'
>
> "If it might not be more properly said, that thou (Venus) belongest to the morning."

Really, this is too soft to crack a joke upon.

"'Sure pledge of day.'

"Pledge is properly any thing given as a security for the performance of something that is to be done."

We will hasten on; for it is something like an imposition upon our readers, to wear their patience with such stuff.

The explanations upon Milton we shall close with as rare a piece of criticism as is to be met with in these critic days.

"'Fountains, and ye that warble as ye flow
Melodious murmurs, warbling tune his praise.'

"This sentence is incomplete. *Ye* refers to streams, or waters; *warbles* is an uncommon expression when applied to water; it might, however, have occurred to Milton from certain puerile contrivances, which were fashionable about the time in which he lived. Water was made to flow into pipes in such a manner as to imitate the song of birds.—Vide Plot's History of Oxfordshire, in which there is an account of very expensive works of this kind at Lovel-Enston, in Oxfordshire, in which an ancestor of the author wasted a considerable part of his fortune."

We could not refrain from giving this precious note at full length, though we fear that, in so doing, we have broken our promise to our readers. But *warble* "is a vile phrase, a very vile phrase indeed." We find in Webster's Devil's Law-Case,—

"And my scriveners,
Merely through my employment, grow so rich,
They build their palaces and belvederes
With musical water-works."

We are not told whether this "ancestor of the author" was one of these; and "Plot's History" is not at hand.

Next in course are detached sentences, with notes hung to them.

"How far yon little candle throws his beams!
So shines a good deed in a naughty world."

Our authors allow this to be natural, but come to the conclusion, that "it is not a very elevated thought, nor expressed in very elevated language." "Naughty," say they, "is a common, and rather a vulgar word."

We have always thought the passage to possess a moral elevation, and did not suppose, till now, that there was any one who could read it, miserably torn away, as it is, from all with which it stands connected in Shakspeare, without being struck with its native and simple air, and without having an humble, but beautiful scenery open about him. "Naughty," it seems, "is vulgar." As we have read it in Shakspeare, and in the Bible, if our authors will allow us, we have loved it for its old simplicity. It is not every shifting of fashion which can change the character of words, any more than that of men, or render that vulgar, with which we have associated so much that is peculiar and delicate. This same term "*vulgar*" has become a very hackneyed phrase. We hear it from the prettily made up mouths of misses, just brought out, who learn, nobody knows where, that Crabbe is vulgar, Wordsworth silly, and Cowper a very good sort of a man, but no poet.

The last that we shall notice are some few of the readings upon Gray's Bard.

"To arms, cried Mortimer! and couched his quivering lance."

Our authors tell their readers what is meant by couching a lance, and then go on to say:—

"If the little pupil who reads this is in London, I hope his friends will take him to the Tower and show him the horse armoury."

If they should do so, we hope that the child, young as he may be, will not behave so unaccountably silly, and out of nature, as did one full-grown Master Harrington, who played mad, fell down before the figure of the Black Prince, and spouted Akenside.

A little farther on, our authors suppose that, by the words "troubled air," Gray feigned that the air, mistaking the Bard's long beard for a meteor, was exceedingly disturbed and frightened thereat.

"No more I weep. They do not sleep."

This line is considered "rather flat." — Our authors acknowledge having made a free use of the notes to one of the editions of Gray. It would have been fortunate for their reputation, and the taste of their "little readers," had they omitted their own criticism upon the above line, and inserted the following, from an edition of Gray, upon the whole passage. "Here a vision of triumphant revenge is judiciously made to ensue, after the pathetic lamentation that precedes it. Breaks, double rhymes, an appropriate cadence, and an exalted ferocity of language, forcibly picture to us the uncontrollable, tumultuous workings of the prophet's stimulated bosom." They should have known better than to criticize the line otherwise than in the connection in which it was written.

There is a criticism upon "bright rapture," quite of a piece with the foregoing, which our readers may examine for themselves. Our authors remark, that it is made with an intention "to caution their young readers against blind admiration of what they do not clearly comprehend"; and it would not have been an ill-timed direction to have added, that they should not, on the other hand, condemn all they may not understand.

*"The following lines, relating to Edward III., we had supposed to contain a picture of the dreadful effects of that conqueror's triumphant progress through France. Before him, the affrighted inhabitants are flying in wild disorder; behind, they are mourning over the miseries and desolation which his ravages had produced.

> 'From thee be born, who o'er thy country hangs
> The scourge of heaven. What terrours round him wait!
> Amazement in his van, with flight combined,
> And sorrow's faded form, and solitude behind.'

"Our authors' explanation is this:—

"'The poet describes the beginning of the reign of Edward III. as full of glory; representing him as attended by *amazement* and *flight*, and the end of his reign, [as] marked with sorrow, and with the desertion of his friends.'

"It is abundantly evident, we think, that this is not a correct explanation. In the first place, it is extremely forced and far-fetched. It supposes the poet to call the early part of a man's career in life his "*van*," and the latter part his "*rear*," which, to say the least of it, is a very unusual manner of expressing one's self; and it creates an arbitrary distinction between the two last lines in respect to the persons to whom they are applied; that is, the *sorrow* and *solitude* are represented as the lot of Edward himself, in the latter part of his reign, and the *amazement* and *flight*, that of *others*, in the

* The following remarks upon the construction put by our authors upon two passages in the Bard, relating to Edward III., were contained in a communication made for our Review. We had already been through the volume before us, when this came to hand. We hope the gentleman, whoever he may be, will pardon us the liberty we have taken, in thus connecting his observations with matter of our own. We should gladly have given way to him altogether, had his remarks extended to the work at large —*Note in North American Review.*

early part of it. If the sorrow and the solitude belong to Edward, the construction requires that the *amazement* and the *flight* should also belong to him. But as it would be false to say, that at any period of his reign, particularly in the beginning of it, he *fled in dismay* before his enemies, it follows that we must have recourse to a different explanation.

" In the next place, the stanza immediately following that in which these lines are found contains a description of the end of that monarch's reign. It begins thus:—

> ' Mighty victor, mighty lord,
> Low on his funeral couch he lies!' &c.

" Now, if the termination of Edward's reign had been previously described, there would be a tautology in this stanza which no correct poet would be likely to commit, and Gray, perhaps, less than any one in the English language.

" The exposition of the following lines is, also, evidently erroneous.

> " ' The verse adorn again,
> Fierce War, and faithful Love,
> And Truth severe, by fairy Fiction dressed.'

" ' It does not,' say our authors, ' at first appear to whom this is addressed; but upon consideration, it seems that fury, war, and love are called upon to adorn verse.'

" We are rather surprised it did not occur to them, that, in fact, this is ' addressed ' to nobody, but that war, love, &c., are the nominative to the verb, and are represented as being *seen* by the prophetic bard *adorning* the verse of some future period; more especially, as this thought occurred to them when explaining the next three lines, which are so perfectly analogous to the foregoing in the order and arrangement of the words. The lines are these:—

> 'In buskined measure move
> Pale Grief and pleasing Pain,
> With Horrour, tyrant of the throbbing breast.'

"Upon this they observe,—

"'The sense is, that pale grief, &c., move on the stage in buskined measure,—that is to say, in the solemn tones of tragedy.'

"But why did they not say that grief, pain, &c., were addressed in these lines, as well as love, war, &c., in the former ones? The truth is, there is no address, no apostrophe, in either case."

Had our authors carefully read the notes to Gray of which they speak, they could not have fallen into these strange blunders. We fear that neither these notes, nor all that have been written, could set them right in what relates to taste in poetry.

The volume closes with some remarks upon Parody; but we have done with it. We presume that enough has been quoted to tire our readers, and to satisfy them, even should they approve of the plan, that our authors were but poorly qualified to carry it out. For ourselves, we think the execution worthy the design. Surely, children so very ignorant as to require many of the explanations in this work are not fit subjects for the kind of poetry it is here attempted to make them understand.

If it is intended to open the feelings and give growth to the imagination of a child, he should read all, that is not in language too obsolete, in Percy's Lyrical Ballads, and works of the kind; and, though in prose, yet, for the same purpose, Pilgrim's Progress, the

Arabian Nights, Æsop's Fables, &c. We are aware of the objection to beasts and birds talking like men; but

> "I shall not ask Jean Jaques Rousseau
> If birds confabulate, or no."

The feeling of kind attachment and fellowship, which the reading of such fables begets for the poor brutes, outweighs, in our perverse minds, all that has been said or written for years on the sad effects of so deceiving innocent and unsuspecting children. To back us in our recommendation of Æsop, we quote, though with some diffidence, considering that he lived in what is now called an age of darkness and prejudice, the words of Locke. "I think," says he, "Æsop's fables the best, which, being stories apt to delight and entertain a child, may yet afford useful reflections to a grown man; and if his memory retain them all his life after, he will not repent to find them there amongst his manly thoughts and serious business." — To works of this sort should be added natural history of birds and beasts, accounts of manners and customs of foreign nations and tribes, and what is peculiar in the scenery of the countries they inhabit or wander over. After all, the soul of poetry lives in the natural powers and qualities of the mind, and must be brought out by the study of circumstances and things about it; yet so far as early impressions from reading go, it must be of the kind which we have just mentioned. It is the delight of poets in years, and what they fed upon when young. With the severer studies of children we have nothing to do at this time. The work before us was written to bring forward and improve the poetry of character in children, and it is all to which we have intended to apply our remarks.

We cannot close without expressing our belief, that Miss Edgeworth wrote but a small part of this book. There is too much feebleness in it to be the production of her mind, though it relates to poetry, a subject upon which, perhaps, she is less qualified to treat than any on which she has written.

Perhaps the expression of this belief makes it unnecessary for us to say any thing in justification of the freedom of our remarks; if, indeed, it were not rendered useless by the manner in which we have so often spoken of Miss Edgeworth. There may be those, however, who, in their zeal, will not discriminate, and because we think her defective in certain qualities of mind, will not allow that we hold her to be the first woman of the age, without any reservation, and the greatest tale or novel-writer of these times, with the exception of that mysterious wonder of the North.

HAZLITT'S LECTURES ON THE ENGLISH POETS.*

CONSIDERING the rank which the works of the late Mr. Hazlitt now justly hold in English literature, the manner in which he is spoken of in this article may sound somewhat strange to readers of the present day. It must be borne in mind, that it was written thirty years ago, when, I believe, little besides these Lectures was known of him in this country. I need hardly add, that, had I now to express an opinion of them for the first time, though that opinion would be much the same as before, my manner of expressing it would, very properly, be modified by the deep respect which a further acquaintance with his works compels me to feel for his great intellectual powers.

Perhaps I should state, that, in the present republication, I have added somewhat to the original review, mainly by carrying out more at full the parts relating to Pope, Thomson, and Cowper.

HERE is a book of large and stately type, and fair and ample margin, which, with eighty pages of extracts, and a good stretch of blank at the beginnings and endings of chapters, leaves, after the deduction of

* From the North American Review for 1819.

Lectures on the English Poets. Delivered at the Surrey Institution. By WILLIAM HAZLITT. Philadelphia: Thomas Dobson & Son. 1818. 8vo. pp. 331.

a general introductory chapter, a little more than two hundred pages in which to treat upon the English poets, beginning with old Chaucer, and closing with criticisms upon those of the present day.

Though we have been thus minute in our calculation, we do not take into our reckoning the marvellously free use which Mr. Hazlitt has made of the orts and ends, as well as the good things, of other authors, with which to patch out his sentences. Indeed, we could hardly have done this if we would; for we soon discovered, that, in many places, he is too much wearied with the task of tacking on marks of quotation, often leaving it to our reading and recollection to find out what may be his own and what borrowed. How far he may have carried this, our memories are too poor to satisfy us. It was not to expose or harm the art of book-making, — without which there would soon be an end to us reviewers, — that we went into this examination, but for the purpose of ascertaining into how small a compass a man of Mr. Hazlitt's powers could bring so important a subject as a treatise on the English poets.

When we opened upon the title-page of this book, we almost envied our author the deep and secret delight with which we supposed he must have been filled while intent upon such a subject. All the philosophy of mind, all that is good in the heart, or worth our regard and love out of our practical duties, seems to us related to it, and making a part of it. It takes us from the hard and jarring road of life to places that lie along the imagination, like bright and still clouds upon the clear air. It smites the heart, and there gush out waters, fresh and pure as ran down from Horeb, which make green and young again the fading and decaying things of earth.

It is not in poetry as in many other pursuits, where the heart grows idle and old while the mind labours and waxes strong; for here mind and heart work together, as our parents once did in Paradise, and gather and store up of all that is beautiful in nature, and feed on its fruits. The commonest thing has a character to a poet's eye, and awakens an individual interest in his heart; and he is never solitary, for the desert place is populous with forms and beings towards whom he feels as a brother. In the world, too, much is open to him from which others are shut out. He knows the movings of our passions, and startles us by showing us what we are. And this distinct and intimate reality casts off its heavy and lumbering form, and is lifted from the earth, to mingle with airy, ideal shapes, and be shone on by the same light which shines on them. He shuts his eyes, and a brightness comes up and spreads itself out through his mind, and beautiful beings float into it, silent as air, from the hollow darkness beyond it.

But the poet is not a creature all of joyous fancies; he knows, as Wordsworth has finely told us,

> "That there is often found
> In mournful thoughts, and always might be found,
> A power to virtue friendly."

The streams of his heart are not always like those of spring, huddling and rapid, and telling out gladness, but sometimes move on slow and murmuring, like those of autumn sounding a solemn chant with the spirit that is moving above them through the changing and falling leaves. He is fond, and he hates; he is weighed down, and lifted up; but it is in a world of his own creating, and with beings moulded and quickened in his own mind, that he suffers and enjoys. Not that reality does not come nigh to him; it touches him, and is changed to his own mood. He sees and studies the world, but with feelings little known to other men, and to give life and motion to his lonely visions. His chief joys are in these dreams. He asks for fame, but it is for fame after death; the dust of earth is not on his possessions, and the things of this world are raised and spiritualized.

We would not be taken too strictly, lest we should be held over-fanciful. It is of the nature of poetry that we speak, and of the tendency merely of its influences upon the heart and mind. For the man is not always the poet, and is often little better than one of ourselves. But though he may be pained by the world's crosses, wish for its wealth, and aim at its honours, yet what is peculiar to him as a poet consists of beauties and associations which we are proud to understand, and has forms of height and grandeur which it elevates and enlarges us to look upon.

Humanity would seem to be strangely made up. We find men with intellects of a second order, who scarcely make approaches to genius, and who are careful to avoid all undue indulgences in conduct and conversation, but who are yet without those deep and solemn tones, those pure and airy sounds, which make secret music in the heart of him who sometimes forgets them and gives himself up to the indulgences of tainted wit or idle pleasantries. Yet even at such times the character may be seen through, and we may perceive that the man has, unconsciously, gone out of his individuality, if we may so speak, as if only to return to himself again, to feel the more distinctly his own peculiar being, and to dwell in the midst of those thoughts and sensations which absence has given freshness to. It seems to be upon somewhat the same principle that a man of still life and retired feelings now and then goes into the riot and bustle of the crowd with an alacrity and relish which his friends smile and wonder at. But the stir and noise are over, and he sits once more by the gentle flickering of his fire, and quiet, low beating of the flames, and the thoughts and feelings from which he had for a while gone abroad give him a kind and cheerful welcome, and he takes his seat among them again happy and at home. Perhaps, too, it is that something of earth about us which will not let us live always in the higher regions of the mind, but sometimes brings us low that our imaginations may not make us vain, and humbles us with healing sorrow for our weaknesses, and mercifully turns our very failings into ministers to us of good.

We are not making excuses for these givings-in to the frailties of humanity; we are simply speaking of men as we find them, and of the fact, that seldom has one been met with so guarded as never to smile at playful follies, nor to take part in what, perhaps, in more serious moments, he would be sorry for having said or done, who had not a self-gratulatory spirit in his shut-up propriety, which stained deeper than those momentary failures which, in more careless and open natures, are not rooted deep in the character, but fall off from it almost as fast as they put forth. So true is this, that there is the same proneness in us to look doubtingly upon that scrupulosity which has never so far forgotten itself as to laugh at the unwashed wit of Swift, as there is to question the intellectual superiority that has never deigned to be amused with his fooleries in verse. He who never lends himself to the follies of fellowship may avoid them quite as much from an ever-present inflated, formal self-complacency, as from a singleness of pure and elevated virtue: — if it be indeed from this ever-sustained virtue, verily, well is it with that man!

If we have gone a little out of our way, it was because the by-path looked green and pleasant. Allowing for its windings, we will be upon the main road again all in good time. It was from thinking how individual, varied, and strongly marked must have been the characters of the older poets, — in times when all men had more of individuality and eccentricity, which asked not what the world would say, than we find in the smooth and even polish of later days, — that we have been led somewhat astray.

We are filling our hot-houses and gardens with plants of the tropics and of either end of the earth; we decompose air, and water, and earths; find the dip of rocks, and mark their strata; voyage into regions of thick-ribbed ice; travel up to the sources of strange rivers; betake ourselves to the mountain-tops; and are bustling and busy in this great huddling and overturning of every thing within our reach, while the delightful mystery within us lives on unexamined and unobserved. But if the pursuit of this mystery has been neglected for objects more gainful or of cheaper fame, it has inward satisfyings and healthful moral uses, which are found only here. We can scarcely look into the hearts of other men without seeing the workings of our own, and learning to know ourselves in studying them. This brings us nearer to each other, and, in opening out like weaknesses and like virtues, teaches us forgiveness and love.

To follow the mind back, and see the most exquisite thoughts and finely touched feelings shooting up in fresh and infant beauty among the hard and rough-grown passions of the early ages, — to hear the tones of love and deep, low plainings of grief come from out a region which we had looked upon as dark and boisterous alone, — to find ourselves going thither for all that is peculiar and poetic in our natures, and cleansing our hearts, and storing them with the sentiments, and laying them open to the moral influences of those times, — is surely something worth our earnest study, and may make us humbler talkers upon the vast mental advancements of this our age.

The study of the works of the older English poets, along with what we can learn of their character and that of mankind in their day; the history of the religion, superstitions, laws, and customs, under which they were born; the unnoticed yet ever-working influences of these on their passions and cast of thought; the vastness and variety imparted to their imaginations by the strange mixture of ignorance, wild conjecture, and bold adventure; the effect of the open simplicity, the close and keen cunning, of the tenderness and hard brutality, of the exquisite delicacy, and what we, sometimes falsely, and again truly, call the vulgarity of those days;—these surely are subjects deserving our attention, and requiring an intellect of more power and variety to comprehend, than those are well aware of who hold poetry to be a matter of mere amusement, and all connected with it a light thing.

The man who would do this well must have a wide taste, and be trammelled by no narrow systems or schools; he must have a nice perception for the minutest beauties, nor must he turn away from them because they may be surrounded by deformities; he should have an imagination which can group and fill out, and throw lights and shades over the scanty materials left us, with the distinctness of a picture; he must love old books even as Southey does, who says that he should be miserable without them, — that they are to him what old pictures are to a painter. He must do more; — he must love a long story, and not count it labour lost, though it take him "from hence to Ertham"; he must have a relish for the quaint and grotesque, without becoming quaint and grotesque himself; he must not mistake simplicity for weakness, nor frankness for coarseness; he must understand and love nature through all her varieties, and have poetical associations, not with her beauties only, but even with her harsh and uncouth things, which shall give them a hold upon his imagination; he must have an ear like Cowper's, to which the noise of a goose in a barn-yard was pleasant, though he confesses he should not care to have the bird hung up in a cage in his parlour.

But in all this let a man beware of pretence; for not only is pretence not love, — it is fatal to love. There are some who read old authors, and affect to despise the new. They are satisfied with nothing since the days of Milton, and would not be satisfied with him did he live now. They want the sanction of posterity for their admiration; and affect to speak lightly of living men whose praises will be upon the tongues of those who shall come after them: —

> "I asked thee oft, what Poets thou hast read,
> And lik'st the best; still thou reply'st, The dead.
> I shall, ere long, with green turf covered be;
> Then sure thou 'lt like, or thou wilt envy me."

Of this number must be reckoned the writer before

us, of whom it is quite time that something was said.

This work is divided into eight lectures. The introductory one is upon poetry in general; the three following on six only of the older poets, ending with Pope, and bringing us to the middle of the volume; and the remaining four, first taking up Thomson and Cowper, close with criticisms on the living poets.

Though Mr. Hazlitt has not gone into the subject with that fulness with which we have just intimated it should be treated, nor followed down the poetry of his country through its changes, as perhaps connected with and brought about by the alterations in society, nor wrought into his work old anecdote, which could be put to uses as instructive as entertaining, still we would make no objection had he carried out his own plan. But from aught we can learn from Mr. Hazlitt, Chaucer and Spenser, Shakspeare and Milton, Dryden and Pope, were about all the poets that lived from the days of the Heptarchy to those of Queen Anne. We should not care to have a lecture devoted to Piers Plowman; but we did expect to meet with the names, and something more than the names, of Ben Jonson, Massinger, Beaumont and Fletcher, Ford, and others of the old dramatists. And a passing word might have been given to the other Fletchers, to Drayton, Drummond, Surrey, Wyatt, and many more, who surely are not so out of date that one need fear being thought pedantic in venturing to talk of them.

The second class of the old poets also were well worthy of his notice, differing as they do from the same class among the modern, as, amidst much that may be prosaic, we meet with beauties choice enough to repay us for our travail, and with this in them to win us, that these beauties are not exotics, but the natural growth of the soil. Had Mr. Hazlitt attended to this, and stopped short of the living poets, it may be that he would have left on us a more favourable impression of his taste, and, what is of more worth, of his feelings. As to his omissions among the modern poets, we have little to object.

Mr. Hazlitt sets out, modestly enough, with what he says is the best general notion which he can give of poetry. Though not quite satisfied with it, we shall not attempt a better, and thus put ourselves in danger of falling into the unlucky situation of the reviewer, who, not content with attempts to raise a laugh at the expense of Mr. Coleridge in a like undertaking, was too eager to show the world how it should be done, and unhappily failing, ended with turning the laugh upon himself. Nor is it our intention, in the few pages which we shall devote to our author, to follow him in course, nor to speak in so small a space of all the poets of whom he treats.

The remark in the outset, that "he who has a contempt for poetry cannot have much respect for himself or any thing else," is a little too sweeping. Yet we find that men who have toiled in those dry, abstruse studies which have little that is interesting or pleasant apart from the mental effort they demand, are apt to be of the belief, that whatever is intrinsically pleasurable may be acquired without labour; and as what they themselves most value was attained with difficulty, they naturally despise what they think is easily won. And although this be only bad reasoning, still, poetry is made up of such soft affections, and enters so deeply into the heart of man, — has so much to do with our sufferings as well as joys, and helps us so in our love of nature, — that he who is not touched by it affects us as a creature somewhat selfish, coarse, and hard. At least we say that there are not to be found in him those nicer and undefinable sensations, — those delicate tints of thought which are for ever gleaming out from finer natures, running through their several movements, and imparting an interest even to the very awkwardness of some. He seems as a stranger to what constitutes the sentiment of man, as a being, in short, of a lower order, whom we should not censure for his wants, but pity because he is not something more.

Perhaps, however, we have brought Mr. Hazlitt farther than he intended going; for he not only makes every thing to be poetry, but all men, too, to be poets; so that to despise poetry, as he defines it, would be, with Falstaff, to "banish all the world."

> "Man is a poetical animal: and those of us who do not study the principles of poetry act upon them all our lives, like Molière's *Bourgeois Gentilhomme*, [a somewhat stale instance,] who had always spoken prose without knowing it. The child is a poet, in fact, when he first plays at hide and seek, or repeats the story of Jack the Giant-Killer; the shepherd-boy is a poet, when he first crowns his mistress with a garland of flowers; the countryman, when he stops to look at the rainbow; the city apprentice, when he gazes after the Lord Mayor's show; the miser, when he hugs his gold; the courtier, who builds his hopes upon a smile; the savage, who paints his idol with blood; the slave, who worships a tyrant, or the tyrant, who fancies himself a god; — the vain, the ambitious, the proud, the choleric man, the hero and the coward, the beggar and the king, the rich and the poor, the young and the old, all live in a world of their own making; and the poet does no more than describe what all the others think and act." — pp. 3, 4.

Now, this tedious detail and poor sophistry is all for

the sake of being striking and original, we suppose. If Mr. Hazlitt only means that certain faculties, common to the poet and to other men, are often put in action in the concerns of life, he has but set forth what is little better than a truism; if more than this, what is an untruth.

A satisfactory definition of *poet* has never yet been given, and, we doubt, never will be, believing that, in his essential, distinctive nature, he is not to be comprehended. Although certain of his qualities and faculties may be named, yet that which underlies these,—that on which they are conditioned, and by which they are modified, and of which, taken together with these, the poet is constituted, — can hardly be brought within the range of the understanding. We feel that there is a difference; and we all feel the absurdity of bestowing the name of poet on the courtier who, in the chase of court favour, has overrated his man, or on the shopkeeper who, in his calculations, overruns his gains. We know well enough that all the while both may be, and probably are, among the most prosaic of mortals, — that although the poet may use them, they may, essentially, have in them as little of poetry as had the post which Pope so simply and tenderly says he could not bear to see dug up, because he knew it when he was a boy. What are these, and all else, but the mere materials which the poet moulds into new and finer forms, and gives new and further relations to, endowing them with passions, casting upon them the bright glow of his own mind, throwing over them his own rich and gorgeous drapery, and bringing them into unison with the one harmonizing principle of his own soul?

There are many such loose givings-out through this lecture; and a good deal of indifference is discovered as to self-contradictions; still, it is written with a certain force which imparts to it an air of originality. We do not know that, in fact, any thing new is broached in it; but there is much that might be useful to people of confined taste, would they look at it impartially.

From our recollection of what has been already written upon Chaucer's characters, there was little left for Mr. Hazlitt to add. Yet he has analyzed them with acuteness. His remarks upon the particularity, and careful, minute verity in Chaucer's descriptions, and his circumstantiality in telling a story, are just and ingenious; and he has noticed what has been passed over by so many, — his pathos, and that love of nature, which, indeed, all the old poets are so full of and so sincere in.

"Chaucer's descriptions of natural scenery possess the same sort of characteristic excellence, or what might be termed *gusto*. They have a local truth and freshness, which gives the very feeling of the air, the coolness or moisture of the ground. Inanimate objects are thus made to have a fellow-feeling in the interest of the story, and render back the sentiment of the speaker's mind. One of the finest parts of Chaucer is of this mixed kind. It is the beginning of the Flower and Leaf, where he describes the delight of that young beauty, shrouded in her bower, and listening, in the morning of the year, to the singing of the nightingale; while her joy rises with the rising song, and gushes out afresh at every pause, and is borne along with the full tide of pleasure, and still increases, and repeats, and prolongs itself, and knows no ebb. The coolness of the arbour, its retirement, the early time of the day, the sudden starting up of the birds in the neighbouring bushes, the eager delight with which they devour and rend the opening buds and flowers, are expressed with a truth and feeling, which make the whole appear like the recollections of an actual scene."

He quotes the passage, and remarks: —

> "There is no affected rapture, no flowery sentiment: the whole is an ebullition of natural delight 'welling out of the heart,' like water from a crystal spring. Nature is the soul of art: there is a strength as well as a simplicity in the imagination that reposes entirely on nature, that nothing else can supply."

The criticism upon this poet shows discrimination and good taste.

It should be a cause of rejoicing to the studious lover of true poetry, to find his pleasant old companions, who had been confined to his study fireside because their dress was a little too much after the antique cut, brought so often as they have lately been into the company of the well-dressed and fashionable. And if he is not disinterested enough to rejoice at seeing that it is for the world's good, let him be actuated by that general principle, selfishness, and be proud to behold the multitude becoming the followers of his own opinions and tastes.

It is ten to one, however, if his selfishness do not work the other way. In natures of finer touch, there is apt to grow about their larger thoughts and more delicate beauties a suspicious and excluding fear, that letting the world in upon them is only soiling and trampling them down. Their peculiarity is their pride; and if they can get hold of a fine old author whom the readers of the day are ignorant of, he is worth more to them than twenty as good who are well known, — there is an exclusive property in him. Besides, the confined acquaintance begets a sort of companionship, and that a complacent sense of a certain equality with him: — Who but he and I! Thus one foible makes room for another, till what was praiseworthy is lost in weaknesses, and the choicest parts of the character are spoiled, from a want of that only fast hold upon what is excellent, a love of it for its own sake.

Yet, looking a little more closely into motives, we may find better principles silently at work. Seeing that the world praises much which it knows not how to value, and admires from mere vogue what it only affects to understand, we are something moved that high excellence should be degraded by an ignorant and vain worship, and that those who pay it should be clothed in the garments of the true priests. Out of this naturally grow sarcasm and contempt; and he who would endeavour to initiate the vulgar into the mysteries of the temple of Apollo is looked at askance, as being ignorant of what he would teach. Leave men to themselves, says one; they have enough daily doled to them for their daily talk, and are satisfied. Why bring forth before them the great of other days, to be stared at like Indians in beaded moccasons on our paved streets?

Having nothing of the superiority, and, we trust, little of the superciliousness of such minds, we would earnestly recommend to those who read poetry the study of the older writers. Next to studying nature itself, they can hardly be better employed. Indeed, the two have so much to do with each other, that their very differences serve to bring their resemblances to mind; and an acquaintance with the one, and attachment to it, will naturally be followed by a knowledge and love of the other. The old authors have this quality in common with nature, — the more they are studied, the closer hold they take upon the mind. They shoot up and overrun us like vines, creeping along the windings of our feelings and twining in among our thoughts with a growth so gentle and silent, that, although our hearts are kept fresh by them, and our minds overhung with their dangling beauties, the grateful sense that they impart to us is hardly noted, and is in us as if it were only our own happy nature. Perhaps it is owing to this very quality that the common run of people are so little drawn toward them. For the greater part of men want something that will take a rude hold upon them, something that will flare upon them like a broad setting sun. Tangled and by-path overgrowings tease rather than delight them; and they lack that infant nativeness of heart which gladly lies down in warm, lighted nooks, and looks with a half-strange delight upon the dancing sun-spots which play upon the grass under the thick wood.

We urge this matter now, being aware, that, with a few exceptions, Chaucer's language puts as many obstructions in the way of beginners as does that of any of our old poets. Yet even in him a little patient and careful reading will overcome them, and what at first looked strange and uncouth will appear natural enough; and the very peculiarity of the diction, obsolete words, and singular spelling, will, in time, form pleasant and poetical associations for us, for the very reason which at first made them distasteful, — because they are not identical with the language of our everyday conversation and reading. We have heard some say, that these differences from our modern tongue have such a baby air, that they can never be reconciled to them. If they have honestly made the attempt and failed, we have nothing further to urge, but must leave them to elegant English and — the Calvary of Cumberland.

As to Spenser, the difficulty in reading him is little more than fanciful. If any one meets him for the first time in the extracts in these Lectures, and can be content without knowing more of him, all we can say is, that we are sorry the gods have not made him poetical.

Omitting quotations, we have here some half-dozen pages upon Spenser, — rather a summary way of treating the author of the Faerie Queene, and of so many beautiful poems, — upon him, too, whom Mr. Hazlitt calls "the most poetical of all poets." Of course, the remarks are very general, yet, for the most part, in good taste.

After mentioning what he considers the best parts of the Faerie Queene, he replies to the objections urged against it on account of the difficulty of comprehending the allegory: —

"But some people will say that all this may be very fine, but that they cannot understand it on account of the allegory. They are afraid of the allegory, as if they thought it would bite them; they look at it as a child looks at a painted dragon, and think it will strangle them in its shining folds. This is very idle. If they do not meddle with the allegory, the allegory will not meddle with them. Without minding it at all, the whole is as plain as a pike-staff. It might as well be pretended that we cannot see Poussin's pictures for the allegory, as that the allegory prevents us from understanding Spenser."

We wish that Mr. Hazlitt's off-hand, cavalier way of treating those who differ from him was never more out of place than in the present instance. The answer is certainly as good as the objectors deserve. But if they are not satisfied with it, we must add, that, be the allegory ever so hidden, the world of prodigal beauties lying about it and overhanging it will take off the sense of toil in searching it out, and that the way leads along by many a shelter from the dust and sun, where the traveller

> "feeds upon the cooling shade, and bayes
> His sweatie forehead in the breathing wynd,
> Which through the trembling leaves full gentle playes."

To the charge which we have more than once heard made, that Spenser wants strength and passion, Mr. Hazlitt answers: —

"But he has been unjustly charged with a want of passion and of strength. He has both in an immense degree. He has not, indeed, the pathos of immediate action or suffering, which is more properly the dramatic; but he has all the pathos of sentiment and romance, — all that belongs to distant objects of terror, and uncertain, imaginary distress. His strength, in like manner, is not strength of will or action, of bone and muscle, nor is it coarse and palpable; but it assumes a character of vastness and sublimity seen through the same visionary medium, and blended with the appalling associations of preternatural agency. We need only turn, in proof of this, to the Cave of Despair, or the Cave of Mammon, or to the account of the change of Malbecco into Jealousy."

Let us add, for force of description, the House of Care, although there are things in it which make us smile; also, the Descent of Night with the Black Steeds, — the scenes of horrour and great darkness, and dreadful noises, through which Guyon voyages to the Bowre of Blis, — the description of Error, at the very opening, — and the "salvage man," of whom it is said, —

> "For other language had he none nor speach,
> But a soft murmure and confused sound
> Of senselesse words, which Nature did him teach
> T' expresse his passions, which his reason did empeach," —

and whose strange, poetical uncouthness brings Caliban to mind.

Though it be true that "Spenser seldom makes us laugh or weep," yet his Mother Hubberd's Tale is a delightfully playful satire, and keeps a smile about the mouth all the time we read. We are affected in the same way by Braggadocio, a fellow something between Pistol and Parolles, — a losel base; and Gule, too, he that "us'd to fish for fooles on the dry shore," amuses us exceedingly, when, by changing from a bird to a "hedgehogge," he escapes from the hand of Artegall. Malbecco in search of his wife, which Mr Hazlitt refers to, is also ludicrous. His uxoriousness, forcing him into dangers which his cowardice makes him tremble at, joint and limb, renders him altogether a most pitiable, yet diverting object.

It may seem singular, yet we are hardly willing to call Spenser's poetry mere fairy land, or to say that we wander among mere ideal beings in another world. True it is, "he takes and lays us in the lap of a lovelier nature, by the sound of softer streams, among greener hills, and fairer valleys. He paints nature, not as we find it, but as we expected to find it, and fulfils the delightful promise of our youth."

And it is just so. The grass is of a fresher green, the fruit hangs heavier and of a brighter gold, and the harvest is fuller, — the sky of a richer glow, and the clouds more gorgeous and piled; yet we feel as if on the same earth still, only in a region of it more fair than we had before visited. The females are not precisely such as those we meet at tea-parties, nor the men just like those we talk with upon business and politics on Exchange. But when romantic boys, we fancied ourselves very much such heroes; and she whom our imaginations bodied forth and our hearts loved with earnest constancy, — she that suffered with us in our fancied disappointments and sorrows, and looked happy when a brightness broke out on us in the close,—was no less beautiful than Florimel, nor less fond than Britomart. Spenser has placed his actors in scenes of nature pictured so truly, only a little more beautiful than we with our every-day eyes can see them,—has scattered through them so much of gentle and kind-hearted affection and sentiment,—that we forget all is so unreal, and feel a good deal relieved when the Red-crosse Knight has fairly slain the Dragon.

But it matters little whether this be true or not,—whether, making due allowance for its being an allegory, he gives so much the impression of reality, or whether his strange forms, iron-toothed dragons, and lighted castles seem to us mere things of air;—if we would be filled with poetry in all its nativeness, and beauty, simplicity, richness, gorgeousness, we must study Spenser. Not to speak profanely, the Faerie Queene should be to the poet what his Bible is to the Christian. How carefully did Milton read Spenser! Compare the description of Sin with that of Error, and the voyage of Satan through Chaos with that of Guyon. How many, too, of his words and phrases, which are ever sounding in our ears and filling our hearts and minds with undefinable sensations and fair images, may be followed home to this work!

And not only has Spenser been the store-house of poetic language to our poets. For nothing is he more remarkable than for his unceasing action, his exhaustless productiveness and variety,—motion upon motion, change upon change! You pass on from one scene to another, perpetual diversity keeping off fatigue, quitting the wild and gloomy for the cheerful and quiet, the large and desolate for little sunny nooks;—from the close, shady forest you come out all of a sudden upon the bright, broad sea and open shore, and at every turn in the wood fall upon some new adventure, and meet some stranger face to face. You are in absolute wonderment that the earth should be so populous! And with what facility all this comes about! Every thing *happens*,—nothing is *made* to take place. Let any one lay down the Faerie Queene, and, as well as he may, go through in order in memory with the different places, persons, and events, from the beginning to the end, and if their countless multitude and contrasting characters do not leave him in wonder and admiration at the intense life and prodigal productiveness of this old poet, it must be because wonder and admiration are states unknown to his mind. Is it too much to ask, whether, in these respects, Spenser has had a superiour in any age or land?

That Mr. Hazlitt should bring the description of Lechery against Mr. Southey's character of Spenser—

> "Yet not more sweet
> Than pure was he, and not more pure than wise;
> High-priest of all the Muses' mysteries!"—

can be accounted for only on the score of a sort of fatality which he labours under of attacking whatever comes from the so-called Lake School. No doubt there are passages in Spenser, which, taken apart, might put toys into young imaginations. But we should think that there was little harm remaining to be done to that mind that could read them in connection with the rest, and having in view their intent, yet find in them only incitements to loose thoughts. Some of the objects met with on the way to the Bowre of Blis. which, had they come from a less pure mind, might have worked evil, partake so much of that abstract sense of beauty, in which Spenser's mind seems so exquisite, that they do not affect us so much like creatures of flesh and blood, as like fine transparencies or forms beautifully pictured within the poem. Spenser is indeed the Palmer who will carry us safely through all such dangers, if we are not lost through a headlong desire for our own wreck: the spirit of Sir Guyon in us, and we need not fear stranding. — But it must not be forgotten how much is before us, and that something must be said of others beside Spenser, — that "inspired infant," as we once heard him beautifully called.

In so cursory a notice as this must needs be, it is hardly worth while to follow our author into his remarks upon Shakspeare and Milton. We will hasten forward, then, to what he says of those about whom the world is less agreed. There is something enlivening in all matters of dispute, and a feeling of self-importance begotten by the mere term "Our side." Were it not for this, we would stop to say a word upon Mr. Hazlitt's sketch of the character of Satan, and somewhat more upon that of Hamlet; for they are both old favourites of ours, — the latter so from our boyhood up.

It is somewhat puzzling to ascertain what our author's notions of poetry really are. At one time neither mere descriptions of natural objects, nor mere delineations of natural feelings, constitute poetry; but there must be imagination and passion, and an uneasy, restless sense of beauty, which is only to be relieved by connecting itself with images of beauty and grandeur, to be thrown off from the mind, and then to come floating before us accompanied by modulated sounds harmonizing with them. Words, too, must be as pictures to our minds. — But presently he overtakes one who has few or none of these qualities, all of a sudden becomes extremely intimate with him, and straightway turns round, contradicts all he had said before, and falls to abusing those who had gone peaceably along with him from his starting. He has now a new matter in hand, and without a very clear notion what he is to do with it. Of course, it is worked into a variety of odd forms, and put to as odd uses. He is a very Gonzalo in matters of poetry; and the latter part of his commonwealth is continually forgetting the beginning.

Thus, when he comes upon Pope, doors are straight shut, curtains dropped, and chandeliers lighted up. How brilliant and fascinating every thing and every body appear! The essence of roses, my Lady, is surely a finer perfume than the rose unexpressed! And those perennial flowers, too, that give such dazzling brightness to the eye, blooming in a light where nothing withers, but all is warmed, — how much happier in their lot than those that perish under the oppressive sun! Yes, so that he can talk of them in taffeta phrases, silken terms precise, he neither sees nor cares that they are paint and rags. Quite natural, too, upon my word! — Yes, the crackling, ill-savoured things, very like to honest out-of-door flowers, and as fragrant of the fields as Pope himself!

It is not merely because Pope wrote so much upon manners and fashions, — upon what we term the artificial, — so many now-a-days deny, that, in the strictest and highest sense of the term, he is a poet; although it is true that a prevailing disposition for such subjects indicates a defective poetic temperament and genius. Without dwelling upon this point, it may be said, that, let the subject be what it may, a poetic mind will permeate it with its own poetic character. Shakspeare is the poet everywhere and in all companies. Whether he argues or moralizes, is witty or sentimental, he dwells in a poetical atmosphere, and whatever he has to do with takes its tone from it. The same may be said of most of his contemporaries, and, with some qualification, of a few of the poets yet living, and of others who not long ago died. But rarely indeed does Pope touch the heart, or awaken our associations with those things to which the mind naturally goes in its poetic moods. And when does he fire the passions, or burst as with a glory over our heads?

No one questions his wit, his keenness, or good common-sense, or denies him the merit of expressing his moral sentiments with plainness and vigour,—although the best apology that is made for the scheme of his Essay on Man is, that he did not understand himself. But these qualifications do not of themselves constitute poetry; and to partake of it at all, they must have had their life in a poetic temperament, must have been moulded by poetic thought, and have been associated with poetic images. Nor will their having been measured into verse make them poetry,—for measured verse is not always the poetic voice.

Among the English satirists, Pope has been generally placed next to Dryden, by some ranked as his equal. Upon the difference between them Mr. Hazlitt remarks:—

"His Satires are not in general so good as his Epistles. His enmity is effeminate and petulant from a sense of weakness, as his friendship was tender from a sense of gratitude. I do not like, for instance, his character of Chartres, or his characters of women. His delicacy often borders upon sickliness; his fastidiousness makes others fastidious."

And again, speaking of Dryden:—

"Mac Flecknoe is the origin of the idea of the Dunciad; but it is less elaborately constructed, less feeble, and less heavy. The difference between Pope's satirical portraits and Dryden's appears to be this in a good measure, — that Dryden seems to grapple with his antagonists, and to describe real persons; Pope seems to refine upon them in his own mind, and to make them out just what he pleases, till they are not real characters, but the mere drivelling effusions of his spleen and malice. Pope describes the thing, and then goes on describing his own description till he loses himself in verbal repetitions. Dryden recurs to the object often, takes fresh sittings of nature, and gives us new strokes of character as well as of his pencil."

Aside from the philosophy of Pope's views respecting man, — if philosophy it must be called, — his Epistles, but more especially the Prologue to his Satires, and his Imitations of Horace, are the most satisfactory to us of all his writings. Beside their fine wit, they are full of capital remark growing out of the observation of a sensible man who had been long conversant with society. To be sure, there is no attempt in them to rise above the world, and this is well; for besides that it would have ill sorted with their general character, it would have been but an attempt, as Pope had not the eagle's wing for such ascents. Subjects like these, when treated in such a form, tend to sententiousness and to plainness of speech; so that here Pope is more compact and logical in his use of words than he is elsewhere. Where all, too, is on a level, that balance and monotony of versification, which so wearies us in his other writings, is less noticed from its falling in better with the general character of the work. How far this compactness, plainness, and logic of words was the result of the paraphrastic and imitative character of these writings, and placed them, in this particular, above his other works, we cannot now stop to consider. That it was somewhat a consequence there can be little doubt, and as little that just so far it detracts from his merit.

As Pope has been denied to possess imagination, Mr. Hazlitt claims for him fancy, — a claim which is immediately allowed, for up starts before us the Rape of the Lock, with its fairy creatures. It would be as unnecessary as difficult to show that these beings are original creations of our poet. It is enough that they are not mere copies of any particular writer, that they are self-congruous, and adapted to their new offices and circumstances.

But allowing its full merit to this extraordinary work of the fancy, we must remember that fancy has its modifications, being sometimes tinged with the ingenious, conceited, and curious; and, again, glowing with the solely and highly poetical, and even so blending with that higher faculty, the imagination, as to be hardly distinguished from it.

Now, with all the lively talents shown in the Rape of the Lock, and sprightly and delicate as its supernatural beings are, its fancy seems to us to be modified by the former qualities of mind, rather than by the latter and higher faculty. Indeed, where the fancy is called out in sprightly satire, it is more likely to partake of the ingenious than of the poetic, though this is not the tendency of graver satire. And in whatever approaches to parody, travesty, or any form of the mock character, still more likely is this to be the case, and fancy to be merged in cleverness and a certain species of wit. Parody, travesty, or the like, however near it may seem to come to poetry, and however generally it may be taken for it, gives no assurance, but rather the contrary, of the writer's success in works of an opposite and strictly poetic kind: it is the product of talents rather than of genius, — poetic genius we mean. Now the Rape of the Lock does partake somewhat of this character; and though we do not intend to dispute its possessing poetic fancy, yet in so far as it savours of the other character will the principle spoken of more or less apply.

The poem is full of life; and it is animating to see how briskly at work the author is, how gay upon fashionable follies, and dexterous in setting out a toilet; how well arranged things are; and what a show there is of beaux and belles, powdered heads, craped cushions, fans and furbelows, ruffs, cards, and tea-cups, with all sorts of washes, and essences too, till the senses nigh ache at it.

This taking of supernatural poetic beings from poetic scenes and relations, and shutting them up in a drawing-room, and associating them with the most anti-poetic form of artificial society, is primarily the work of wit rather than of fancy; and while we would not, for a moment, question the predominance of fancy in the poem, yet is it fancy quickened by the former faculty, wit, and working in its service and wearing its badge: it is fancy owing much of its activity to wit. It is the very reverse of the fairy parts of Midsummer Night's Dream, where what there may be of wit is salient from and subordinated to poetic fancy, — poetic fancy in its amusive mood.

And how do Shakspeare's little creatures divert themselves with honest Bottom? Why, with fanning the moonbeams from his sleeping eyes with the wings of painted butterflies, caught in their airy chases. Some kill cankers in the musk-rose buds; some war with rear-mice, and others keep back the clamorous owl; — all their duties and all their language bring before you poetic beings of substance as delicate as the soft air they play in, and doing the offices of poetry. They are not tied up to the leading object, — a comic one, — as in Pope, but are seen coursing among flowers and silver dew-drops, or just coming into sight through the moonlight, with some trophy of their skill and spirit; yet the main purpose is not neglected. Drayton's Nymphidia, too, partakes of the ludicrous, — but how subordinated to the poetical! Considered in reference to its *poetical* character solely, is it inferior to Pope's work? — While we would not detract a jot from the really great merit of Pope's poem, we would make what we think to be a well-grounded distinction respecting it.

But the English moralist, as he has been styled, has produced one work — at least so says Mr. Hazlitt — in which "the tears shed are drops gushing from the heart: the words are burning sighs breathed from the soul of love." And can Mr. Hazlitt come away from reading the old poets, or the better poets of this day, and take up the Epistle of Eloisa to Abelard, and feel his eyes moisten and heart move? We doubt whether even Mr. Hazlitt is so tenderly constituted as ever to have shed a tear on the occasion.

We quarrel with no one on the point of taste; but it is something more serious when a man can come directly before the lady and gentleman auditors of the Surrey Lectures, with an intimation of a certain sort, and in language so warm, upon a poem on so gross a subject as this. Yet how can we speak thus, when we find the Rev. Joseph Warton saying of the most offensive line in this licentious poem, — "And then follows a line exquisitely passionate, and worthy the sensibility [sensibility!] of Sappho or Eloisa." — And so they wrap it up, and call the *furor* of appetite passion and sensibility in these dear creatures!

The truth is, Pope's frequent allusions of a certain kind, in his works, show that his mind was tainted; and this, together with the disgusting nature of his subject and his lack of truly poetic sentiment and passion, has made the poem what it is. Fuzeli has well termed it "hot ice." For, with the exception of a few lines of simple passion, — and we must remember that most of these are gathered from the original prose, — it is hot with lust, and cold with false sentiment, vague generalities, sought antitheses, forced apostrophes, and all sorts of artificialities, in the place of natural feeling and plain truth.

But we must leave Eloisa; for the lamps are dying around, a voice from a shrine summons her to prepare for death, and she bursts away in the following rhapsody: —

> "I come, I come! prepare your roseate bowers,
> Celestial palms, and ever-blooming flowers."

We have spoken of Pope's general closeness and correctness of language in the imitative, satirical, and didactic portions of his works. With that same want of discrimination which has been shown in other points, he has been praised for these qualities, as if his writings at large partook of them. On the contrary, few poets of high rank have been so defective in this respect as Pope, when he has left satire and moral teaching, for nature and subjects strictly poetical. Here he felt less vividly and saw and thought less distinctly, and, of course, uttered himself too often in generalities, less logically, with less life, definiteness, and adaptedness of terms; for words are the manifestations of the spirit within. In what commonplace tawdriness is the couplet just now quoted dressed, with its "roseate bowers," and "ever-blooming flowers," — which, we suppose, mean pretty much the same thing. And here, again, we have "bowery mazes," and "sequestered scenes," and "surrounding greens": —

> "Ye sacred Nine! that all my soul possess,
> Whose raptures fire me, and whose visions bless,
> Bear me, O, bear me to sequestered scenes,
> The bowery mazes, and surrounding greens."

Not so talked the veritable Eloisa!

> "But e'en those clouds at last adorn its way,
> Reflect new glories, and augment the day."

Who ever talks of clouds *augmenting* the day? or of any thing else doing so? Nor is *elevates* a fitting term in the following connection: —

> "Is it for thee the lark ascends and sings?
> Joy tunes his voice, joy elevates his wings."

And of a piece with it, or worse, —

> "Or under southern skies exalt their sails."

Exalt a *sail!*

> "Come, with one glance of those deluding eyes
> Blot out each bright idea of the skies."

Beside the illogical combination of words, we ask whether any small compounder of amatory or complimentary verses could be guilty of the manufacture of flimsier tinsel? — "deluding eyes," "glances," and "bright ideas." But this is called Eloisa and passion. And so, we suppose, is this: —

> "And waft a sigh from Indus to the pole."

And this: —

"Yet here for ever, ever, must I stay;
Sad proof how well a lover can obey."

"Unequal task a passion to resign."

Resign a *passion!* But not only so; flames, too, must be resigned:—

"Here all its frailties, all its flames resign."

"The transient landscape now in clouds decays."

Better still, we have *decays* as a noun plural, which we hold to be singular, and which would hardly have found place here, but for the rhyme's sake:—

"These ever new, nor subject to decays,
Spread and grow brighter with the length of days."

Mr. Hazlitt has noticed the frequent recurrence of *sense* as a rhyming word. There are a few others quite as great favourites with our poet, coming in full as often, and rather more inappropriately; such as *display*, *survey*. Then we have *greens* in abundance.

We wish that some one had the patience and curiosity to ascertain the number of times these words occur! For, poor things, they seem to have been kept like a family drudge, to do the service of all or any who happened not to be at hand. We have already quoted lines, for another purpose, in which *scenes* and *greens* occur as rhymes; and here are more:—

"To paint anew the flowery sylvan scenes,
To crown the forests with immortal greens."

"Call forth the greens, and wake the rising flowers."

How is one to wake flowers that are already *rising*, unless they get up in their sleep?

"Her gloomy presence saddens all the scene,
Shades every flower, and darkens every green."

Here we have "gloomy," "saddens," "shades," "darkens," all in the space of a couplet. And this, too, is called "close writing," we suppose!

And now for a *display.*

> "New graces yearly like thy works display,
> Soft without weakness, without glaring gay."

> "Beneath the shade a spreading beech displays
> Hylas and Ægon sung their rural lays."

> "Here waving groves a chequered scene display,
> And part admit, and part exclude the day."

And, next, for a *survey* of other couplets.

> "The face of nature we no more survey,
> All glares alike, without distinction gay."

> "There at one passage oft you might survey,
> A lie and truth contending for the way."

> "Stretched on the lawn his second hope survey,
> At once the chaser, and at once the prey."

> "Methinks already I your tears survey,
> Already hear the horrid things they say."

How would a lad, who had written such lines, have fared, had he fallen into the hands of some old master Bowyer? — Helicon and the Pump! But enough of such instances!

Much has been said of the melody of Pope's verse; and, if the term be taken in its most limited sense, as implying the smoothness of single lines, we will not question it. But what can be more wearisomely monotonous (to say nothing of the closes of every line) than the ceaselessly regular return of the cæsural pause? We remember meeting somewhere with examples of this from Pope, in which lines were drawn by the side of the cæsura through long passages, and almost without a bend. But is there not a melody better than this, and with more of rhythm and varying flow? Surely, he had never prayed, or had prayed in vain, —

> "Lend me your song, ye nightingales! O, pour
> The mazy-running soul of melody
> Into my varied verse."

As to "linked harmonies," he was incapable of perceiving them in music, — much less could his spirit utter them in verse. Bowles has said of his Pastorals, what he might have applied to his other poems, — "Warton does not seem sufficiently to discriminate between the softness of individual lines, ... and the general harmony of poetic numbers." And again, — in too limited a way, however, — "His nice precision of every line prevented, in a few instances, a more musical flow of modulated passages." We may well apply to his versification his own lines, —

> "In wit, as nature, what affects our hearts
> Is not the exactness of peculiar parts;
> 'T is not a lip, or eye, we beauty call,
> But the joint force and full result of all."

It is not this mechanical meting out of the lines alone which wearies you. The effect is increased by the over-frequently inverted form in which the lines are made to terminate in verbs, for the sake of rhyme.

> "Meanly they seek the blessing to confine,
> And force the sun but on a part to shine,
> Which not alone the southern wit sublimes,
> But ripens spirits in cold northern climes."

> "'T is not enough your counsel still be true;
> Blunt truths more mischief than nice falsehoods do."

A sufficiently clumsy inversion this last, yet in some degree emulated by the following: —

"With his own tongue still edifies his ears,
And always listening to himself appears."

"Made for his use all creatures if he call,
Say what their use, had he the powers of all."

"(Her guide now lost) no more attempts to rise,
But in low numbers short excursions tries:
Content, if hence the unlearned their wants may view,
The learned reflect on what before they knew."

Another defect in his versification is the nearness to each other of couplets terminating in the same rhyme. Yet, notwithstanding this fault and that of the very frequent endings in verbs, his rhymes are, after all, allowed by Mr. Hazlitt to be frequently imperfect, and rather to the eye than for the ear.

"Who now reads Cowley? If he pleases yet,
His moral pleases, not his pointed wit;
Forgot his Epic, nay, Pindaric art,
But still I love the language of his heart.
Yet surely, surely, they were famous men!
What boy but hears the sayings of old Ben?
In all debates where critics bear a part,
Not one but nods, and talks of Jonson's art,
Of Shakspeare's nature, and of Cowley's wit:
How Beaumont's judgement checked what Fletcher writ."

And again:—

"F. See libels, Satires,—here you have it,—read.
P. Libels and Satires! lawless things indeed!
But grave Epistles, bringing vice to light,
Such as a King might read, a Bishop write,
Such as Sir Robert would approve ——
F. Indeed?
The case is altered,—you may then proceed."

"Where towering oaks their growing honours rear,
And future navies on thy shores appear,
Not Neptune's self from all her streams receives
A wealthier tribute than to thine he gives.

No seas so rich, so gay no banks appear,
No lake so gentle, and no spring so clear."

In this latter extract we have again an instance of the terminations in verbs.

"Think what an equipage thou hast in air,
And view with scorn two pages and a chair.
As now your own, our beings were of old,
And once inclosed in Woman's beauteous mould;
Thence, by a soft transition, we repair
From earthly vehicles to these of air."

"And I not strip the gilding off a knave,
Unplaced, unpensioned, no man's heir, or slave?
I will, or perish in the generous cause:
Hear this, and tremble, you who 'scape the laws.
Yes, while I live, no rich or noble knave
Shall walk the world, in credit to his grave."

It will be observed that the fault reaches to the repetition of the very words. We might go on multiplying instances, to the surprise of any who have not taken particular notice of this defect; for no poet has sinned oftener in this way. Should any one doubt it, let him examine more strictly the poems that do not come under the head of the satirical.

This repetition may occur over-frequently in some writers, from their relucting at the labour of correction. But Pope, it is boasted, was the most patient and painstaking of men at this work.—It is apparent how much this frequent falling of similar sounds upon the ear must add to the wearisomeness of the general monotony.

While on the subject of rhymes, we may as well set down some instances of identical rhymes which we chanced upon.

"Why not with equal ease
Confess as well your folly, as disease?"

"Who sent the thief that stole the cash away,
And punished him that put it in his way."

"The doubtful beam long nods from side to side;
At length the wits mount up, the hairs subside."

"But this bold lord with manly strength endued,
She with one finger and a thumb subdued."

Pope himself would hardly have been inclined to plead some of the older English poets in justification of a practice which, if we mistake not, had nearly ceased in his own day; and which, however in conformity to French and Italian usage, is not agreeable in our own language to an English ear.

In speaking of his inverted form of bringing in his verbs, we would not be understood as laying the inverted structure of sentences under the sweeping condemnation which many pass upon it. For, undoubtedly, it is often the natural utterance of impassioned and lofty thought, and where it is so it adds force and grandeur. But where it is evident that its frequent occurrence is simply for the rhyme's sake, and in poetry, too, as unimpassioned and as far from sublimity as Pope's, its only effect is to weary us with its sameness and offend us with its artificiality.

In his Moral Essays, we meet with much exaggeration, and with perpetually recurring antithesis, that in its effect may be often called a form of exaggeration, and which young minds are apt to run into, but from which the matured mind should have freed itself so far as to use it sparingly.

"While the gaunt mastiff, growling at the gate,
Affrights the beggar whom he longs to eat,"

is an instance which, however witty some may think it, is inconsistent with the general spirit of a passage that is among Pope's best descriptions.

"But on some lucky day, (as when they found
A lost bank-bill, or heard their son was drowned)."

And again:—

"Narcissa's nature, tolerably mild,
To make a wash, would hardly stew a child."

This is a striking example, and the more so as it is a work of supererogation, not being in the Satire of which it is an Imitation, and which surely goes far enough.

"A few gray hairs his reverend temples crowned,
'T was very want that sold them for two pound."

A goodly price, truly, and a part of which we should have guessed to have gone for the rhyme, had it not been for the spirit of exaggeration of which we complain, and that the verse is made to halt with the weight of "two," when it might have carried *a* pound easily enough. Though there is not wanting authority for such a use of the noun singular as we find in the above and following couplets,—

"Or in pure Equity (the case not clear)
The Chancery takes your rents for twenty year,"—

still it would hardly be looked for in Pope. And we believe that, notwithstanding his sanction, good writers have nearly or quite given it up, on account of its certain air of vulgarity.

We cannot but ask, in passing, what must have been the reading of the lovers of poetry in that day, when one could think of stealing from the Comus without fearing immediate detection.

"By grots and caverns shagged with horrid shades."

Now Pope:—

"Ye grots and caverns shagged with horrid thorn."

And, alas! with the "shades" fled the imaginative character of the pöetry. Again,—

> "Above the smoke and stir of this dim spot
> Which men call Earth, and with low-thoughted care
> Confined, and pestered in this pin-fold here."

And now for Pope once more:—

> "O Grace serene! O Virtue heavenly fair! ["O" indeed!]
> Divine oblivion of low-thoughted care."

Every one feels immediately that Pope never could have used such an epithet but by an act of memory,—that no length of time could have made it his own to his mind. There were no *mento*-chemical affinities for it to combine with there.

We have dwelt awhile on particulars which may seem to some of small importance; yet they are not so. Besides, the consummate skill of Pope, his mastery over his art, his faultlessness as a writer, have been urged upon the world, till those who do not class him with the few poets of highest rank have conceded to him these merits almost without qualification, and notwithstanding such marked defects after all his labour at finish. Is not much in his art, for which he has been so praised, a very little way removed from mechanic art? The smoothness of single lines is dearly bought, when obtained by such monotony and inversion, and by Latin terms ill sorting with their context, and rendering vaguely general what should be particular, confounding the abstract with the concrete, and effacing the image where there should be distinct picture. If such things be, as Byron and some others would have us believe, the consummation of Art, we can only say, give us Nature, then, in her ruggedest form, and we will be content. We well remember, after having travelled on, page after page, to one unchanging tune, with what a sense of surprise, with what a rousing effect, the close of the following passage from the Imitation of Horace broke upon us: —

> "Loud as the wolves, on Orca's stormy steep,
> Howl to the roarings of the Northern deep."

It calls up the sounding close of Campbell's couplet,—

> "And waft across the waves' tumultuous roar,
> The wolf's long howl from Oonalaska's shore," —

and certainly goes sounding on with a grandeur surpassing that of the woods and waters of the original: —

> "Garganum mugire putes nemus, aut mare Tuscum."

From what we have before said, our remarks, especially where they bear upon his language, will be understood as intended less for the satirical and didactic portions of his works, than for those of which the subjects are of a more strictly poetical nature. While he confines himself to naked satire, or plain moral or critical teaching, he is, for the most part, clear, apt, and logical in his use of words.

But as soon as he turns to a strictly poetic subject, or would illustrate a plainer one by a passing poetic image, clear and appropriate words seem to take their flight, and vague and unapt ones to light in their places, as if a sudden dimness had fallen on his mental vision, blurring the imagery, and a confusion of speech had happened to him. He has a deal too much of what was wont to be called poetic phraseology, for no better reason than that it would make intolerably bad prose. He was for hanging the inner room of the Muses' Temple in the ill-shaped imagery of a worn and faded tapestry. He was a trained and worthy servitor in its courts, but no Aaron to burn the heaven-ascending incense before its shrine.

We all know on what nicety and exact truth of terms the entire living form of poetry depends. Yet Pope's notions about poetical language went but little beyond a Frenchman's. Seldom are there any attachments or poetic associations with his words; nor have they more power over our emotions than the sing-song of his metre. They are, as we have said, rarely pictures, but rather cold abstractions, too often loosely and unphilosophically combined. Place his poetical passages by the side of our old poets, or by the better poets since his day. Take, in his translations, the much talked of description of Night, the meeting of Hector and Andromache, the description of Polypheme, or, indeed, most of the noted passages of Homer, and put them along-side the "bald and naked" version of Cowper, as it has been called, and you see at once how wanting in the peculiar eye and tongue of a poet he is.

Says Cowper, in a letter to his friend Hill,—"I have two French prints hanging in my study, both on Iliad subjects; and I have an English one in the parlour, on a subject from the same poem. In one of the former, Agamemnon addresses Achilles exactly in the attitude of a dancing-master turning Miss in a minuet: in the latter the figures are plain, and the attitudes plain also. This is, in some considerable measure, I believe, the difference between my translation and Pope's; and will serve as an exemplification of what I am going to lay before you and the public."

Had Coleridge applied his hand to analyzing Pope's poetic language, as he has done to analyzing that of some others, with what dust and chaff would his sifting of words have filled the air, and how small a heap of golden grain would have been left behind! The passages which we have already quoted furnish instances enough, and make it needless to encumber ourselves with more.

This mere difference of style between the treatment of his satirical and didactic subjects, and of his strictly poetical ones, is of itself something more than an indication that Bowles is not far from right in denying to Pope the character of poet, in its highest and strictest sense. Nor will Byron's clever, savage, but superficial letter alter the matter with any one who is clear of party, and has a right apprehension of the distinctive attributes of poetry.

While we think there is little in the objection, that Pope produced no one great poem approaching the epic, we do think that the light amount of his original poetry, compared with his Translations and Imitations, is presumptive of a secondary order of poetic power. When language, and verse, and all the mechanics of art are appropriated to *turning out* modified expressions and forms of the thoughts and images of other minds, we may be well assured that there are within no great multitude of living forms struggling to break forth, nor many emotions of the soul striving for relief in voice. Real poetic genius may be unproductive, through constitutional indolence, and find ease in musings and day-dreams; or the sorrows or cares of life may weigh upon it, and the man may endeavour to forget his higher and complete self in the exercise of any faculty save this supreme one; — he may not have the heart for it. As Coleridge once replied to a friend, — "I am too unhappy for that." But when one, to the neglect of original working, continues to busy himself about his art with manufacturing and finishing off verse for the conveyance of others' thoughts, the suspicion will arise, that he has more fondness for the use of the instruments, than he possesses substance in those attributes of the soul for whose organs of utterance the instruments were meant.

Another point is, that the pathos of the true poet is not dependent upon his personal interest in the event or individual that gives it birth. But events lying far off in place or time, hints which the formative principle in him seizes upon and gives expanse and shape to, things acting through the creative faculty, — these the true poet utters in tones of tenderness and deep passion. But Pope's heart must be first touched, not through the ideal, but by some fact or person near and tangible, something relating to himself, before he can utter the language of simple pathos: — it must be his mother, or Gay, or — for we will not here question its true and simple tenderness — the Unfortunate Lady. And this has enabled many a one, of no high poetic character of mind, to express himself in pleasing and moving verse. Unless it had its origin in the *pride* of pity, the Death of Villiers may be taken as an exception, as, so far from its being introduced from personal attachment, it was to censure and to warn that it is spoken of. It is one of the most touching things in this poet, more touching to us than Mr. Hazlitt's bewept Eloisa and Abelard, — from the line

> "In these deep solitudes and awful cells,"

> "He best can paint 'em who shall feel 'em most."

Rarely is Pope's thought illustrated by any thing from nature; and when so, it is with the faultiness which we have spoken of. His early attempts in verse — his Pastorals and Windsor Forest — are drawn from books, not from fields and woods that surrounded him at his

17*

birth, and amidst which he was then living: — little of eye had he for nature, and, even then, less of heart.

We have just spoken of his pathos being dependent upon something personal to himself. And it is well worth remarking how much of his satire even, in which he was more at home, rests upon it, and owes its dexterous vivacity to a double personality, if we may so express it, — to the love of himself and his personal hatred of another. With what keen and malign glee does he seize upon the weapons of Horace, and turn them upon his own enemies! — and they were legion; for with him party opposition was too much personal enmity, especially towards his superiours in rank and wealth. But the highest poetic genius, though it may sometimes make use of its near enmities, loves, and interests, as of other things, does it seldom, and never owes its life and power to these. It embodies from itself, and finds in its own world the objects of its passions, and its ideal is its real state. This habitual indulgence in personalities argues a mind limited, and dwelling more upon small particulars than upon great principles, and constitutionally wanting in lofty thought. Accordingly, passages of high moral indignation are but thinly scattered through Pope's works, — such passages, for instance, as are found in the Epilogue to his Satires, and in his lines on the Unfortunate Lady, — which, from their seldomness, bring with them a certain sense of surprise.

His mind and affections wanted expansibility. He talks much about his right and duty to castigate the vices and follies of the age, but loved rather, we fear,

> "To make Vice sit for purposes of strife,
> And draw the hag much larger than in life."

He seems to have been moved by an unkind delight

at the failings of others, and to find more amusement in showing up the fool than the folly. His perpetual recurrence, also, and in gross forms, to Lady Mary Wortley Montague, indicates that spite towards her was seldom out of his mind; and an asp-like venom seems to be infused into the pertinacity of his hate. How different the general character of his satire from the broad view and the moral loftiness of that of Cowper and Young, which, in the very act of making us ashamed of our weaknesses, imparts to us strength, and cleanses our hearts in making us feel our pollution! — We rise from their satire with our natures not degraded, but ennobled.

But does not all this show a lower poetic action in Pope? He tried to deceive himself in this matter, and, with the help of his friends, succeeded but too well, we fear; and the darts dipped in the poison of his own gall were called the honest weapons of an open warfare waged against vice. So, in his eternal splenetic flings at courts and kings, like many others, he mistook envy for scorn; and with a consistency like theirs, while seeking anxiously to make out a pedigree from noble blood, talked loudly of owing all to self. Among the greatest of egotists, the melancholy part of it is, that he discovered it more in his enmity towards others, than in honest boasting of his own powers. Surely this is not favourable to poetry in its beautiful and grander forms. The groundwork of his Essay on Man and his Moral Epistles is not only false philosophy, but, what is the important point here, is contrary to a deep poetic nature. The poet of the higher order may hold to a mistaken philosophy, but then it will be of a mystic character, with something in it congenial with our profounder spiritual being, moving with our more mysterious emotions and blending with our aspirations after things unseen. But Pope's adopted scheme indicates that pathos and sublimity were not the elements of his soul.

If we have gone somewhat particularly into his defects, and have said comparatively little upon his undoubted merits, it has not been from any party feeling, — for we hope that we like whatever is good in its kind, and relish as much as others that in which he excels, — but for the purpose of pointing out how indiscriminate has been the praise bestowed upon him, and with how little propriety he has been classed, in strictly poetic qualities, in the first rank of our great poetic worthies. The keen satirist and plain-sense moralist must needs be set up as the first of poets. Our poetic language, the language of Shakspeare and Milton, had not, we have been told, attained its perfectness till he spoke. And the full organ-tones of Milton, and the varying and mellifluous harmonies of Shakspeare, and Spenser, and the singers of old, must be hushed, for all the world to stand listening to the one unvarying note from the pipe of Pope.

No wonder that such notions should have prevailed in his time, and that Warburton and others should have lauded him in ludicrously bad taste. For the tide of the poetic sea had then run out, and little was to be seen or heard but the dull flats and the warm dribblings through the gullies of the shore. But now, when the channels have so far filled again with the returning waters, it is strange indeed that any should maintain there was at that day no ebbing of the tide.

Of the effect left upon a thoughtful mind after a long-continued reading of Pope, we fear we must say that it is by no means a grateful one. We pass by his choice of such subjects as Eloisa to Abelard, the loose character of his selections from Chaucer, his Sappho to Phaon, and his many gross allusions,— for greater minds than his have sinned more or less in this way, and something must be set down to the times. But the personalities of his satire, with all its wit and cleverness, at length make us heart-weary; and the absence of an elevated spirit, and of a yearning after something higher than we possess and better than we are, depresses us with a sense of the littleness and poorness of the world, without quickening us into a purer life by awakening our finer emotions, or making us feel the strength of life by stirring the loftier passions which have being within us. We pity the man who can read Pope for any length of time, and not feel his need of the restoring and elevating influences of our older, yes, and of some of our later bards, — who can say to himself, "I 'm content." We have dwelt overlong on this part of our review, and yet have left much unsaid.

It is narrowness of mind, or pride of system, which takes from some men a relish for the exercise of the intellect through all its varieties. One tires and yawns at sentiment; another recoils from wit as undignified, and, wrapped up in the dull and vulgar, yet smile-provoking dignity of his own importance, puts from him all humour, as so much buffoonery.

The man who likes widely, for the most part, likes truly. Confined taste comes from some defect in us, which weakens our relish and warps our judgement even of those things which we like best. He who has sentiment and humour is more thoroughly possessed of both, than he who has a feeling of but one of them can be of either. Where we are moved violently, we are moved strangely. Through the over-shadowings of affliction images the most grotesque are passing, now dimly, now distinctly, before us; and even into the depths of a sorrow which seems to have driven out from the heart all that is impure, and to have made it the dwelling of heavenly visitants, unholy thoughts, seemingly formed from without us and on which we shut our eyes with loathing and horrour, make their way.

With this show of contradictions mocking us in the very sincerity and earnestness of our passions, and with all the changing images and shifting lights of our minds, a singleness of taste, which puts aside every thing that is not modelled to its own notions, is punished for its warring with nature, by being cut off from its rich and healthful varieties.

Yet every mind has something which it turns to as especially its own, and each thing connected with it is looked on with a peculiar fondness. It has its society of thoughts and feelings, which are as old friends to it, and though it may find entertainment abroad, these are of its household. Now, surely, it will not be said, No matter what their character, so there be enough of them. Minds of the higher order, — minds that have a heart in them, — look up to lofty objects, go out over broad nature, and hang over its simple and lasting beauties. With such, ill-humour is not seriousness, nor vain laughter cheerfulness. They have moral elevation, and deep and sober sympathies,

> "That steal upon the meditative mind,
> And grow with thought."

Their gayety has the pure gladness of morning in it; and their associations are with what is stable and good.

Allowing something to the modifications of our natures, such were the old English poets, and such are the modern, compared with those who shone and sparkled in the age of Queen Anne. The early poets did not think to make us moral by cold teaching, or to change the corrupt heart to soundness by ridiculing the fopperies of fashion. They worked with instruments of more power and with mightier hands. They were not little, and brisk, and smart, but of large minds, full and various. They are as another race, of a taller growth and broader spread, and stand among those who shot up after them like old oaks among slender and prim poplars, rough, irregular, gigantic, and dark.

Speaking generally, the poets of Queen Anne's time, and a little before, were men of wit; and those of them who had something of decency now and then talked morality, but appeared hardly to feel it. They seemed to write rather for a well-dressed party of ladies and gentlemen, than for the man of sentiment and genius in his study; — they were society poets, and looked at little more than the outside of things.

Though such men may entertain us for a while, they awaken no sense of inward satisfaction. They may speak truths, but in such a way, and of such a nature, as not to fasten upon us; and of their conventional wit we soon weary. We feel relieved when we have again returned to ourselves, and to what almost make a part of us, the works of those who tell us what is in our hearts, and help us to see and love the earth on which God has placed us. It is indeed a reviving thing to quit London, and "sin and sea-coal," as Sir Roger hath it, for the open country and pure air.

No wonder, when, in such a state of things, Thomson appeared, he so speedily reached that popularity he well deserved. The young and the old, the rich and the poor, the learned and the ignorant, all crowded out of the city to meet him. He was the high-priest of Nature, and he showed them her grand and simple works, and taught them to understand and love them. He turned their eyes upward to the moon and the pure stars, and, again, bade them watch the shifting forms and changing colours of the clouds, as they floated in the sunlight. The green hills and brown mountains, that looked so visionary in the mists, opened upon them, and harts were seen drinking at the water-brooks. They were filled with a strange joy at "the silent looks of happy things," and felt their minds expanding under new and far-reaching associations: —

> "Here littleness was not; the least of things
> Seemed infinite."

The old trees on the earth were as their ancestors unto them; and hills and valleys, and even the smallest things, seemed types and figures of eternity. They had a sense of a nobler and kindred nature within them, and of wiser and soberer purposes taking root in their minds.

Thomson was one of the first to bring about this wholesome change; and, as he made himself in a good measure, though not entirely, independent of the writers of his own day, so did he, too, of those who had gone before him. He must have the credit of originality. They say that he copied from the Georgics. That he has here and there made use of them is true, but is little to the purpose. Virgil, before him, stole, and Milton was a noted thief. Great minds read books as they read things, and do not go to them, like children and the common folk, to get a lesson by rote. If they have in themselves that fire of genius, into which all that is thrown, be it from where it may, is melted down, and comes out fresh cast and new shaped by their own mould, it is enough.

The faults of Thomson's style are of quite an obvious kind. There is scarce a passage in which you are not annoyed by some objectionable phrase; and his diction is so cumbrous, that you read with a wearying weight upon you. He abounds in words that should seldom be met with except in a dictionary, or a court letter of compliment, and that are for ever thrusting their unmeaning faces between you and the picture.

Mr. Hazlitt must not be allowed to treat this as a matter of little consequence, and in a manner accidental. He knows well enough that there may be as much poetry in the use of a particular word, or in a certain arrangement of common words, as in a set description, and sometimes much more; and that often it is one simple word, which, from its place in the passage, so strikes our minds, that a thousand associations are started, and feelings set in motion, such as the most laboured circumlocution never could awaken.

Not mainly, but partly, from this suggestive quality in a poetic use of words, from these hints, if we may so say, in descriptions, it often comes to pass, that,—having for some time laid by a work, portions of which we call to mind with peculiar delight, and which, according to the impressions left upon us, we think of as prolonged and abounding in particulars,—if we turn to these again, the first effect will be disappointment at finding how little is actually set down, what were pages in our minds having diminished to a common paragraph, and how few the beauties actually made out, where, according to our remembrance, the passages were thronged with them. There is no less vital power in them, however; indeed, there is more. For they not only gave to our minds so much as was put down, but also imparted of their own suggestive action to us, so that, when we shut the book the second time, the same feelings and the same scenery return, in spite of our momentary disappointment.

Neither can we set Thomson's principal faults of style to what Mr. Hazlitt is pleased to call his easy temper and careless indolence; they have quite a different origin, and are far-fetched and laboured. Or rather, without meaning to take from his poetic genius, his mental constitution was not strong enough, nor his taste pure enough, to throw off the diseases with which the poetry of that age was infected.

Is what follows a specimen of this easy temper and careless indolence? —

> "Eager, on rapid sleds,
> Their vigorous youth in bold contention wheel
> The long resounding course. Meantime, to raise
> The manly strife, with highly blooming charms,
> Flushed by the season, Scandinavia's dames
> Or Russia's buxom daughters glow around."

Now this is as watery and showy as the thin and gaudy colours which are duly set in a druggist's bow-window. There is nothing beyond it, unless it be our standing toast, — "The fair daughters of Columbia"!

Whether it was from a predilection for the enfeebling term *around*, or that he found it to be a convenient expletive, we cannot determine; but of this we are sure, many a fine passage in his works is spoiled by it. *Immense*, too, is another favourite; and it is not seldom that we meet with these pets pacing on together, hand in hand: —

> "The bursting prospect spread immense around."
>
> "Through the black night that sits immense around."

Were it not for this silly form of expression, the passage of which the latter line is a part would be one of much grandeur.

One would frequently be led to suppose he went upon the principle that poetic diction, *par excellence*, lay in terms as far as possible from natural ones, and should express a thought or image with as little of distinctness as might well be attained to. There is, likewise, so much of the vulgar dread of being thought vulgar, that he goes about the commonest offices of life in full dress; and you come upon him amidst half-naked, sweating harvest-men, or wet and hungry fishermen, in his gold-bound hat and laced coat, with rake and sickle, or hook and line, in hand; while the elegant *Amanda* "amusively" "walks the smiling mead," as she

> "Beholds the kindling country glow around."

Here he is among the country clowns, — we ask pardon, among the "spotless swains," "rustic youth," "generous band," — getting in hay? O, shocking! a question not to be asked. As far from it as possible; they are only disporting themselves as

> "They drive the dusky wave along the mead."

And now he betakes himself, thus accoutred, to the water, and, as may well be guessed, not for ordinary fishing, but for something every way finer, — to "draw the copious fry"!

Even birds are any thing but birds; they are "feathered youth," or "tuneful nations," or "gentle tenants of the shade," who "indulge their purer loves."

When, to ordinary people, it rains,

"The full distended clouds
Indulge their genial stores."

And a horse which breaks loose, it is said,

"Springs the high fence; and o'er the field effused,
Darts on the gloomy flood."

The next use of this latter term, though not illogical, like the other, is affectedly fine enough:—

"The glittering court effuses every pomp."

How poor is this compared with the Scripture-like grandeur of the often-quoted passage of Cowper!—

"To see the stir
Of the great Babel, and not feel the crowd;
To hear the roar she sends through all her gates
At a safe distance, where the dying sound
Falls a soft murmur on the uninjured ear."

Again,—

"Where simple nature reigns; and every view
Diffusive spreads the pure Dorsetian downs."

And this is "simple nature"!

"Lead me to the mountain's brow,
Where sits the shepherd on the grassy turf,
Inhaling healthful the descending sun.
Around him feed his many-bleating flock,
Of various cadence; and his sportive lambs,
This way and that convolved, in friskful glee,
Their frolics play. And now the sprightly race
Invites them forth; when swift, the signal given,
They start away, and sweep the massy mound
That runs around the hill, the rampart once
Of iron war."

Here be epithets enough and to spare!—"Many-bleating," "various cadence," "convolved" flock of sheep, "sportive lambs," "friskful glee," "frolics play," "sprightly race," — and all these in the narrow space of four consecutive lines.

We next meet with him in Hagley Park; and were it not for occasional felicities of description, we should gather, from the general namby-pamby character of the lines, that he had never been out on the other side of its pale. For there he is with thee "O Littleton," "courting the Muse" in "thy British Tempe."

> "Perhaps thy loved Lucinda shares thy walk,
> With soul to thine attuned."

And now, again, he sits with Pitt, in one of those specimens of what for centuries could not but have been effete classical fooleries, — "The Temple of Virtue," — ominous of the time when he was to "draw the tragic scene." But if wise men wasted wealth in building such follies, we may well pardon Thomson the cheaper deed of putting them into verse.

We sometimes meet with a half-way personification of abstract qualities, through which the true sense is lost, no image presented to the eye, and so indistinct a state of mind induced, that, if not careful, we read on without any definite notion of what we are about. This fault may not happen often; it should not at all; for it would seem to be one especially reserved for those who, not being blessed with poetic powers, take upon them to contemn plain prose.

One thing which we would urge somewhat doubtingly as a fault, and which, at any rate, may be called the excess of a particular excellence, is an over-accumulation in describing. We are filled almost to repletion, so as to be in momentary danger of stagnation taking place. Thomson crowds his descriptions so closely upon us, that there is no opportunity to look at them severally, or to give them their proper places; so that, after going over a few pages, it is hardly possible to recall his scenes, and we must turn back again, and take them, as well as we may, one by one. We do not carry them about with us in our memory, or call them up when in a musing mood. He has given us a kind of poetical map of the world, but with a surface so closely dotted over, that the eye longs for a few deserts, a little *terra incognita*, and the sweep of an ocean or two, in way of relief. Then we have such careful and numerous observations upon the clouds, and changes of the air and seasons, as to amount to a very tolerable poetico-meteorological table.

Another fault involved in the foregoing, in part the cause of it, is the want of relief from this almost continuous description by the spontaneous outflow of moral reflections, — we do not mean such as Crabbe's gentle Vicar utters, — and by the bringing in of the heart and mind of man, as they might be supposed to be moved and carried forward by what was present to them. We are aware that a mere image, coming from a mind in a true condition of moral sentiment, may awaken another mind to that same state, just as well as if there had been a sentiment tagged to it.

But Thomson too seldom does more than put us into that pleasurable state into which we are brought by looking upon the material world, without going deep, and into its spiritual forms. And when he does throw out remarks, it is ten to one that they are some sage observations upon affairs of state, having as little natural connection as possible with the subject in hand, and rather attached to than forming a part of the web of the work. And when he leaves inanimate nature and the brute creation, and ascends to man, he almost always fails.

His episodes are, for the most part, abominable. Yet the time was when these gave him no small portion of his popularity: — It was the "Lavinias," the "Amelias," and "Amandas" of the day that smiled upon him, happy man! We are clear, too, with Mr. Hazlitt, that he should not have meddled with the story of Ruth. And for doing so we blame him, and not for his failure; for in that he only shares the fate common to all who have attempted to improve upon the Bible stories, or to turn them from their original purpose or form. It is a sacrilege to attempt to change the voice of native pathos, or to interfere with the patriarchal simplicity of the holy men of old; and verily whoever does it hath his reward in the figure which he makes in comparison.

We have dwelt upon these faults, both because due discrimination required it, and because Mr. Hazlitt would make light of them, that he might, in way of contrast, impart more liveliness to his ineffectual attempt upon Cowper. It is for these reasons, and not, we trust, from a disposition to speak lightly of our superiours. We leave that to Mr. Hazlitt and whoever else may affect it.

Yet with all these faults, Thomson hardly had a contemporary who wrote with such happiness of poetic diction, or with such poetic feeling and thought. There are now and then turns of expression reminding you of Milton, — sometimes, perhaps, too like him not to be directly borrowed, — and here and there we happen upon the exquisite felicities of our old dramatists. The opening pages of Winter, for instance, though much harmed by his peculiar defects, have touches of grandeur almost Miltonic, and that not only in the words, but also in the images and the movement of the verse.

"Hung o'er the farthest verge of heaven, the sun
Scarce spreads o'er ether the dejected day.
Faint are his gleams, and ineffectual shoot
His struggling rays, in horizontal lines,
Through the thick air; as clothed in cloudy storm,
Weak, wan, and broad, he skirts the southern sky;
And, soon descending, to the long, dark night,

. . . . .

Meantime, in sable cincture, shadows vast,
Deep-tinged and damp, and congregated clouds,
And all the vapoury turbulence of heaven,
Involve the face of things."

The opening of the following passage has a Shakspearian turn, both of thought and expression: —

"The reeling clouds
Stagger with dizzy poise, as doubting yet
Which master to obey; while rising slow,
Blank, in the leaden-coloured east, the moon
Wears a wan circle round her blunted horns.
Seen through the turbid, fluctuating air,
The stars obtuse emit a shivered ray;
Or frequent seem to shoot athwart the gloom,
And long behind them trail the whitening blaze."

We have spoken of the Shakspearian opening of this passage: and is not the following epithet, given to the clouds, beautifully so? —

"The youthful sun
Shot his best rays, and still the gracious clouds
Dropped fatness down."

The streams,

"In glassy breadth, seem, through delusive lapse,
Forgetful of their course."

And how delicately touched is this coming on of the rain!—

> "The clouds . . . . .
> . . . . . softly shaking on the dimpled pool
> Prelusive drops."

And in Spring, he calls the south wind,—"full of every hope and every joy,"—"the wish of nature."

The following pause, then rush, has a truly Miltonic propriety and force:—

> "Then issues forth the storm with sudden burst,
> And hurls the whole precipitated air
> Down in a torrent."

And again,—

> "Or into vacant chaff,
> Shook waste."

In the well-known description of the "swain," as Thomson loves to call him, lost in the snow, there is a finely rapid accumulation of fearful images before the mind of the way-bewildered man:—

> "Then throng the busy shapes into his mind,
> Of covered pits, unfathomably deep,
> A dire descent! beyond the power of frost;
> Of faithless bogs; of precipices huge,
> Smoothed up with snow! And what is land, unknown,
> What water, of the still unfrozen spring,
> In the loose marsh or solitary lake,
> Where the fresh fountain from the bottom boils."

And there is felicity in the almost impersonation of the hills, and pathos in the epithet bestowed upon them, when it is said he

> "sees other hills ascend,
> Of unknown, joyless brow."

What a pity that such a description as this is should be almost spoiled by two paltry little words, and that, too, where it was intended to be particularly touching,—

where the little children peep out into the storm, and "demand their sire." Again, the ox, lowing for his fodder, "demands the fruit of all his toil." But such was the taste of the times, and Thomson should not have the whole laid on his shoulders.

Here comes a sounding passage, in which heaven and earth seem astir. We are almost tempted to give, along with it, one from the Poly-Olbion.

> "Or where the Northern Ocean, in vast whirls,
> Boils round the naked, melancholy isles
> Of farthest Thule, and the Atlantic surge
> Pours in among the stormy Hebrides;
> Who can account what transmigrations there
> Are annual made? what nations come and go?
> And how the living clouds on clouds arise,—
> Infinite wings! till all the plume-dark air,
> And wide-resounding shore, are one wild cry?"

Take his description of the commerce of the Thames:—

> "Then Commerce brought into the public walk
> The busy merchant; the big warehouse built;
> Raised the strong crane; choked up the loaded street
> With foreign plenty; and thy stream, O Thames,
> Large, gentle, deep, majestic, king of floods!
> Chose for his grand resort. On either hand,
> Like a long wintry forest, groves of masts
> Shot up their spires; the bellying sheet between
> Possessed the breezy void; the sooty hulk
> Steered sluggish on; the splendid barge along
> Rowed, regular, to harmony; around,
> The boat, light-skimming, stretched its oary wings;
> While deep the various voice of fervent toil
> From bank to bank increased; whence ribbed with oak,
> To bear the British Thunder, black, and bold,
> The roaring vessel rushed into the main."

Here is a description representing things as they are, and not unlike any thing ever seen before, or so scattered and general as to present nothing at all to the mind. The poetic effect is here produced by a selection from the actual, and by grouping and contrast; — the big warehouse, — he is not afraid to call it "big"; the old-fashioned crane, — a picturesque object; the choked-up street; the sluggish, sooty hulk; the splendid barge, rowed regular; the boat, light-skimming. It would be well to compare this strong, plain, distinctly pictured description with Father Thames, in his own proper person, making the speech so much admired by Pope's commentators. Being, like most speeches, rather long, there is not room for it here. Yet Thomson must needs make

> "the bellying sheet between
> Possess the breezy void."

And instead of multitudes of muscular, deep-voiced *men*, crowding and calling out at their work, which would mean something, we have a dainty, affected, half impersonation of "fervent toil" with its "various voice." This is just the inappropriate, vague phraseology that we should expect, in such connection, from Pope.

And should not such eyes as these have saved the modernized Ruth from the hard things we have said of her? —

> "Her eyes,
> Still on the ground dejected, darting all
> Their humid beams into the blooming flowers;
> Or when the mournful tale her mother told,
> Of what her faithless fortune promised once,
> Thrilled in her thought, they, like the dewy star
> Of evening, shone in tears."

And, in another place, what is there more exquisite than this, — and, alas, alas, more rare! —

> "Disordered at the deep regard she draws."

In describing the earth, he animatedly calls the

"leafy woods,
Her liberal tresses."

In his close and apt description of the precious stones, Spring moves airily: —

"Nor deeper verdure dyes the robe of Spring,
When first she gives it to the southern gale,
Than the green Emerald shows."

"The sun, ... with various ray,
Lights up the clouds, those beauteous robes of heaven."

Then comes the soothing sound of waters, —

"the plaint of rills,
That, purling down amid the twisted roots
Which creep around, their dewy murmurs shake
On the soothed ear."

We find him imparting life and reality to a description by a single epithet. In the midst of nature we come upon the abodes of men: —

"And spiry towns by surging columns marked
Of *household* smoke."

In his Latinisms he is not unfrequently happy, as may be seen in passages already quoted, and in the following: —

"Nor is the stream
Of purest crystal, nor the *lucid* air,
Though one transparent vacancy it seems,
Void of their unseen people."

"Thus passed the time,
Till through the *lucid* chambers of the south
Looked out the joyous Spring, — looked out, and smiled

"Prime cheerer, Light!
. . . . . Nature's resplendent robe!
Without whose *vesting* beauty all were wrapped
In unessential gloom."

The fault of the last passage is, that the whole of it is too close an imitation of Milton; and from him, too, may be borrowed the beautiful epithet which changes his "hills" into urns of light.

> "Up springs the lark
> Shrill-voiced and loud, the messenger of morn;
> Ere yet the shadows fly, he mounted sings
> Amid the *dawning* clouds."

In the finely wrought description of the Plague, the term applied to the winds comes in with great effect, making them spirits indeed, and the deathly scene more deathly, by contrast:—

> "Man is her prey,
> Intemperate man! and o'er his guilty domes
> She draws a close, incumbent cloud of death,
> Uninterrupted by the *living* winds."

> "The circling sky,
> The wide, *enlivening* air, is full of fate."

And how does a single epithet open the following scene, and breathe its fresh air upon us!—

> "Or, on stupendous rocks,
> That from the sun-redoubling valley lift
> Cool to the middle air their *lawny* tops."

And in the northern regions:—

> "While through the gloom,
> Far from the bleak, inhospitable shore,
> Loading the winds, is heard the *hungry* howl
> Of famished monsters, there awaiting wrecks."

And in the foregoing description of the Plague:—

> "The sullen door,
> Yet uninfected, on its cautious hinge
> Fearing to turn, abhors society;
> Dependents, friends, relations, Love himself,
> *Savaged* by woe, forget the tender tie."

And though most at home in nature, he is sometimes, although not often, happy in his turn of expression when speaking of man:—

> "Now the distempered mind
> Has lost that concord of harmonious powers,
> . . . . . and all
> Is off the poise within."

How delicately and closely he expresses this beautiful thought,—

> "The tender heart is animated peace."

And,—

> "Progressive truth, the patient force of thought."

> "The smooth barbarity of courts."

> "A lustre shedding o'er the ennobled mind,
> Stronger than summer noon; and pure as that,
> Whose mild vibrations soothe the parted soul,
> New to the dawning of celestial day."

The following brings to mind the form of thought and expression so peculiar to our older dramatists,—a form which pleases us, we can hardly tell why, as scarcely any other ever does:—

> "Sweeter than Spring!
> Thou sole surviving blossom from the root
> That nourished up my fortune! Say, ah, where,
> In what sequestered desert, hast thou drawn
> The kindest aspect of delighted Heaven?
> Into such beauty spread, and blown so fair?"

And this, again, is Ruth!

We must pass on from Thomson, one of the most minute and accurate, as well as wide, observers of nature among our poets, in an age when, to other eyes, nature was almost blotted out; rich, too, in poetic diction, when the true poetic was nearly a lost tongue, yet blending with it the factitious taste of the age along with a taste as factitious, peculiar to himself; so that it is no exaggeration to say, that not a dozen consecutive lines can be found in the "Seasons," in which, whatever there may be of beauty of diction, there will not also be something to offend. Perhaps there is not an author in all our literature, who, from this remarkable entanglement of good and bad in language, would make a more useful study for the young, under the guidance of a discriminating critic.

It is the easiest thing in the world to criticize one poem by its difference from another, but it is not very philosophical to censure it on account of that difference. Because Thomson's views spread over a wider surface than Cowper's generally do, shall we forget how distinct Cowper's are, and how close to nature, how varied, beautiful, and sunny, and what a "summer feeling" they send to the heart? It cannot be admitted, however, that narrowness in his descriptions amounts to a fault in Cowper. And if it did, it is hardly for Mr Hazlitt, just let out from Pope's bandbox of caps and ruffs, to perk about in Cowper's fresh gravel-walks, and under his colonnade of solemn trees, and complain of want of room and air.

Indeed, this difference, for which Mr. Hazlitt praises Thomson so much, is oftentimes Thomson's fault. His scenery, as we have before suggested, is apt to be too broad and general, with a multitude of things in it, but without a leading object in the prospect for the eye to rest upon, or to which all else stands subordinated and related, and by which its varieties are harmonized and held in unity; and for want of which we come away with an indistinct recollection of something quite beautiful, — we forget what.

Not so with Cowper's descriptions. Take, as one

or two of a thousand instances, his Postboy, his Wagoner, his Wood-cutter and dog. They are as distinct upon the memory as if cut in with a graver. And this is not simply because he saw clearly and minutely, but because he saw things in their characters, and therefore in their parts as related to a whole, and suggestive of other parts not expressed, but implied, in the idea of that whole.

His descriptions of nature have life, too, for our minds, because they were something more than mere material objects presented to his. He looked upon them from a moral position; his moral nature required them, and held them as by a mental sympathy, imparting to them of its own life, and modifying them by it, till they reflected back that life upon him and us. They had higher offices to fulfil than the gratification of his sensuous being alone, — higher than even mere taste for beauty, or for the pleasurable exercise of what, for want of a better term, we must call religious sentimentality. Nor did he begin in these. He tells us, —

> "In his works,
> Though wondrous, he commands us in his word
> To seek Him rather where his mercy shines."

> "Full often, too,
> Our wayward intellect, the more we learn
> Of nature, overlooks her Author more;
> From instrumental causes proud to draw
> Conclusions retrograde and mad mistake.
> But if his word once teach us," &c.

It may be true that the relation of man to nature, of the creature to the Creator, and the fact ever present to his mind of a personal God governing all, and to whom all intelligential beings stood accountable, was so near and solemn and self-concerning a reality, when taken in connection with the theology he held, as sometimes to weigh upon the free action of the poetically ideal, in so far as his mind partook of the higher forms of this. Yet it may not be uncharitable to suggest, that, with many, the want of sympathy with the religious seriousness and earnestness of his mind may have checked their full sympathy with its poetic processes, and made them slower to feel the poetic power and beauty of its productions.

Simple in his tastes, and finding his pleasures in the ordinary circumstances and scenes of his daily life, — the most affectionate of beings, and, from his deeply moral and religious cast, connecting with these mental qualities all that engaged his affections, — through these, the near and familiar necessarily became objects of earnest concern, and, however small, had in them that meaning and importance which are seen in the least of things by a thoughtful mind. Therefore it is that Cowper so domesticates nature. The places he leads us through are our own homes; the barn-yard, and the cattle in "unrecumbent sadness," are ours; we fed the barn-door fowls when we were children, and whittled our bows and arrows under the sunny side of that green hedge.

In the midst of all this, our hearts are opened to the kindliest influences, and there are happy emotions within us, of a nature gentle as that home-feeling of which we hardly take note till the sick sense of its loss comes over us in a strange land. It is true that mere description is not a product of the higher powers of poetry; and it was because Cowper had so much of the spirit of poetry, and breathed it into and over his objects, that they touch us so deeply, and look so beautifully in the light which they stand in.

And could these things be done without a single and entire love of what he was about? Could a man who "shakes hands with nature with a pair of fashionable gloves on, and leads 'his Vashti' forth to public view with a look of consciousness and attention to etiquette, as a fine gentleman leads a lady out to dance a minuet," — could such a man link us so closely to all he sets before us, and make us so familiar with it too? Indeed, so ludicrously inapplicable to Cowper is Mr. Hazlitt's illustration, that we are left only to look at it as a pet of his from the nursery, his commonplace book, which, like other eager and fond parents, he inconsiderately and untimely thrusts upon us.

If man ever loved nature with sincerity, Cowper did; and it was because of this sincerity that he connected it with his fast attachments, which were domestic, and made it one with them.

What says he of himself?

> "The country wins me still.
> I never framed a wish, or formed a plan,
> But there I laid the scene. There early strayed
> My fancy, ere yet liberty of choice
> Had found me, or the hope of being free.
> My very dreams were rural, rural, too,
> The first-born efforts of my youthful Muse."

> "No bard could please me but whose lyre was tuned
> To Nature's praises."

Never was a more preposterous charge than this made against a man. If any one might say with truth, —

> "In my soul I loathe
> All affectation," —

Cowper might. Yes, all affectation, under all forms, conditions, and relations. Mr. Hazlitt may be resolutely lively, if he so chooses, at the expense of his judgement, and, we fear, of his better feelings; but no one can seriously think that he is the man destined to lessen the well-deserved popularity of Cowper.

Mr. Hazlitt, indeed, points out a few passages of general description, but need not have so limited himself in his list. And could he read the Time-Piece, and not feel a touch of awe from the power that moves through its vast and terrible scenes? Yes, he could. Even here he could step forth the "spruce philosopher," even with the warning voice of its prophet sounding in his ears, — here, where Cowper seems as if inspiration had imparted a strange power to him, and bestowed upon him the speech of sacred writ.

Speaking of the calamities that fell on Europe, and holding them up as warnings of greater evils to come, with what a compassionating, solemn thoughtfulness does the poet begin! —

"Sure, there is need of social intercourse,
Benevolence, and peace, and mutual aid,
Between the nations, in a world that seems
To toll the death-bell of its own decease,
And by the voice of all its elements
To preach the general doom."

Upon this soon follows the description of those calamities, beginning "Alas for Sicily!" — a description which, for concentrated strength of language, and for grandeur the more awe-inspiring because bare of ornament, is hardly to be matched, out of God's Book. Take a specimen: —

"The very elements, though each be meant
The minister of man, to serve his wants,
Conspire against him. With his breath he draws
A plague into his blood; and cannot use
Life's necessary means, but he must die.
Storms rise to o'erwhelm him: or, if stormy winds

Rise not, the waters of the deep shall rise,
And, needing none assistance of the storm,
Shall roll themselves ashore, and reach him there.
The earth shall shake him out of all his holds,
Or make his house his grave; nor so content,
Shall counterfeit the motions of the flood,
And drown him in her dry and dusty gulfs."

When this moral teacher speaks of the Great Capital with that high feeling and thoughtfulness blended with graphic distinctness so marked in him, with almost a single word he not only puts the scene before us, but bears it in upon our moral natures, and awakens us to a kindred thoughtfulness: —

"No rattling wheels stop short before these gates,
No powdered pert, proficient in the art
Of sounding an alarm, assaults these doors
Till the street rings; no stationary steeds
Cough their own knell, while, heedless of the sound,
The silent circle fan themselves, and quake."

And where his purpose is merely to rebuke the extravagance, ostentation, and glare of fashionable life, in doing it he surprises us by a figure which rises into magnificence: —

"Just when the drawing-rooms begin to blaze
With lights, by clear reflection multiplied
From many a mirror, in which he of Gath,
Goliath, might have seen his giant bulk
Whole, without stooping, towering crest and all —— "

So is there a sudden sense of artificial, transient splendour mingled with the calm and solemn breaking of day: —

"All catch the frenzy, downward from her Grace,
Whose flambeaux flash against the morning skies,
And gild our chamber ceilings as they pass,
To her," &c.

But his whole invective against

> "Excess, the scrofulous and itchy plague,"

is in a noble strain.

With the exception of Milton, there is no poet, perhaps, who illustrates his thought from Scripture with so much of the Scriptural spirit of poetry and expression. Take, for example, the prisoner in the Bastile:—

> "There, like the visionary emblem seen
> By him of Babylon, life stands a stump,
> And, filleted about with hoops of brass,
> Still lives, though all its pleasant boughs are gone."

We must be pardoned adding, from the same passage, words which have in them the force, truth, and aptness of the best days of our tongue:—

> "To turn purveyor to an overgorged
> And bloated spider, till the pampered pest
> Is made familiar, watches his approach,
> Comes at his call, and serves him for a friend."

If it be said that this is mere description of an outward thing, we must be allowed to deny it. If the extract immediately preceding it awakens a sense of the mystical in us, so does this loathsome creature not only remind us of our loathing and antipathy, but it also instances those feelings subdued, and a most abhorred form of sensation and life cherished and petted with solicitous care, because the mind must have witness of sensation and life out of itself, or perish in fatuity. It tells us that life is sympathetic, and that the living mind will have this sympathy answered to, though it seek it through what it most abhors, and find it in the dungeon-spider or the toad. A poet, now-a-days, must needs philosophize upon this, all out. And let him do so if he will, but let him not set that man down for no poet who does not do so too.

Give us the result, and in such words, — words that cling to us, — and we are content.

There is, probably, no poem which brings out so unstudiedly as the Task, and so as a matter of course, what from time to time had been passing through the writer's mind as influenced by the casual circumstances and scenes of his daily life, or as that mind, deeply and habitually reflective, evolved itself in its customary meditations; no poem so alive with the life of the individual, yet so unegotistic; so familiar, yet so poetic; — so unegotistic, because the man forgot himself in his sympathies, or recognized himself only in them; so familiar, yet poetical, because, to the sincerely poetic nature, nothing can be so familiar as to become common.

We seem to be overhearing the man holding converse with himself, rather than to be reading what he has formally written down. He does not observe, and think, and work himself up to feel, in order to write; but having long seen, and thought, and felt, observation, thought, and feeling, in due time, and unpremeditatedly, run into words. Or if he may be said to talk to us, it is as if he and we had chanced to fall in company while footing it along the road, — where every kind man feels that he owes another a kind word; as he has somewhere said, with that happy facility so peculiar to him, —

> "The world and I fortuitously met;
> I owed a trifle, and have paid the debt."

No doubt the desultory character of these poems helps to this impression. But we think that they took this character, not from design, — not because, with some little pains, he might not have moulded them into set forms and connection, — but because of the predominance of a certain downright sincerity and plainness, which unconsciously made poetry assimilate itself to the settled habits of his life and character.

We do not say, that, abstractly considered, this mode is the best for poetry to be presented in. But the principle of compensation takes place here, as it does in other things. And if we miss the beauty of form, the fitness of method, and the sense of pleasure which the success of mere art imparts, on the other hand we have that agreeable feeling of naturalness and ease which a mind, moving nearest in accordance with its usual action, experiences in itself, and, in doing so, necessarily transfuses into others. Besides, with more or less of the abstract character that must belong to all literary productions, here the individual is brought nigh to us; the whole natural man is before us, speaking to us, looking upon us, and we on him; and there is superadded somewhat of that power which the simple presence of man has on man.

Then, again, there is the ineffable grace of transition from object to object, and from thought to thought, unpremeditated, — not linked together, but flowing together, — where the soul, by its mysterious power, is harmonizing things the most unlike as it courses on, at the same time that itself is taking the impress of all differing forms, and is tinctured by their several hues.

This likeness amid unlikeness, this unifying principle pervading variety, is not made obvious in these cases, as it is in works modelled more according to rules of art. In them we see the connections and proportions whole and at once, and are pleased. But where there is a more hidden, yet real unity, from being longer occupied in tracing it out, from living as it were in a state of continuous discovery, and meeting with beautiful surprises at finding things akin which had been thought to be foreign to each other, and from working in these processes deeper and deeper into the subtile operations of the laws of mind, does not one experience as much enjoyment as where the work is done for him at hand? and is there not a longer continued freshness of novelty? — We suggest these things as bearing upon the principle of compensation, and not with the purpose of depreciating Form.

Of the grace and ease of his transitions we have an instance, where, availing himself of the mention he has made of the gout, he slips away with us from his mock-heroic history of joint-stools, chairs, settees, and sofas, and we find ourselves all at once with the truant boy, "far from home," feeding

> "On scarlet hips and stony haws,
> Or blushing crabs, or berries that imboss
> The bramble, black as jet, or sloes austere."

But sudden and unlooked for as this transition is, we are not sensible of any abruptness or break, nor do we think of asking ourselves, In the name of wonder, how came we here?

> "The sofa suits
> The gouty limb; but gouty limb,
> Though on a sofa, may I never feel:
> For I have loved the rural walk through lanes
> Of grassy swarth, close cropped by nibbling sheep."

And take, a little way on, this picture, beginning, —

> "The grove receives us next;
> Between the upright shafts of whose tall elms
> We may discern the thresher at his task."

How soon and how naturally does he pass out of this into the reflection, —

"By ceaseless action all that is subsists.
Constant rotation of the unwearied wheel
That nature rides upon maintains her health,
Her beauty, her fertility."

Read on, and see how it proceeds, thought unfolding after thought, through all conditions of life, through country and through town, ever varying yet ever related, growth upon growth.

Poor crazy Kate is brought in after the same natural manner. After his Crabbe-like description of

"The common, overgrown with fern, and rough
With prickly gorse,"—

"There wanders one, whom better days
Saw better clad."

Observe with what facility he passes from the splendour of his Winter Morning into a familiar and thoughtfully amusive glance at his own figure; and mark how it grows out of the scene:—

"His slanting ray
Slides ineffectual down the snowy vale,
And, tinging all with his own rosy hue,
From every herb and every spiry blade
Stretches a length of shadow o'er the field.
Mine, spindling into longitude immense,
In spite of gravity and sage remark
That I myself am but a fleeting shade,
Provokes me to a smile."

We trust that these passages are too well remembered to make it necessary to cite any more than their beginnings.

Most thoughtful of poets, his eye was ever ministering both nourishment and activity to his mind; or, rather, he sought nature and the world of man as that on which he might pour out of the fulness of his moral and mental life. Would that this feverish and restless age would read Cowper more. For we may say to him, as, in his beautiful and calm address to Evening, he says to her, — "Composure is thy gift."

We have left ourselves very little time to speak of his satire. Like every literary production that has life in it, and, because it has, will continue to live, it partakes of the peculiar individuality of the writer. There is nothing in it of the splenetic and captious spirit of a disappointed and selfish man.

Cowper had no personal revenges to gratify, no poor and craving hates to appease. His was a mind of true principles; and it was what in the world was at war with these that he warred with. Such a mind could not contract itself into a state of personal hostility. It was no alembic into which a principle of right could be cast, and, by a process of hellish alchemy, come out a concentrated extract to touch the darts of satire with, and send their poisoned heads home to the heart of any man. The mind of a man of leading principles is of too large capacity for that; and with due allowance for human infirmity, the disposition of such a man must partake of this same quality of largeness. Great principles have their roots in great hearts, and air their leaves in open natures.

Even in an instance where Cowper's rebuke takes the personal form, the individual has passed away, and it is for the world and of the author that he speaks. Young was never more lofty in his rebuke; nor was rebuke ever more terrible or more just. And how do mere brilliant talents shrink under the moral power that lays its chastising hand upon them!

"Petronius! all the Muses weep for thee;
But every tear shall scald thy memory:

The Graces, too, while virtue at their shrine
Lay bleeding under that soft hand of thine,
Felt each a mortal stab in her own breast,
Abhorred the sacrifice, and cursed the priest.
Thou polished and high-finished foe to truth,
Gray-beard corrupter of our listening youth,
To purge and skim away the filth of vice,
That, so refined, it might the more entice;
Then pour it on the morals of thy son, —
To taint *his* heart was worthy of thine own!"

After reading this, one is ready to exclaim, with the old gentleman who was scrupulous not to exceed the moral law in his anger, — "Well, well! there's such a thing as holy indignation, and I thank God for it!"

Where shall we look for such concentrated strength as in the last of the following couplets, taken from his rebuke of the conduct of England towards her Eastern possessions? We can give no more than

"With Asiatic vices stored thy mind,
But left their virtues and thine own behind;
And, having trucked thy soul, brought home the fee
To tempt the poor to sell himself to thee!"

Do not such lines as these make a man feel himself growing strong throughout his moral nature?

In describing the inconsiderateness, follies, or low tastes of other men, there is a kind-hearted playfulness which finds its way through his own wise and stricter life and straiter moral principles, which permeates his reader so that he, too, is ready to make allowances, and to forgive while he blames. As showing somewhat of this spirit, as well as for the facility and liveliness with which it is told, and for its sagacity in detecting human workings, we must be pardoned in calling to the reader's mind the following touch of character: —

"Poor Jack — no matter who, for when I blame
I pity, and must therefore sink the name —

Lived in his saddle, loved the chase, the course,
And always, ere he mounted, kissed his horse.
The estate his sires had owned in ancient years
Was quickly distanced, matched against a peer's.
Jack vanished, was regretted and forgot;
'T is wild good-nature's never-failing lot.
At length, when all had long supposed him dead,
By cold submersion, razor, rope, or lead,
My Lord, alighting at his usual place,
The Crown, took notice of an ostler's face.
Jack knew his friend, but hoped in that disguise
He might escape the most observing eyes;
And whistling, as if unconcerned and gay,
Curried his nag, and looked another way.
Convinced at last, upon a nearer view,
'T was he, the same, the very Jack he knew,
O'erwhelmed at once with wonder, grief, and joy,
He pressed him much to quit his base employ.
His countenance, his purse, his heart, his hand,
Influence, and power, were all at his command.
Peers are not always generous as well-bred,
But Granby was, — meant truly what he said.
Jack bowed, and was obliged, — confessed 't was strange
That, so retired, he should not wish a change,
But knew no medium between guzzling beer,
And his old stint, — three thousand pounds a year."

And was ever any thing so admirably hit off as the talk theological of bottle-companions, beginning, —

"Adieu, Vinosa cries, ere yet he sips
The purple bumper, trembling at his lips"?

Where he is severest, as when dealing with gross and hardened vice or premeditated wrong, his severity does not degenerate into asperity. He does not fall into one of the commonest forms of self-delusion, that of mistaking the indulgence of acerbity of temper for an honest expression of one's abhorrence of vice. So truly is this the case, that, where we may be disposed to think he went too far in his censures of certain amusements and the gratification of certain tastes, we do not attribute it to harshness and moroseness of temper, but to an over-scrupulous view when applying to particulars the general principle of self-denial. For he did not enough consider that temperance is a distinguishing trait of Christianity, and is not to be confounded with that cheaper one, abstinence, whose tendency is to impart one-sidedness to character, instead of forming the complete man, and to compensate itself for its forbearance from gratifications harmful only when in excess, by a secret indulgence in "grave vices," as in craft, in acrimony, or in eagerness for gain.

Cowper is a religious poet; and to this some have ascribed his popularity. But if it has gained him popularity with certain readers, are the great reading public of so religious a spirit that this quality should make him a general favourite? We fear not,—and that what he has gained by it with one set of men he has lost with another. Particularly has it tended to his being too little regarded in a distinguishing trait of his mind, his satire. For while many of the latter class of readers have taken it for granted that he must be too prosy and serious for them, most of the other class pass by his lighter satire, and know little of the rest, except as they find it mingled with the graver and more religious portions of his works.

But, to our minds, his satirical poems are not inferiour, taken in the rank of satires, to those by which he is better known. And we would advise those who have paid but a slight attention to him as a satirist to study him for a while in that character. The first thing that strikes one in it is his variety. He seems to possess almost every quality of satire, except that of bitter personality, — from an affectionately amused spirit, in his Fables, to that graphic and ludicrous specimen of it, John Gilpin; and thence, yet blended with the same kindly spirit, to his keen, wise, and various views of a world diversified by all modes of follies, infirmities, and vices; thence, again, ascending with it from the plainest form, as best suited to ordinary life, up to the grandeur of scorn, or sublimity of sorrow, when, with a voice like the prophets, he utters his warnings and lamentations over a nation's sins.

We think we have not here given too extended a character to his satire; but that we may go so far as to say, that, not only does it also show itself clearly in short passages occurring in the higher and more poetical portions of his works, but its spirit may be felt, permeating these, where, perhaps, it is not easy distinctly to point it out. If it be so, who of our satirists can be compared with him in this last and high style of it, unless it be Young? Young, however, has too much of stage stateliness; his gait is too measured a tread; and with mannerism there is forecasting for effect.

But Cowper's satire is the natural working of a vigorous spirit, varying its actions according to the subject before the mind, and, through an adaptedness thus brought about, attaining to a completeness of control over that subject, and, through a nice susceptibility to impressions, making deeper the impress upon us.

And further, his style is downright English, strong, plain, and fitting; and few are the passages in which one would not find himself at fault in an attempt to change his terms for the better. This home English air imparts a character of ease in bringing about his effect; which, again, heightens that effect by the feeling of superiority produced by that appearance of ease.

The same may be said of his verse in the heroic couplet; — we are not aware that his blank verse is found fault with; — for, although his heroic verse has been objected to as rough, it has a character of freedom helping to deepen this sense of superiority. Though it is the result of careful correction, its air is as easy as if it had not cost a moment's toil, and was but the involuntary expression of the passing impulse or thought. This is overlooked by the mechanical critics, and the admirers of mechanical verse, who, confining themselves to a regular alternate accent, and to as regularly measured pause, never have conceived of verse as the varying utterance of varying living emotions within. But Cowper has said, "Such mere quarter-strokes are not for me." And the last man in the world would he be, for the sake of "a creamy smoothness," —

"To sell his living sense for lifeless words.
My thought 's the fittest measure of my tongue;
Wherefore I 'll use what 's most significant."

He felt the significancy and force which such lines as these give to the thought: —

"God . . . . .
Strikes the rough thread of errour right athwart
The web of every scheme they have at heart."

"Till the foe found them, and down fell the towers."

"And bears the brand of blasphemy burnt in."

Cowper worked understandingly.

We are no apologists for lawlessness in versification, any more than in graver matters; but we have a hearty contempt for martinets in every thing. Delightful indeed is it to meet blended, pleasing melody, rich harmony, and exquisitely apt and meaning words. But, since "the days of good Queen Bess," these are seldom found combined. And if we must choose between Cowper's verse and that made popular by Pope, we have not a moment's hesitation. For Cowper will at least save us from that weariness with which the latter's monotony oppresses us, in spite of his sense and wit.

His superiority appears again in his comprehensive brevity, and the consummate skill with which he completes his work by one quick, short master-stroke: —

> "Quevedo, as he tells his sober tale,
> Asked, when in hell, to see the royal jail;
> Approved their method in all other things;
> But where, good Sir, do you confine your kings?
> There, — said his guide, — the group is full in view.
> Indeed? replied the Don, — there are but few.
> His black interpreter the charge disdained, —
> Few, fellow? — there are all that ever reigned."

> "Gives liberty the last, the mortal shock,
> Slips the slave's collar on, and snaps the lock."

> "Thus often unbelief grows sick of life,
> Flies to the tempting pool, or felon knife.
> The jury meet, the coroner is short,
> And lunacy the verdict of the court."

If brevity be the soul of wit, Cowper was possessed of wit's very soul, — no English satirist surpassing him in this.

We have spoken of his true and logical use of words in his poetry, on which the very life of poetry depends; — if we add to it the term *aptness* in a certain sense, and not shortly to be defined, we shall have said no more than is due to the language of his satire.

Perhaps the readiest and surest way of satisfying ourselves as to the purity of his language is to call to mind what was the effect upon us of the few instances in which he has failed.

In that passage, so Shakspearian in spirit and expression, beginning, —

> " 'T is therefore sober and good men are sad
> For England's glory," —

we read, —

> " Such were they not of old, whose tempered blades
> *Dispersed* the shackles of usurped control,
> And hewed them link from link."

Had the reader met with the word here Italicized, in a similar connection, in Thomson, for instance, he would probably have passed on without particularly noticing it; but in Cowper he immediately feels its defect. And when we come upon such expressions as the following, let it be observed, we are not only offended, but surprised too: —

> "The season smiles, resigning all its rage."

Any one who did not recollect that this line was Cowper's would immediately ascribe it to Thomson. And as surely would he set down this couplet to Pope: —

> " So withered stumps disgrace the sylvan scene,
> No longer fruitful, and no longer green."

For although it has the fault of language common to both these latter poets, it has also Pope's favourite rhyme of *scene* and *green;* and, besides, the two lines

> " Like the two figures at St. Dunstan's stand,
> Beating alternately, in measured time,
> The clock-work tintinnabulum of rhyme."

It is quite time that we closed our remarks upon Cowper; and we do so, expressing the conviction, that not only will he be more and more valued as a poet generally, the more he is studied, but particularly in his rhyming poems, and as a satirist; and that he will yet take his place in this latter character by the side of the two or three to whom it has been the custom to confine the honour of that name.

Mr. Hazlitt next speaks of Bloomfield. And it is pleasant to find a modest man, who is not without some merit, introduced into such company. He is now relieved from the excess of both praise and ridicule, which was for a while bestowed upon him. Some were in admiration, not at his poems, but at the fact that a shoemaker should make verses. But an extraneous circumstance such as this, however extraordinary, in time ceases to be a wonder; and so the shoemaker and his works were before long forgotten by them. Those who ridiculed him did it on account of that very fact for which others praised him. And as the same timely end, for the same cause, comes equally to either ill-applied ridicule or admiration, he soon passed from the minds of these also.

Bloomfield is a poet of humble pretensions, but of a certain placid tenderness and simple beauty. With that due sense of his own powers which almost always waits on merit, how would he have turned from the gross flattery of Mr. Hazlitt, which places him by the side of Crabbe! It is not a part of our duty to find reasons for another man's opinions; but however uncertain Mr. Hazlitt's taste may be, it can hardly be the mere accident of that uncertainty which led him to a decision so preposterous.

Some good reasons are given by Mr. Hazlitt why uneducated genius does not succeed as well in a polished age as in earlier and ruder times. But the poetry of the present day happens to contradict his conclusion, "that all that the ambition of the highest genius can hope to arrive at, after the lapse of one or two generations, is the perfection of that more refined and effeminate style of studied elegance and adventitious ornament, which is the result, not of nature, but of art"; and that, "in fact, no other style of poetry has succeeded, or seems likely to succeed, in the present day."

On the contrary, the poets of this day, and some of those who were alive yesterday, have most of them been travelling back up the heights on which our old poets dwelt, and from which those of our Augustan age, as it is styled, had descended low enough. They are carrying up with them, too, the taste of the public, which in this seems to let drop the "adventitious ornaments," fastidious refinements, and unmeaning restraints, with which more polished society is too much cumbered.

As, upon the whole, we agree with Mr. Hazlitt in his general remarks here, and are unwilling to be always at points with him, we will pass by Crabbe at present, to say that we like the observations on love of the country. They not only discover ingenuity, but soundness too, and are written with a feeling and simplicity seldom shown in these Lectures: the subject seems to absorb him so much, that he quite forgets himself.

The observations at the beginning of the sixth Lecture, on the idiomatic prose style, are just, as are those, in part, upon the so-called Johnsonian style. But when the Doctor's heart was in his subject, he uttered himself in rich harmony of sound, which rose upon the ear like organ-notes. His words sometimes breathe forth sentiment, and rise even to the poetical; and there is a deep tone of thought over his language, which makes us feel all the seriousness of him who utters it. His style, though artificial to us, was probably the natural one of such a mind. And it is when that mind acted in its full vigour, that it comes sounding out, as we should listen for it from such a source. When he goes exhausted to his work, it is laboured and unwieldy, and his words are cumbrous and tiresome. He has suffered from a host of imitators, because his style was so much easier of imitation than that far better one, the natural, idiomatic English. These mimics have stolen his faults; but as they did not chance to possess themselves of his temperament and intellect, they have unluckily missed of his excellence.

Mr. Hazlitt's character of Swift's works shows a right understanding of that extraordinary and singular mind. It is high praise, but not too much.

Notwithstanding there seemed to be only one opinion about the genius of Swift, and all were reading him, and "As Swift says" was in many mouths, it was but a few days ago that a distinguished reviewer, on the other side the water, undertook to tell the world that it had all along been quite out in its judgement of him, — that, to be sure, he was an entertaining companion, and clever and witty withal, but that he had been thought too much of, had taken airs upon himself in consequence, and that it was high time he was made to know his proper place.

Now, though this must have struck people as singular, and have led them to ask whether any one would seriously set about breaking down a character so long and well established; yet it was done with so much confidence and smartness, — taking folks by surprise, too, — that it was reported a good many began to have suspicions that they had not been quite right as to Swift. A state of doubt is an uneasy state, especially if the multitude do not doubt with us. So, to relieve themselves, those who were startled by what they had heard began by passing Swift without giving him "Good day," and when his back was turned would shake their heads, whisper those next to them, and by their givings-out, such as "We could if we would," and so forth, contrived at last, as we are told, to have him received with coldness wherever he went, and, in the end, to be fairly shut out from much of the good company he had been in the habit of keeping.

Many in this country, who had been on terms of intimacy with him, no sooner heard what had happened to him in Edinburgh, than they exclaimed, "Well, who would have thought it! We always considered Swift a first-rate fellow, and, with all his coarse jokes, a gentleman at heart, and of good breeding; — many 's the hearty laugh that we have had with him!" "Now do you, indeed, think so?" some one would reply. "For my part, though I never thought him wanting in good sense, I took him for a vulgar fellow, and only bore with his jokes that I might not hurt the feelings of those who relished them; and I am glad he is run out." Another would affect an utter ignorance of him, and, looking you full in the face, would ask you, with consummate composure, "Of whom were you speaking? Swift, I think you said? Swift, was it not? Pray who is this Swift that they are making all this noise about?"

People should be careful lest they be overhasty in shaking off one suddenly cast down from fortune; for should he chance to rise again, and become something more, perhaps, than our equal in prosperity, it would really be a little embarrassing to meet him in the return of his golden day, and have him put out his hand and wish us cheerfully "Good morning." We have been credibly informed that matters did not go quite so hard with Swift as it was represented,—that he continued through the whole affair to keep the best company, though, for a day or so, to be sure, his levees were less crowded, and that he is now as much as ever a general favourite. We mention this for the sake of our friends, that they may be prepared to receive Swift as every gentleman should be received.

Swift's satire differs from Pope's, not only in appearing to be thrown off without effort and painstaking, but in a certain manliness of character, also,—to say nothing of its being occasionally associated with scenery and images of a somewhat picturesque aspect, and not like what we meet with in the Dunciad. He seems honestly conscious of his merits and powers, yet, be the fact as it may, does not affect us as writing like one fretted at their poor rewards. It appears rather as if the world's heartlessness and selfishness, and its littleness, making itself important through much bustling and many words, had worn on a mind strong, and sagacious, and hating hypocrisy and pretence, and loving the workings of strong passions, till, hurt where it was most sensitive, it had sheltered itself in unsocial eccentricities, and forced itself to seek relief in making mock at what it secretly held most dear.

For the disappointment of those feelings which lie deepest, and out of which springs up what is most beautiful to the mind, is apt to break down a sensitive spirit, or turn what is best in it into bitterness and scorn. It quarrels with itself for its own shortsightedness and folly, and revenges itself in its sneers at other men's weaknesses, and comforts itself in the reflection, that they are at least as great as its own. This is not Christianity, but we fear that it is humanity. It grows evil to very rankness, yet may have had its root among our virtues.

Though it may sometimes be the self-complacency of external correctness which censures our infirmities, still we must not confound right with wrong in making excuses for errours. Yet, in reading of the sufferings and melancholy deaths of the two females who loved Swift with such passion, there presses upon the mind a disposition to find something to extenuate his conduct, and, instead of cursing him, we are moved to pity him. And where this is the effect upon a firm and right mind, we may be sure that there is a true cause for it, though hid under too many obvious faults for us ever to trace it out. Particularly is this likely to be the case with one like Swift, — that "hypocrite reversed," — who would sooner treat his friend with coldness, than let him see the tear that parting cost him. O the depth of that heart which a rough, or hard, or cold exteriour sometimes hides!

Swift took a scornful pride in not letting the world see what there was of good in him. Judging it, too sweepingly, to be without feeling, he was himself ashamed that he should feel while in it, and made jest at his own heart and the hearts of others. When, in this state, he met with a being that loved him, it was like coming out of death into life; and that vague yet strong desire, — which knows not its own purpose, — to make sure to ourselves what is the hold that we have upon the heart of another, took possession of him. Little thinking in the outset to what it was leading him, he went on torturing, not from cruelty, but because, in seeing the sufferings and workings of another, he felt with more and more certainty with what a passion he was loved, and could brood in secrecy over the sympathetic emotions in his own bosom. Then, again, recollecting his estrangement from the world, he would become ashamed of what he held to be a weakness, and would cast it from him, till at last those who were fitted to open his heart and make him a better man sank away under the sufferings which he inflicted upon them, and left him alone, ill at ease with himself and impatient of the world, till the sense of all things was lost to him, and his mind went out in "dreary vacuity." At least, it is not for us to judge hardly of a mind that so perishes. What can we know of him who long before, pointing to a tree with its sapless top, would say, — "That will be my fate"? Charity, nay, more, — justice bids us hope, that what would have been another's vice was perhaps his disease. We have been unwarily led from the works of Swift to the man himself, and feel little disposition to return to them now. Here we part with him.

Collins, the most delicate of creatures, one who saw every thing through a refining medium, which, emanating from his own beautiful mind, surrounded him like a finer and exquisitely tinted atmosphere, we are thankful to say, not only still lives, but has recovered of the injuries he received by rough usage from Dr. Johnson. The Doctor meant no harm; it was only that his was too clumsy a touch for the handling of any thing so delicate.

About Gray the world is still divided. He is no favourite with Mr. Coleridge. And there is truth in the remark, that his personifications too often depend more upon their capital letters than upon any property they possess of producing a distinct personality to the mind. Not unfrequently they would have stood but a poor chance of being distinguished in our old books, where each noun is complimented in the same way. There is no doubt that Gray sometimes deceived himself, as well as his readers, in this particular, and that they both fancied they were moving in a crowd of individual figures, when, had they looked into the state of their minds, they would have found there nothing but undefined and vague generalities.

His tenderness and sentiment are genuine, and his moralizing neither formal nor lifeless, because it springs from the affections; and there is often a truly poetical character, taste, and richness in his epithets and combinations. And although he has stolen more, perhaps, than any one who has written so little, and, from a certain fastidiousness, may sometimes have injured what he has stolen, still he has enough of the temperament of a poet to resolve it into himself, and to impart to it his own life, so that the product is not a cento, but the one expression of a single mind.

Mr. Hazlitt says of the Ode on a Distant Prospect of Eton College, — "Though mechanical, it touches on certain strings about the heart that vibrate in unison with it to our latest breath. No one ever passes by 'Windsor's stately heights,' without thinking of Gray."

We can hardly believe that his Pindaric Odes are generally given up at present; and we think with Gray himself and Beattie, against the opinion of Mr. Hazlitt and others, that his Elegy is not his greatest production. We would rather have written The Bard. It required another and a higher order of mind. It is a poem of large and imposing conception, and is sustained with a spirit equal to that conception. Nor can we allow that there is any thing of conceit in the startling abruptness of its opening, which seems to us in proper agreement with the state of superstitious dread, and to be the only form of terrour fitted to move the bold and barbarous minds upon whom it was supposed to act.

The situation of the Bard, and of Edward and his army, opens as wild and grand a scene as ever lay before us. It is not made out by nice delineations or a multiplication of particulars. But one or two grand, leading circumstances, told in close, energetic, and picturesque language, all of a sudden turn our light imagination into a gloomy region of bare and rough mountains, wandered over by giant forms: —

> " Such were the sounds that o'er the crested pride
> Of the first Edward scattered wild dismay,
> As down the steep of Snowdon's shaggy side
> He wound with toilsome march his long array.
> Stout Glo'ster stood aghast in speechless trance:
> ' To arms!' cried Mortimer, and couched his quivering lance."

It is in vain to say that any other than a mind of lofty, poetical, and impassioned conception could have so imagined and expressed this. It is true that there are instances in the Bard of the faults we just now mentioned; but all and more than we have said of it, or have time to say, is due to it. To Gray's character, and to his prose writings, Mr. Hazlitt has done justice. We have still better authority to the merits of his Letters; for Cowper, himself one of the most delightful of letter-writers, somewhere says, that "they have all the wit, without any of the ill-nature, of Swift's." He is one of the few of whom it may be said, his wit alone makes the heart better.

We should not have said thus much upon Gray, — and, as it is, we have been able to do no more than hint an opinion, — were not his situation particularly unfortunate. Those who call themselves of the school of genuine English poetry say that he is not of them; that he wants truth and closeness in description, so that the eye may dwell upon it or run over its parts; that he is too general; that he does not seem to be fairly in love with nature and his fellow-man; that he gave himself to these too little, and to books too much.

This is not without truth, but it is carried too far. And those of the present day, who are so inveterately natural, are in some little danger of putting nature herself to school. They may have looked at nature closely; but they have looked at it rather too much from one point of view, and with a set of feelings and associations that want variety; and when another man, without doubt a poet, works in a way differing from their system, they shut him out from their number. With all Gray's faults, they are wrong in this.

Perhaps, however, this treatment of him was to have been expected from them. But, surely, it was a matter of surprise, that those who are not of the vulgar, who never soil their shoes in muddy lanes, nor in the wet grass of a morning, who make mouths at their mother tongue, and have only "fed on the dainties that are bred in a book," should turn their backs upon a man who was as classical and fastidious as heart could wish; who "spoke scholarly and wisely," and was ever in his best apparel. We see no reason for this, unless it be that the true native genius of English poetry was discoverable through these disguises. We think it was so. And for this we like him; and for this he should fare better with the English school. Though Milton's learning was the occasion of certain faults of manner, he had a mind strong enough, not only to bear up under it, but to put it all to use. Had Gray been less of a scholar, he would, perhaps, have been a better poet.

Of Goldsmith's poetry Mr. Hazlitt has said too much; but he has made up for it by saying nothing of his Good-natured Man. Why this is not a stock play we cannot tell. It is amongst the easiest and most entertaining of modern comedies in the reading, and, we should think, well adapted to the stage. Cumberland's affected interest and condescending pity for Goldsmith are ludicrous enough. He could not have produced such a play, had he written pen and fingers to the stumps.

But the popularity of Goldsmith's two principal poems was owing more to the times in which they appeared than to their intrinsic merit. It was the recoil from art to nature, from artifice to simplicity. There are many commonplace lines in them, and not many at which you are made to pause, from something in them peculiarly poetical. And he too often falls into those generalities and those faults of expression which we have complained of in Pope.

> "Sweet Auburn! loveliest village of the plain,"

is rather a soft beginning; nor is it strengthened by

> "Sweet smiling village, loveliest of the lawn,"

or by

> "Sweet Auburn! parent of the blissful hour,"

> "Do thine, sweet Auburn, thine, the loveliest train."

And of whom the following lines remind one we need not say:—

> "Ye bending swains, that dress the flowery vale."

> "Those healthful sports that graced the peaceful scene,
> Lived in each look, and brightened all the green."

And take, as a further specimen, the first dozen lines at the opening, on Italy, in The Traveller:—

> "Could Nature's bounty satisfy the breast,
> The sons of Italy were surely blest.

Whatever fruits in different climes are found,
That proudly rise, or humbly court the ground;
Whatever blooms in torrid tracts appear,
Whose bright succession decks the varied year;
Whatever sweets salute the Northern sky
With vernal lives, that blossom but to die;
These here disporting own the kindred soil,
Nor ask luxuriance from the planter's toil;
While sea-born gales their gelid wings expand
To winnow fragrance round the smiling land."

What Gray says of Addison's versification, we are sorry to add, too well applies to Goldsmith's also, which scarcely has "above three or four notes in poetry, sweet enough, indeed, like those of a German flute, but such as soon tire and satiate the ear with their frequent return." Goldsmith played this very instrument: it was significant.

One also is ill at such dim generalities, and unmeaning and false elegances of phrase, as we find in these extracts. But many pictures there are definite enough, and of much tenderness and beauty, and which were a novelty in the poetry of that day. And withal, he produces that effect which a kind-hearted man never fails of, when he is not afraid to express himself as he thinks and feels. You love him, and are pleased with yourself that you do so. His prose style is most delightful, and not injured by the defects which we find in his verse. His fame must mainly rest on his two plays, on his Citizen of the World, and on his Vicar of Wakefield.

The criticism upon Burns, save in the manner of it, is in good taste. Few of the readers of Burns would object to any part of it, except the doubts expressed as to the merits of "Scots wha hae wi' Wallace bled." Nor need Mr. Hazlitt have given us the whole of Tam o' Shanter, nor so much of the Cotter's Saturday Night, to prove the truth of his remarks. It is too barefaced book-making.

We wish that more had been said upon the old Ballads. As Mr. Hazlitt has enough of nature to like them, and his Lectures have been much read in this country, it might have put those upon reading them who, we fear, now know little about them.

On quitting the Lectures relating to the dead poets, we regret that, imperfect as are Mr. Hazlitt's enumeration and notice of them, we have been able to do no more than make a few passing remarks upon only a part of those he speaks of. They form a subject much too full and varied to be treated hastily, or in a small compass. It is painful parting from them, even after so short a talk.

Thinking of them in the order in which they lived, and especially of those far back, and seeing them drop off from us one after another, throws a funereal sadness over the train; and we feel as if all nature were going down with them to the tomb. The low grass and the small flowers, which were as a feeling to them while they lived, have taken root by their graves, and the tall trees have grown up by them and spread their dark shadows over them; the stream sends out a sound of mourning as it passes by; the sun takes his farewell there, and the stars of night look down and talk with their spirits there: The whole earth was theirs while living; and now that they are dead, their tomb is the place

> "Where all the perfumes and precious things
> That wait upon great Nature are laid up."

When these men, who once imparted a new and peculiar being to all things, for whom there was a gladness in the flower, who saw a beauty and a spirit in what is common, unnoticed earth to us, and whose souls blended with every thing that grew or moved, are thought of as being now shut up in darkness, outward things begin to droop about us, and our hearts sadden in the midst of the sad decay. Yet this is but a passing feeling. For as they lived in the minds and passions of their fellow-men, and were kindred with nature, so will they go along with us, and have an existence and presence in all that we see.

The recollection, that some of them lived so far back, in times indistinct to us, when society was so different and the very earth scarcely looked as it now does, — and that they are best suited to lead us through the obscurity, and are just as we are in what we most value and love, — all this brings them nearer to us than if they were only of yesterday. The distance we pass over, and the unknown objects lying through it, make their resemblance strike us with the more force; and they become more fixed in our minds, and take a firmer hold on our affections: It is like the sound of our own language in a strange land. We do not think of them as we do of other men of whom we read, for such are little more than a part of history to us. But we take up the works of these, and are let immediately into their secretest thoughts and affections; they make us merry or serious along with themselves, show us what they have seen, and tell us what they like and what offends them. And that which makes this feeling of intimacy more to us is, that we go to them when we are tired of the talk of men about us, and would be quiet, and, in a sense, alone. So that they become as a part of ourselves; and there is no sound in their communion with us, but it is in our very hearts. What engaged their thoughts has little concern with the petty and perplexing cares of our daily life. It has to do with our moral and intellectual being, apart from these outward annoyances; and by teaching us to look beyond the notice of present society for our happiness, and higher than its honours for our rewards, begets in us a steadiness, and hence a calm of mind and a just self-estimation, which will carry us right onward in youth, and be the support of our old age. It is like Cambina's Cup:—

> "A drinck of soverayne grace,
> Devised by the gods for tő asswage
> Hart's grief, and bitter gall away to chase,
> Which stirs up anguish and contentious rage;
> Instead thereof sweet peace and quiet age
> It doth establish in the troubled mynd."

We are quite tired of discoursing in the very general way we have been obliged to do upon the old poets; and as we have not room to be more particular upon the living, we shall close with a few remarks, hoping to have other opportunities to speak of them at large.

We have no disposition to profane the passage with which Mr. Hazlitt begins this portion of his labours, by the application which he has made of it. To come immediately from those who lived after Milton, but so unlike Milton, into the society of the poets of this day, with the following quotation upon our lips, would savour a little too much of false taste, self-sufficiency, and a want of kind feeling:—

> "No more of talk where God or Angel guest
> With man, as with his friend, familiar used
> To sit indulgent."

The living poets, however, should take it friendly of Mr. Hazlitt, that he makes so many consolatory reflections, in the introduction to his dissertation upon them, relative to the denial of its proper reward to living merit. He has elsewhere said, that the world is a spurner of living, and a patron of dead merit; and, lest his assertion might turn out false, has done what lay in his power to establish its truth. It was frank in him, also, to acknowledge that he could not speak of them with the same confidence that he could of the dead, as he had not the sanction of posterity for his opinion. Never, till this confession, had we suspected him of a want of confidence, nor, indeed, does his depreciation of the living seemingly savour of it. As it is, we may as well go on without particular regard to the remarks of one who, if we take his own word for it, can come to no decided opinion in the matter.

Of Hannah More Mr. Hazlitt says, — "She is another modern poetess, and, I believe, still living. She has written a great deal which I have never read." This is condescending! Mr. Hazlitt must at least know that her reputation does not rest on her verses, but on her prose, — which, if he has never read, we assure him he had better read, as from its plain, vigorous style and religious principles some good is to be gathered.

Miss Edgeworth, it is true, is not a poet, — we dislike the feminine of this noun, — nor can she share, if she would, in the particularly flattering praise which is bestowed upon Mrs. Barbauld. Mr. Hazlitt cannot make compliment to her, and say, "She is a very pretty poetess; and, to my fancy, strews the flowers of poetry most agreeably round the borders of religious controversy"! He has noticed Mrs. Radcliffe, and Madame D'Arblay, or Miss Burney, as we like to call her, — and had he no place for Miss Edgeworth?

We cannot speak of Byron and Moore now. And of "The Pleasures of Memory," — while we confess that we are unable to give it the rank assigned to it by many, — we can only now express our regret, that it has been made the occasion of so unfeeling an attack upon such a man as Mr. Rogers.

For a good while, Campbell's Pleasures of Hope had a popularity beyond its deserts; every body was quoting and reciting it; and there being an affluence of compounds and loud-sounding epithets, the good and the bad went equally well with the many. Passions and abstract qualities of the mind are all personified, and few stopped to ask how; for poetry was not then read with so critical an eye as it has since been. There is also too much of that language which, with no definite meaning, is styled elegant, and which is better suited to a morning call among the "accomplished," than to the quiet study of the poet.

These faults, however, are nearly all confined to the Pleasures of Hope, and to the author's youthful days. Neither are subjects like that of this poem happy ones for poetry. They have a tendency to generate a sort of prize-poem character. Notwithstanding its failures in taste, there is energy, and an air of eloquence, in the Pleasures of Hope, — real eloquence, and some touching passages; figures, too, formed by a truly poetic mind, and lines which almost any one might be glad to have written. Take the mother who "weaves a song of melancholy joy" over her sleeping boy; the maniac girl who lights the pile of fagots on the steep to guide her lover home from sea; the destruction of Pharaoh in the Red Sea, the closing line of which alone should almost save a poem; the sufferings and deaths of the Swedish soldiery under Charles; and the birth and destination of the soul. The following passage, too, is plain, compact, and spirited: —

"When front to front the bannered hosts combine,
Halt ere they close, and form the dreadful line;
When all is still on Death's devoted soil,
The march-worn soldier mingles for the toil;
As rings his glittering tube, he lifts on high
The dauntless brow, and spirit speaking eye,
Hails in his heart the triumph yet to come,
And hears thy stormy music in the drum."

To be sure, there are passages bad enough in this poem, and figures looking as if cut out of wood. We have

"Friendship weeping at the couch of Woe."

"Come, bright Improvement! on the car of Time."

Then we have two such lines as the following, which one would guess to have been pilfered from the Rape of the Lock, or from the Epistle of Eloisa to Abelard. But we doubt whether Campbell has any others so bad.

"Ecstatic throbs the fluttering heart employ."

"While woman's softer soul in woe dissolved aloud."

But neither his many faults in this poem, nor Mr. Hazlitt's indiscriminate attack upon him, are enough to kill his beauties. His permanent reputation will not rest on his Pleasures of Hope, — which, after all, is perhaps more rhetorical than poetical, — nor, it may be added, on his Gertrude of Wyoming; although many, both friends and enemies, have called the latter the best of his works. There are, of course, fewer faults in it than in the Pleasures of Hope, the production of his youth. And there is a tender emotion slightly felt in reading it, — very slightly, however, for the character of fiction is ever present to the mind. There are rather beautiful descriptions; but as a whole it is thin and watery. If O'Connor's Child may be classed with the longer poems, it is the best of them. Nothing seems to be got up for effect; it is wild without extravagance, is in the spirit of true pathos, and the fire of poetry shines brightly through it. — Lochiel's Warning comes nearer to that class of his poems which distinguishes Campbell from his contemporaries. It is marked by daring and passion, and the Wizard is finely visionary. — Hohenlinden is all astir with the spirit of battle; and the fire and roar of artillery are kept up till the sudden pause at the last melancholy stanza, in which passion, wrought up to its intensest state in the immediately foregoing lines, sinks down, exhausted, into instant stillness and death. The night scenery also, and, afterwards, the coming up of the sun upon the dun war-clouds with which the fiery hosts are overcanopied, impart to the fight a something which sets it above a contest between mere men. — The Battle of the Baltic has even more expanse and solemn grandeur, with an air of simplicity almost that of the old ballads. We wish that a poem, unequalled in its kind by any in our tongue, might be fairly rid of so commonplace a line as

"To anticipate the scene."

—What more can be said for Ye Mariners of England, than that, in spite of our politics and national jealousies, it is sung all over our land. — Mr. Campbell need not fear. Let him but give loose to his genius, and write more stanzas after the manner of these, and no builders-up of narrow systems in poetry can ever harm him.

If variety in production be accounted genius, who, among our later poets, shall be placed before Crabbe in this respect? By variety is not here meant that certain quickness and aptitude for any thing, no matter what, by which some men perform pretty well whatever it may be their fancy to undertake, or by which, like Bunyan's Talkative, they can discourse you what you will; "will talk of things heavenly or things earthly, things moral or things evangelical, things sacred or things profane, things past or things to come, things foreign or things at home, things more essential or things circumstantial." This is what we call cleverness, or sometimes dignify with the title of talents. But such a quality is rather a misfortune than a blessing to the man who possesses it, and to his neighbours too. For he must needs have an active part in whatever is said or done, while all that comes from him is, at best, but second-hand. Still, his versatility astonishes the bystanders, who exclaim, What might he not be, would he but devote such powers to a single pursuit! It may be answered, Only a second-rate man still. His changes come of his defect, — a want of a particular bent of mind, arising, not from an intense universal love, but from a knowing of many things superficially, and from a caring little for any one thing in particular. We mean not that disposition to variety which leads a man to turn poet, politician, divine, artist, mathematician, chemist, botanist, with the alterations of fashion or whim, but that by which one feels and sees, in all its changes and relations, the particular purpose or object for which Heaven made him.

This quality has Crabbe. And we think that such a variety of characters, with the gradual changes and growth of each individual, the slow coming out of the secretest thoughts, the course of the passions, from the first stirring of the calm to the most violent tossings, together with the strange humours of men, can hardly be found so fully brought together and distinctly made out, since the days of our old dramatists.

Nor is this done by a cold, anatomical process.

Though each variation is well marked, there is no apparent labour, nor are we left standing as mere lookers-on. It is not a dissection of character, as has sometimes been said of it, but the unfolding of character as by a power within. The men and women are living, suffering, or happy beings; we are interested in their concerns, and are moved with them to fear, or grief, or smiles. The dramatic form alone could more perfectly embody them, or unite us more closely with them. Notwithstanding, also, the multitude of characters, confined, with few exceptions, to the lower class of society, and engaged in none but ordinary pursuits, there is no repetition. As in life, though some have general resemblances to each other, particular differences keep them apart. Where is there a completer mastery over the passions? Peter Grimes, the Patron, Edward Shore, the Parish Clerk, — and so to the end of the list, — take hold of us with a power scarcely felt in poetry since the time of our old poets, except now and then in Byron, and in such pathos as that of Wordsworth's Michael, and his Weaver's Wife.

There is a marked character in Crabbe's sarcasm and humour, — dry, shrewd, playful, and unforced. Take the bland Vicar, whom "sectaries liked,— he never troubled them," moved to complainings by nothing save innovations in forms and ceremonies; who distilled moral compliment from flowers, for the ladies; the fire of whose love burnt like a very glowworm's, and who declared his passion with the uncontrollable ardour of Slender when protesting to Mistress Anne Page that "he loved her as well as he loved any woman in Gloucestershire." The story of this once "ruddy and fair" youth, whose arts were "fiddling and fishing," is well sustained, and one of the most delightfully sarcastic and humourous of tales.

In his descriptions of nature there are the same verisimilitude, particularity, clearness, and nice observation as in his characters, and here, too, without marks of the tool. And in these qualities in description he may be said to bear a resemblance to Chaucer, as in his character-drawing he may, with due allowances, be styled the modern Chaucer.

What adds to his character as a poet is his having introduced into poetry scenery new to it, or, where not altogether new, so modified by his peculiar manner of describing, and so associated and conditioned, that we know not where to find its like, save in such scenes in nature itself. We have only to remember the Borough and its neighbourhood. Here, perhaps, appear most distinctly the originality and independent working of his mind.

The principle of unity in that mind is shown in his scenes being the very places in which his men and women should be set down, or, rather, such as they seem to have grown up in; so that their occupations, their characters, and the scenes amidst which they live, are in keeping, and brought together just as they should be. And this, again, remembering how living the characters are, gives reality, sentiment, and feeling to his descriptions. Where else could Peter Grimes have been placed than where he is, — here all alone, for his passion to grow and feed upon that on which he gazes?

> "When tides were neap, —
> There anchoring, Peter chose from man to hide,
> There hang his head, and view the lazy tide
> In its hot, slimy channel slowly glide."

But we had almost forgotten that Peter Grimes — for developement and power of the passions unequalled by any other character Crabbe himself has drawn, and placed in the midst of scenes so new in poetry — is shut out by the poet's earliest and warmest admirers, the Edinburgh Reviewers, because it was thought a clever thing to write a dissertation under the term "Disgusting," and was found convenient to sacrifice Grimes to it, by way of example. For an exemplification of their principle, they might almost as well have taken Macbeth or Iago; for Peter Grimes, as well as they, raises emotions, and manifests quite enough of energy and power for poetical effect.

Crabbe's versification has been likened to Pope's; but the resemblance is much less frequent and near than has been supposed. It is easy and familiar, more varied than Pope's, though not so broken as Cowper's rhyming verse, and when his subject rises, rises with it into a fuller and more sonorous tone. His language is idiomatic, and strikingly free from false terms; and at times becomes eloquent or poetic.

We do not place Crabbe in the very upper region of poetry; but we do assure Mr. Hazlitt, that if he and master Leigh Hunt undertake to turn such gentlemen as Crabbe into the kitchen, they will soon have the parlour all to themselves. They may compliment each other as much as they like, and admire their own forms and the tie of their cravats in the full-length mirrour; — there will be but four of them, after all, — Hunt and Hazlitt in the glass, and Hunt and Hazlitt out of it, all equally interesting.

What with the variety of faces we have seen, and what with much mixed and continued talk, we are not in heart to say more than a passing word upon Mr. Wordsworth. Besides, it is getting late, and our readers must be growing as weary as ourselves. We must take another time, when we can begin fresh and with the day before us. We hope that it will not be long before Mr. Wordsworth will give us a new occasion for it; when we shall be glad to visit him and his country friends, and take a seat by him in his retired dwelling, "green to the very door," and "in the plain presence of his dignity" experience that satisfaction which respect for what is great inspires, and becoming pure through his teaching, have our minds opened to the beauties which make happy thoughts for him.

Mr. Wordsworth appeared in good time, with a marked, original mind, an imagination filled with forms of beauty and grandeur, and with a profound spiritual philosophy, so universally pervasive, so predominant, and partaking so much of system and form, that he may be said to have presented poetry under a new phasis.

Yet has he such an air of thoughtful truth in his stories and characters, and the sentiments put into the mouths of his people, though so elevated, have such a simplicity of expression, and so distinct are his descriptions and so like to what we see around us, that we do not stop to consider we are taken out of the world and daily reality into the regions of imagination and poetry. We are absorbed into what we are about in this new condition of things, and are unobservedly brought into that state of seriousness into which the near concerns of life put us when they enter into our better and interiour nature.

It may at first seem strange that the poetical interest should be so deep, where there is so slight a departure from plain experience in the circumstances. But it is the silent change wrought in ourselves, through the great depth of the sentiment and the utter, beautiful simplicity of the language, that awakens it in us. We learn that it is we, and the pleasures, the businesses, and the desires of our lives, that have been the illusion, and are made to feel a serious concern in that which we find in him; and what had been too much our great reality becomes idle and unimportant.

Mr. Wordsworth stirs up right thoughts and pure wishes within our minds and hearts, clears our dim imaginations, and the poetry of our being becomes its truth. In a certain sense, he may be said to have given birth to another creation. The mountains and valleys, the rivers and plains, it is true, are the same, and so are the trees and smaller plants, and the bright passing clouds,—to our mere eye, they are the same as seen yesterday. But a new sense is opened in our hearts, and from out it new and delightful reflections are springing up, running abroad over the earth, and twisting themselves about every little thing upon it that has life, and uniting its being with our being: With a higher meaning do they now live to us, for they have received a higher life from us. A moral sense is given to things; and the materials of earth, which had hitherto seemed made only for homely uses, become teachers to our minds and ministers of good to our spirits. Here the love of beauty is thoughtful, and touched with a moral hue; and what we had esteemed as little better than an indulgence in idle imaginations is found to have even profounder and more serious purposes than the staid affairs of life. The world of nature is full of magnificence and beauty, and all in it is made to more than a single end. The fruit we feed on is pleasant to the eye too, that we may find in it a second and a better delight. Purifying and lasting pleasures are awakened within us, and happy thoughts and images take life. In the luxury of this higher existence we find a moral strength, and from the riot of the imagination comes a holier calm.

It is true that other poets have given this twofold existence to creation, imbuing with a moral and intellectual being the material world; but most of them have done it by rapid and short hints only, and with other purposes in view. But in Mr. Wordsworth it is a principle that pervades his whole mental structure, and modifies all its workings. He carries us carefully along through its windings; and touching the strings of our hearts, their vibrations make us feel that they run upon and connect themselves with every thing in nature.

If poetry of this kind has its peculiar beauties, Mr. Wordsworth must remember that it is only a small class in society that can see or feel them; men are too little familiar with their inward being for that. Nor must he be impatient if the larger portion, that they may not be out of favour with themselves, give the name of mysticism to that which they were not born to understand. In truth, those things which one poet sees to be the choicest parts of another poet are not those which the world at large think of turning to. The more obvious, which, to be sure, may be very good in their way, are what please them, and enable them to be gratified with the belief that they have a sense of the whole. Shakspeare's plays are more read than any work, except the Bible; yet how many understand a tithe of Shakspeare?

No poet is more truly imbued with the spirit of our old English masters, or, it may be better said, more essentially in affinity with them. And whether we go with him in his essay on poetical language, or take sides with Coleridge, we can have no doubt, as Coleridge himself has, in substance, said of him, that, however it fare with his theory, his own language is essentially poetical. Imbued as he is with the spirit of the tongue of our earlier and better days, there is not and cannot be any affectation in the use of it. There is no ill-sorting of old and modern phrases, but his words fall naturally from him. His versification is sweet, and of a varied harmony, though sometimes — in the Excursion, for instance — somewhat slow and languid, we think; a fault, which, from a proneness to dwell overlong on the sentiment in the dialogues, occasionally pervades the entire expression of the thought. We sometimes feel, that, though thought is everywhere present, there is a lack of life and energy, from a want of compactness; too often is it thought diffused, not concentrated.

Mr. Coleridge's critique upon Mr. Wordsworth contains more of philosophy, subtile analysis, and good taste, than does any other criticism upon him, or, indeed, upon any other man whom we can call to mind. In fact, our better criticism owes its birth to that. But we must be allowed to dissent from his objections to the Pedler. The rule laid down by him may be true in the general, but fails, we think, in its particular application, and only shows, with hundreds of other instances, how hard it is to lay down rules at all for true genius. There must have formerly been, in parts of Scotland and England, characters enough like this Pedler to serve, as here, the purposes of poetry. He is in agreement with the scenery, and moves among those simple people like a half-familiar, half-patriarchal friend, and surely he possesses an interest for the imagination which it would have been difficult to impart to another accomplished gentleman; for we already have two, and a trio of them would have been rather too much.

We regret closing thus abruptly with Mr. Wordsworth, and are, indeed, ashamed of this sketchy manner of touching upon him. We would at least have looked upward for a moment toward those superiour regions into which, as in his supernal Odes, his thought ascends and voyages on luminous in their light. But the subject is too mighty for us now.

We are scarcely less sorry that we cannot find place for Mr. Coleridge. But such minds are not to be discoursed upon in haste.

Though Mr. Hazlitt frequently shows taste and great talents, still, he hardly seems to have been qualified for his task. Along with much that is true, he sometimes so mistakes as to raise the suspicion that he had no settled principles by which to make up a judgement, and that he must have often picked up his better opinions from others, as he has done his better phrases; and that, when he fails, it is mostly where he has relied upon himself. While it would be idle to call in question his uncommon talents, we should remember that he lives amidst men of genius in London, from whom it would be no hard thing, with the help of cleverness, a good memory, and a due unscrupulousness about thefts, to put together such a book as this.

Were one bound to make up a judgement upon Mr. Hazlitt from these Lectures, he would be compelled to say of him, that he was too loose in his views upon some points of moral conduct, and too splenetic where there was any thing to call his spleen into play, to treat, with a correct understanding, and a right delicacy and truth of feeling and sentiment, upon such a subject as poetry, — a subject which concerns all that is moral and refined in our natures. When he has pen in hand, he seems much too full of himself to have a sincere love and single interest in what is abstractly good and great; and appears to be more intent upon displaying his own fine parts, than upon spreading before his readers the high qualities of others. He is a sort of my Lord Boyet to the Nine, — has "kissed away his hand in courtesy" to his lady-auditors of the Surrey Lectures, and thinks to be at the top of favour with his fair hearers by superciliousness toward his superiours. An alert gentleman he who gets upon Parnassus, whips his boots with his ratan, and, with a negligent twirl of it, cuts off the flowers smooth by the head.

If the want of uniformity of style constitutes liveliness, Mr. Hazlitt must be a most sprightly writer. For his style is neither the familiar, the classical, the old, nor the new, but an odd composite of all these. Sometimes a mock dignified, then a contemptuous negligent, and, again, the tame modern, may be met with; and amidst the last kind, you will occasionally happen upon a fine old English word or phrase, about as much in place as a slab of dark, rich mahogany set in pine. And, lest this should not be enough, we are sometimes relieved of the wearisomeness of prose by a sentence of very tolerable blank verse. After all, Mr. Hazlitt shines most in quotations: — "he has been at a great feast of words and stolen the scraps," — "he has lived long on the alms-basket of words," — we "marvel" the lady-auditors "have not eaten him for a word." One sentence begins, and another ends, and a third is kept together in the middle, by a quotation. It is a curious piece of joinery, and well worth examining.

These things may afford entertainment. But when we reflect upon the manner in which he has brought before those who attended his Lectures some of his old acquaintance and their friends, we feel little else beside disgust, and are put in doubt of the true refinement of an age in which a polite and educated audience would permit such personalities. If Mr. Hazlitt is blind to the beauties of the living poets, it is of little consequence to them or to us. But we must needs be offended at the coarseness of the attack upon the characters of Wordsworth and Coleridge; nor does he rise in our estimation in seeking to make, out of the failings of Burns, a defence for licentiousness and a rude attack upon a well-principled man.

We trust that the English are not losing their reserve, or their reverence for domestic and individual privacy. Strangers who visit them may find it sometimes inconvenient, and coarse-minded people may rail about it. It is connected, however, with their surest principles and best feelings; and should they become the mere creatures of society, they will have put off those traits of character for which they have hitherto been most respected.

THE SKETCH BOOK.*

WHEN Launcelot Langstaff, Will Wizard, and Anthony Evergreen first appeared before the public, they made known that "they should not puzzle their heads to give an account of themselves, for two reasons; first, because it was nobody's business; secondly, because, if it were, they did not hold themselves bound to attend to any body's business but their own"; and the most that could be gotten from them was, "There are three of us, Bardolph, Peto, and I." This cavalier air, together with the mystery, and the bold declaration, "We care not what the public think of us," put the public upon guessing and thinking about them and little else.

Whether it was the sagacity of the people, or that eagerness to be found out which we see in little children at hide-and-seek, which discovered them, we cannot tell; but it was not long before the authors of Salmagundi were as well known as their writings. Probably the secrecy was a mere matter of sport, and after it had served its turn, they cared little whether they were known or not. It is now well understood

---

* From the North American Review for 1819.

The Sketch Book of Geoffrey Crayon, Gent. Nos. I. and II. New York: C. P. Van Winkle. 1819.

who the gentlemen were, and that Mr. Washington Irving was the principal contributor to the work. Knickerbocker, which was published not long after, was written wholly by him, as are also the numbers of the Sketch Book which have just appeared.

Though the surest way of judging of a man's talents is from his writings, it is a very uncertain one by which to form an opinion of his moral character. Yet we have as little doubt about the good principles and kind-heartedness of the author before us, merely from reading his works, as we could have, had we known him for years. The interest which he makes us feel in him personally is one reason why we now go back to his early productions. Another reason is, that we like the leading papers of Salmagundi, and the greater part of Knickerbocker, quite as well as the Sketch Book. Besides, we have all along intended to notice such American works, whether late or early ones, as may add to the reputation of our literary character.

In doing this, we hope to be free from any disposition to sneer at a book because written while our literary reputation is so low. On the other hand, we shall not care to flatter the vanity of those who think to raise themselves and the country to a high rank in authorship through much and earnest talking about it. We shall examine a work without any home feelings; our only business is with its merits and faults. We have many times forborne making amusement for ourselves and our readers from the trashy works which are daily turned out, as there is little danger of their doing much harm. When one considers how pleasant and easy a thing it is to sport with the follies and vanity of our neighbours, we may be allowed to take some credit to ourselves for this self-denial, especially when it is known that we are now lying under the displeasure of a multitude of authors for this very silence, which is all from our good-will towards them and regard for our country.

Though there has been much abuse abroad of our literary character, and too little allowed to circumstances, yet that abuse is rather in the spirit in which facts have been stated than in a falsifying of the facts themselves. Would we give our anger time to cool, place ourselves in the situation of England, consider the number of men of learning and genius who have risen, clustering like stars, to be her light and glory since we became a nation, and then look over our own land at the few dim, blinking lights, with only here and there one of steady and bright blaze, so distant that "fire answers not fire," we should allow something to the sound of triumph and rejoicing, which is heard from the midst of her splendour, and we should be moved with the spirit of forgiveness if we considered what would be our language of boasting were our situation hers.

Without any regard to this, we at once become exceeding angry, — begin to talk in large and general terms of American genius and enterprise, forgetting that first-rate authors are not as easily made as prime sailors and soldiers. We do not stop to ask ourselves whether this universal talent for action in our country may not be inconsistent with that abstract, ideal, and reflective cast of mind, which marks those whose lives appear to be unmixed thought, whose intellectual being seems kindled, and whose passions work strongest in worlds of their own creating. In the eagerness of defence, we urge the necessary employment of the talents of a young country upon the gainful and useful; and looking forward to the time when we shall no longer be rovers through wild regions, but settled down quietly, and full of wealth, we speak of that as the period when we shall have our host of scientific men, great scholars and poets, moralists and novelists, to be our boast and delight. But if the English superciliously tell us that they can furnish us with intellectual nourishment till these ends are accomplished, we forget the very argument we were using as a reason for our deficiency, and deny our need of their aid,—run over our small list of writers, good, bad, and indifferent, and make up with long and heated declamation for what is wanting.

Some have been so far gone in their zeal, as to utter a cry of affected mourning over the decay of learning and genius in Europe, and with that happy talent of making the future present, so common to us, and which has been scoffingly called our "figure of anticipation," have congratulated our country upon having become the home of the intellectual greatness of man; while others hold a lamentation over the thraldom of mind in England, and talk of our letting it out from its dark, close prison-house.

We should be happy to learn of these men what there may be in religion, politics, the sciences, and literature, which has not been discussed by her authors often and freely. In political and religious freedom, we may have put in practice what they have taught, but they have left us little in the leading principles of these to discover.

A short time ago, when the world was talking of discoveries in politics as familiarly as of discoveries in geography, it was curious to look into the older writers of Europe, and see with how many of these new-found wonders they were acquainted. Society at large may have gone forward rapidly, but great minds have always reasoned and felt very much as they do now. And granting that their vigour of thought was sometimes turned from its right action by the prejudices and superstition of the age, still they have been our instructers in much wherein we have fancied ourselves self-taught. At any rate, we cannot as yet believe, that, because the people of England are living under old institutions, they are so enslaved in body or mind as to stand in need of our pity. We think that it will be time enough for us to give utterance to our mixed feelings of triumph and grief, when the scholars, philosophers, and poets of America shall furnish study for one's life; when their views shall be so broad and liberal, that, in comparison, the authors of England will be dangerous to our freedom of mind, and, having been hitherto our teachers in what is moral, lofty, and pure within us, must be shunned as corrupting and degrading our natures. Indeed, it is not yet time to empty our shelves of European lumber to make way for American writers,— there is still room enough for these in the vacancies left. An American library would, we fancy, be rather a sorry and heart-sickening sight to a literary man.

Such notions are almost too ludicrous to be hinted at. Yet if we examine nakedly those which have so often of late been forced upon us, we shall find them the same, only curiously stuffed out and dressed up. This sort of contest deserves no better name than squabbling, and we are sorry to find men engaged in it who are fitted for better things.

The class of men abroad who affect a vulgar triumph over us, with an exception or two, are not those who add to that superiority of which they boa t. Of those at home, who will not stay to consider how much there may be of truth in charges so ungraciously urged, some are restless through wounded vanity and from feeling their own importance lessening with that of the order to which they belong; while others, with more generosity and no less zeal, enter into the contest because their country is assailed.

We do not affect to be wholly unmoved by either of these feelings; yet it is more in sorrow than in anger that we read the contemptuous reflections upon our literary character, because, with all their colouring, there is too much of truth in them, and because even the hope that a brighter day is breaking upon us loses something of its gladness at the thought of how small a change even literature makes in the tempers of its followers.

A man who cares at all for his own nature may well forget all distinctions of place in the sense of pain and disappointment, that minds, whose labours and joys would seem to lie apart from the confused strugglings and evil envyings of the world, who are left to love the beauties of ideal excellence, and to study the deformities of vice only to show them to the world, whose toils are for the world's uses, and whose dreams of delight give it purifying pleasures, — that such minds should turn away from all these, to be heated and depraved by petty bickerings and low strife. He who values literature for its moral uses, for its cleansing of the heart and exalting of the mind, and not from the vanity of scholarship, — who loves it for its own sake more than for its distinctions, — cannot but lament to find it degraded to the service of false pride and sour malignity. Genius of the first order, in comparison with that of a lower class, is seldom cursed with this spirit; and wherever the two are found united, it is to that mind's essential hurt. Every taint of vice is a dimming of intellectual brightness, and the taking away of one good feeling from the heart is the shutting out of countless visions of beauty and delight from the mind. Could this language of boasting on the one side, and of contempt on the other, be kept up without harm, a war of words would never raise us to distinction, nor make us deserving of it. We must take another course to bring us to a level with the literary men of Europe.

In the first place, to have learned men, it would be fortunate if half our colleges, or universities as they are sometimes called, were turned into good schools, and the funds of the rest given to one or two large institutions for fellowships and other purposes. As this cannot be effected, men of wealth must make their donations to those institutions which have already the greatest advantages. Nor let them consider this to be granting a favour or conferring an honour. It is for their own glory, without which they will live with no other distinction than the poor one of wealth, and when they die their names will go down with them to their graves, and they will sink from the memory of man faster than they rose into his notice.

We are not of those who think mere scholars useless. They deserve praise for the example of industry which they set before us, and for the helps which they afford not only to the world at large, but to men of genius in a thousand ways. Neither is it of good tendency to underrate those who are thorough in any calling, in a country where each one does every thing, and nothing well. True, they have their reward; for if their merits are not understood, the mystery of their calling makes them the gods of the ignorant, and if holden lightly by some, they have a consolation in their own self-esteem. It is true that mere learning does not give a nation its great name; and what would England have been with her Bentleys and Porsons, without her Shakspeare and Milton? Neither have many of those works which make a nation's reading been written within college walls; and some of those which are most familiar to us are from men who never wore a gown or square cap. Still, the influence of literary institutions upon society reaches to the uneducated, and the effect of their early discipline is felt by the educated after they go into the world. Suppose such institutions at an end, or, what would be as bad, with just science enough to instruct head-workmen in the mechanic arts, or a sailor how to take a lunar observation, or, according to a system of intellectual economics, "to teach no more than can be turned to some account," how long would there be left any reward for mental toil, or any excitement to peculiar genius? — Those who are most fond of trying things by their usefulness know least of the great uses of life.

More is necessary to our literary character; and changes must be wrought in society at large; without which all arbitrary institutions will first become mere things of show, and then decay.

If we allow society to have any effect upon first-rate minds, perhaps genius is nowhere more likely to die at its opening than in this country. The peculiar fitness of our state for general talents and for activity of character is that which is most in the way of individual genius. Men of genius are a sort of outlaws, because too few as yet to form a class in our society, and because, for the most part, they want that *getting-along* faculty which is naturally enough made the measure of a man's mind in a young country, where every one has his fortune to make. This call for business talents may continue to put a check upon the higher kind of literature, as by the division of property the sons of men of wealth are turned down from books into the order of watchful and eager men of business; and the common way must be, that the works of genius, if not wholly laid aside, will no longer fill up hours of lonely thoughtfulness, nor keep a strong hold upon their hearts. Men of acute minds, to be sure, yet uninformed, take place of the learned rich, and in this continual shifting, the exalted but silent movements of great minds are crossed and broken in upon.

This, at least, seems the natural course of things. Without a rivalry which might stimulate men of newly acquired property to raise themselves to the level with hereditary wealth, by building up some part of their character along with that of a man of genius, they feel distinctly what has given undisputed consequence to themselves, and would make that the rate of his importance too. The luxuries of sense are new to them. Lofty rooms and gay furniture still draw their attention and make their pride, and it is hardly yet forgotten how fine a thing is a fine coach: Satiety of outward wealth has not turned them to the riches of the mind.

Let us not be misunderstood. If there be any thing of truth in our loose suggestions, still we do not mean to quarrel with our political institutions, or the general circumstances in which we are placed, because their influences may not be so favourable as one could wish to the mental state of which we speak. Besides, it often falls out that facts run counter to theories; and experience and prophecy seldom meet. It may be, that with the wealth of the country will come in a better taste, and that, instead of growing more sensual, we shall become more intellectual, — that we shall, one day, buy pictures as well as looking-glasses, and that, in good time, an author will be set as much by as an Argand lamp or an imported chimney-piece. Even now, there are many well educated among the wealthy, and some have laboured to improve themselves later in life; and in most of them there is a generosity of character needing nothing but a right direction. All that has been done of late for public institutions has been by rich individuals; and when they shall have learned how to value original, creative minds, these, too, will receive their respect and support.

This must be brought about by a middle class, — men of improved intellects, who are labouring in the different callings of public life. And here the evils from change of property may, perhaps, find their cure. A young man of cultivated mind, thrown into that order of society, which, after all, is the most efficient, will have an influence over those who have succeeded him in the rank of wealth, which will lead them to support and encourage those whose powers they still may not clearly understand.

Our scholars, though a little apart from society, have an influence in it which might be used to the same end. Here, again, there is something in the way of the mere man of genius. Our scholars, though less learned than those of Europe, hold properly enough a high rank in society. They form a numerous class, and being in many ways connected with the world, have that authority which mental acquirements carry with them. In Europe the scholar has only a portion of power and influence; for there, genius has kept pace with learning and holden as wide sway. Here we begin with the learned, of whom it is asking a little more self-sacrifice than is often found in humanity, to give up into other hands a part of that power which they now exercise alone. The European scholar, when he has an eye to see, has nothing of this to take from his admiration, when the brightness of a new mind breaks upon him; for suns have for ages been coming up in that horizon, making a noonday blaze, and never has he thought to see them quenched in his own borrowed and fainter light. But those here might not only feel that self-estimation which undivided power gives sinking away; the fear of losing their influence might startle them, to find a man of untaught powers suddenly rising to a height which they can never reach, or one, like Milton, with as much of other men's knowledge as they, using it as the stuff of his own mind, building a temple in which they may be the worshippers, but can never be the gods.

It would be a narrow prejudice to suppose men, whose studies from childhood have been fitted to enlarge the mind, and bring them acquainted with its beauties, so moved by selfishness as to shut the doors upon all outward excellences, and live in complacent contemplation of themselves. We speak of that which is natural to all of us, — of that which is common to the learned and the ignorant, the man of genius and the fool, — a proneness in favour of our own sect, which leads us, unawares, to judge hardly of those not of it, to be quicksighted to their defects and careless of what is good in them, to feel our own importance growing with that of those we belong to, and, unconscious of our motives, if not pleased, yet not sorrowing at the ill success of others.

We need not go thus far to find why mere scholars (we mean those whose reputation rests on their acquisitions and studied correctness alone, and not those amongst us who have laid open to the world the rich veins of thought in their own minds) are so slow to see and acknowledge what is good in a new author. The habit of referring to certain rules makes them doubtful of every thing that cannot be tried by these; and reading under old authority, with the mind at school, takes away from their freedom of judgement, and leads them to consider every thing new as dangerous innovation, and to look upon it with a mixed feeling of superiority and alarm. Besides this, an exclusive study of the classics is much like living in a foreign country, with which we can never become so intimate as to have the feelings of a native, and must always be in some degree on the outside of its society, at the same time that our old associations are fading and dropping off. Early familiarity with the thoughts and feelings of home may make them appear vulgar to such men, — and from the mistaken notion that a knowledge of what is best there can be reached without toil, they let it fall into neglect.

Besides, what is foreign always has so much of show and dress in our eyes, that we cannot but look upon it as something a great deal finer than any thing we ever saw at home; and because attained with more consciousness of toil, and never so completely absorbed as to be unnoted by us in ourselves, there comes to be attached to it the notion of superiority over that which is made more completely our own. But if, when we go to books, we give up the delights, fears, and superstitions of our childhood, all that we connect with the thoughts of our ancestors, and all that has helped to form what is peculiar in ourselves and the society in which we have grown up, our minds will pass into too artificial a condition to perceive, even in those authors of whom we are most fond, their greatest, because their most natural and simple, beauties: — little knowing how variously nature works, every thing will be moulded by us into our own forced state.

We have hinted at the evil effects of confining the mind to the classics, from no foolish wish to lessen the study of them in this country. No man of good taste, who had begun to be acquainted with them early, and has neglected them in after life, but will regret his neglect; and the greatest consolation which he will find is, that some of their words and thoughts are still in his mind, and some of their images still floating there; and that, even though most of them may be forgotten, the labour of once acquiring them has given a lasting vigour and elasticity to his mental powers.

If the danger we have spoken of really exists, there is an easy and delightful way of avoiding it, by adding to the classics a thorough acquaintance, not only with modern, but early English literature. The literary man in England is familiar with it. Her poets and great prose-writers, who for the most part have been classical scholars, made the early literature of their country their study. Milton, to say nothing of Gray, was almost as well versed in it as in that of Greece and Rome, and turned it to good account; and Burke, the most poetical of the late prose-writers, did not forget it through all the heat and contest of political life.

If we have spoken freely of the failings of scholars, it is not from a disposition to fault-finding, nor from a blindness to their use and merit. Each class has its errours: to the wealthy is pride; to the poor, envy; and to the favoured of mind, an impatience of the talk and a supercilious indifference to the opinions of ordinary men. Through the large variety of life, there never will be wanting something to put in motion the evil as well as the good of our natures, and, while trusting to the strength of our virtue, we shall be ever failing through its weakness.

Whatever we have said has been from anxiety for the literary character of our country. We would warn those who are to encourage and support it, against a narrowness of taste, — a taming down by confined notions of faultlessness. Original minds will be peculiar and individual; and it is not for us to haggle at every thing new, but to look at it with care, and see if there may not be some beauties in its novelties, and whether what at first appeared a deformity may not have its fair proportions, and movements no less graceful and natural because all its own. We must be careful not to complain too much of that of which, after allowing something to the eccentricities of genius, we may not approve. Those who have produced what is lasting have been fond of working in their own way. For the most part, we should be content with them as we find them, lest, with that obstinacy so common to such minds, they run more into the fault, or lest, in the endeavour to remove it, they tear away some beauty which was more closely connected with it than we were aware. Some have complained of Milton's inversions, and perhaps they are now and then overstrained. Had he begun to correct them, who can tell where he would have stopped? had he listened, some pedant critic might have spoiled the loftiest and most varied harmony of English verse. In the same way, Cowper's rhyme might have lost all its spirit; and had Wordsworth, in the Excursion, given more compactness to his thoughts, where they are sometimes languidly drawn out, he might have lost something of that calm moral sentiment, of that pure shedding of the soul over his world of beauties, which lie upon them like gentle and thoughtful sunset upon the earth.

The giant minds of England grew up in times when there was less of order in society, — no critics, and few rules. They have their absurdities, affectations, and conceits; but what are all these, when we feel the breathing upon us of that spirit which was given to them alone. Sir Joshua Reynolds says, "Deformity came in with the dancing-master"; and if too great constraint upon the body's movements not only takes from them their elegance, but gives to them an awkwardness in its stead, it is the same thing with the mind. How would the studied graces of Chesterfield appear by the side of a well-made savage? and who can remember without laughter Hogarth's Frenchman, with head erect and toes turned out, telling the grandly formed Antinoüs, with his finely curved neck and firm-set foot, to hold up his head and look like him?

It is strange to see how the motions of the body give the character of the mind; and there is something besides ingenuity in the remark of Sterne, — "There are a thousand unnoticed openings which let a penetrating eye at once into a man's soul, and a man of sense does not lay down his hat on coming into a room, or take it up when going out, but something escapes which discovers him." The French tied up their writers, with the little inspiration they had, as if they were madmen, till well might Madame de Stael ask, "Why all this reining of dull steeds?" At the same time, they taught the world to hold as uncouth the movements natural to man, and to admire sudden, sharp, angular shootings of the limbs, as the only true lines of beauty. Yet the polite world not long ago read and talked nothing but French, and "went to church in a galliard, and came home in a coranto."

Our analogy, perhaps, is hardly in place, and we will run it no further; but will close our general remarks by once more urging those who may have an influence over our writers to use it with liberal minds, honestly looking for what is good, and not dealing harshly with what is doubtful. We do not mean that the eccentricities and faults of a man who shows some talents should be passed over in silence, for this would be no compliment to his intellect; but that the good may be weighed against the bad, fairly and openly, without bitterness or ridicule, and above all, that he may not be shackled by "those rules by which little minds fancy they may be able to comprehend great things."

With the exception of a few editors of magazines and reviews, Mr. Irving is almost the only American who has attempted to support himself by literary labours. Mr. Walsh began with a book of very respectable size and excellent matter, but that was political, and we were all politicians then. He, too, soon thought best to undertake periodical works, but they came to the same end with others, after much toil, little praise, and less money. Brown wrote novels, but was obliged to turn to the making up of political registers and magazines. It is true, that the English, who are thought to be slow enough in giving us praise, had his novels in their libraries, and that Godwin spoke of them with commendation; while we at home, who talk so much about the literary character of America, knew little or nothing of them. They were read in New York and Philadelphia by his personal friends, and there were some half dozen in this part of the country, a few years ago, who had seen one or two of the works, and liked them much, but took them up, and laid them down, for English. The first edition of Franklin appeared abroad, and there are one or two other works of merit which are waiting for notice from the same quarter.

We must not forget, however, to make one exception from our general neglect of American authors, for therein is our boast, — our very liberal patronage of the compilers of geographies in great and little, reading-books, spelling-books, and arithmetics. It is encouraging to our literary adventurers, that, should they fail to please the public in works of invention, they have at last this resort, and the consolation, that, if they are not to rank with the poets and novel-writers of the day, they may be studied and admired till Pike and Webster are forgotten.

Jesting apart, we have to thank Mr. Irving for being the first to begin and persevere in works which may be called purely literary. His success has done more to remove our anxiety for the fate of such works, than all we have read or heard about the disposition to encourage American genius.

Mr. Irving's immediate success does not rest, perhaps, wholly upon his merit, however great. Salmagundi came out in numbers, and a little at a time. With a few exceptions, it treated of the city, and what was seen and felt, and easy to be understood, by those in society. It had to do with the present and real, not the distant and ideal. It was pleasant morning or after-dinner reading, never taking up too much of a gentleman's time from his business and pleasures, nor so exalted and spiritualized as to seem mystical to his far-reaching vision. It was an excellent thing to speak of in the rests between cotillons and pauses between games at cards, and answered a further convenient purpose, inasmuch as it furnished those who had none of their own with wit enough, for sixpence, to talk out the sitting of an evening party. In the end, it took fast hold of people, through their vanity; for frequent use had made them so familiar with it as to look upon it as their own; and having retailed its good things so long, they began to run of the notion that they were all of their own making.

It was fortunate, too, that the work made its first appearance in New York, "where the people — Heaven help them — are the most irregular, crazy-headed, quicksilver, eccentric, whim-whamsical set of mortals that ever were jumbled together." Had it first shown its face in any other part of the country, how soon would it have been looked out of countenance, and talked down by your "honest, fair, worthy, square, good-looking, well-meaning, regular, uniform, straightforward, clock-work, clear-headed, one-like-another, salubrious, upright kind of people"!

New York being a city of large and sudden growth, with people from all parts of the country, and many foreigners, individuals there do not feel every chance sarcasm or light ridicule of some foible in the rank or set they belong to as a personal attack, as is the case in smaller cities, where sets must be small too, or as in cities of less rapid growth, where they are more distinctly marked. Neither have they enough of clanship in the different classes into which society will always be in some degree divided, to allow any lady or gentleman authority to dictate what a man shall be taken into favour for, and for what he shall be put down. One there, who can do it well, may laugh at follies, as well at those in fashion as at those out; nor will any wait to be told whether they are to laugh too. If ladies of all sizes and complexions, in heat and cold, choose to wear red, he may ridicule it, though all the rage, and that in print, too; nor will the female patrons of Mrs. Toole and Madame Bouchard banish him from society because he ventured to say that muslin walking-dresses in wet weather were not quite the thing.

In hinting what there might be in accidental circumstances to help to the early popularity of Salmagundi, we must not be understood as questioning its right to all and more than it obtained. To say that it was out of all comparison the ablest work of wit and humour which we had produced, would not be saying much; for we had done but little before this. McFingal is just enough like Hudibras to remind you that it was intended as an imitation of it, and The Foresters, though written by a man of rather uncommon talents, and in a clear, familiar, natural style, and such as we scarce meet with at home now-a-days, is remarkable only for a careful ingenuity in keeping up its allegorical character. It professes to be nothing more than the application of Swift's John Bull to the concerns of this country with Great Britain. And except in the wit and quick fancy of that work, it is a close copy; but it is about as guiltless of its wit as it is of its indelicacy; for there are but two or three places to shock the most sensitively refined, and not many more to make the merriest laugh.

Mr. Irving has taken the lead here in the witty, humorous, and playful cast of works, — those suited to our happier feelings, — while Brown harasses us with anxiety and strange terrour. He has not modelled himself upon any body, but has taken things just as he found them, and treated them according to his own humour. So that you never feel, as when looking at the works just mentioned, that you have gotten a piece of second-hand furniture, scraped and varnished till made to look fine and modern, that it may be put to a new use. His wit and humour do not appear to come of reading witty and humorous books; but from the world acting upon a mind of that cast, and putting those powers in motion. There are parts, it is true, which remind you of other authors, not, however, as imitations, but as resemblances of mind. In Knickerbocker, particularly, though it may be hard to point out in what the likeness consists, you frequently think of Sterne. Yet it would have been the book it now is though Sterne had never written.

Amidst the abundance of his wit and drollery, you never meet with bilious sarcasm. He turns aside from the vices of men to be amused with their affectation and foibles; and the entertainment he finds in these seems to be from a pure goodness of soul, — a sense that they are seldom found in thoroughly depraved and hardened hearts. The mind is relieved when it can shake off the secret malignity, hard hate, proud oppression, and unsparing selfishness of man, and look at him with his follies showing themselves in a vain, but honest, ostentation upon the outside of him, — pleased with himself, and fancying the world pleased with him too, and wishing well to it from his very illusion. For though foppery seems the most selfish thing in nature, yet a fop, for the most part, is the best-tempered creature in the world; so that old-fashioned censoriousness, which has lived upon the diseases of others' minds, — for ever finding something bad in what is mainly good, till tired of itself and all else, — is ready to give over its calling in despair, and turn fopling too, that it may be reconciled to itself and the world again.

Amiableness so marks Mr. Irving's writings as not to allow you to forget the man; and the pleasure is doubled much after the same manner that it is in a lively conversation with one for whom you feel an attachment and esteem. There is in it, also, the gayety and airiness of a light, pure spirit, — a fanciful playing with common things, and here and there beautiful touches, till the ludicrous becomes half picturesque.

Though many of the characters and circumstances in Salmagundi are necessarily without such associations, yet the Cocklofts are not only the most witty and eccentric, but the most thoroughly sentimental, folks in the world, like some of the characters in the Spectator, and like Trim, and that best of men, my Uncle Toby. And here we would notice a resemblance in our author to Sterne, — that, with few exceptions, his sentiment is in a purer taste, and better sustained, where mixed with witty and ludicrous characters and circumstances, than where it stands by itself. He not only mingles the contemplative and sentimental with the witty and droll, but, what is rarer, blends with them the wild, mysterious, and visionary. Glimpses of this appear in his Rip Van Winkle, — a combination like that found in Mr. Allston's "Two Painters" and "The Paint-King," and a no common union of qualities.

It looks a little like impertinent interference to advise a man to undertake subjects of a particular sort, who is so well suited for variety in kind. Nor do we wish that Mr. Irving should give up entirely the purely witty or humorous for those of a mixed nature. We would only express our opinion of the interest which such writings excite, and of his peculiar fitness for them;

and at the same time suggest to him the advantages he gains by changing from one to the other. For ourselves, we have no fear of being tired of his wit or humour, so long as they come from him freely. He is more powerful in them, we think, than in the solely sentimental or pathetic.

We give him joy of making his way so miraculously as not to offend the dignity of many stately folks, and pray him go on and prosper. It was a bold undertaking in a country where we are in the habit of calling humour buffoonery and wit folly. The notion is singular enough; but there are many who hold, that for a wit to be a gentleman, there is nothing more strange. It is in course that people ignorant of its nature should fall into this confusion. The misfortune is, that they should commit themselves by expressing an opinion uncalled for. We have seen some curb up at light wit let off in their presence, as at an unbecoming familiarity, and others amusingly vehement against it. So that mother wit would, in all likelihood, have been banished genteel company, had not Mr. Irving, in a lucky moment, given her his countenance. We ourselves have our fears of being unduly sprightly, and have forborne many a good thing lest we should be taken to task for sacrificing our dignity and decorum. The commission of this offence is considered in our country more heinous in writing than in conversation. For being rather raw in authorship, and feeling all the while as put upon our good behaviour, and not knowing well how to distinguish between freedom and coarseness, and avoiding the former lest we fall into the latter, we become very proper and very common.

The style of Mr. Irving's lighter productions is easy, idiomatic, and well suited to the matter. He has not thought it necessary to write the history of the family of the Giblets as he would that of the Gracchi, or to descant upon Mustapha's Breeches with the formality of a scientific lecture. We have observed a few slight errours, proceeding probably from the hurry in which such works are commonly written; and we find an Americanism or two. Upon the whole, however, it is superiour to one instance that we can call to mind of the familiar style in this country. "The Foresters" may be freer from faults, but is not so rich.

A main defect of the humorous pieces is a multiplicity of epithets, — continued sometimes to the confounding of distinct qualities, and the deadening of that vivacity which they are intended to produce. Another fault is the employing of certain worn-out veterans in the service of wit. But we owe it to him to say, that we presume he has disbanded them, as we have met with none of them in the Sketch Book, as well as we can recollect. We set down some of them: — Dan Homer, Dame Nature, Dame Fortune, Gaffer Phœbus, Daddy Neptune. And what affects us as false, mock gravity is the use of such antiquated phrases as "eftsoons," "ycleped," "whilome," &c. Mr. Irving, having no further use for them, after the manner of certain German princes, must have let them out for that unfortunate expedition up Mount Parnassus, under the conduct of the famous "Backwoodsman," in which disastrous undertaking they must have perished with their leader. This is the more probable, as, so far as we were able to follow them, we observed they were put to unremitted and hard service.

Another fault, which is found here and there in Knickerbocker, is that of forcing wit as of set purpose; running it down, and then whipping and spurring it into motion again, — as in that part upon the different theories of philosophers. Wit must appear to come accidentally, or its effect is lost. The moment we see any forecasting, it is all over with it. The great superiority of Swift lies as much in the manner in which his good things come from him as in the things themselves. If he keeps you laughing, you are persuaded that he could no more help it than a dull man could help putting you to sleep. And where it is not continuous, but comes in here and there amidst his fine, plain sense, it is always a part of the fabric, and never patched on. It is needless to say, that, were this defect frequent in Mr. Irving, it would be fatal. No doubt, a good deal might be taken from Knickerbocker, which would leave it more sustained and vivid; yet, after the witty and humorous works of a few of the English standard authors, there are no books of the kind in the language so entertaining, in which the circumstances are so ludicrous, and the characters so well sustained, as in Mr. Irving's.

It was our intention in the outset to have given several extracts, throwing in, as we went along, such remarks upon each as might occur to us. But becoming interested in the subject, and discoursing upon it loosely and generally enough, to be sure, it has grown under our hands so as to leave little room for selections. We will only refer our readers to a few places, therefore; and in order to get over the bad first, we will remark that we have been able to find very little wit, and no poetry, in what pass for the poetical articles. The attack upon Dr. Caustic is petulant and coarse, and is an exception to the good-nature which is found in the other parts of Salmagundi. We know not what wonders the Doctor performed to throw the gentlemen so off their guard, but doubt whether they were, in reason, enough to raise the anger of such men as the authors of that work.

Notwithstanding the length of it, we must extract a good part of Will Wizard at a ball. His character is a masterpiece, full of drollery, oddity, and good feeling, with an unsated appetite for long stories, and a most ludicrous uncouthness of person.

"On calling for Will in the evening, I found him full dressed, waiting for me. I contemplated him with absolute dismay. As he still retained a spark of regard for the lady who once reigned in his affections, he had been at unusual pains in decorating his person, and broke upon my sight arrayed in the true style that prevailed among our beaux some years ago. His hair was turned up and tufted at the top, frizzled out at the ears, a profusion of powder puffed over the whole, and a long plaited club swung gracefully from shoulder to shoulder, describing a pleasing semicircle of powder and pomatum. His claret-coloured coat was decorated with a profusion of gilt buttons, and reached to his calves. His white cassimere small-clothes were so tight, that he seemed to have grown up in them; and his ponderous legs, which are the thickest part of his body, were beautifully clothed in sky-blue silk stockings, once considered so becoming. But above all, he prided himself upon his waistcoat of China silk, which might almost have served a good housewife for a short-gown; and he boasted that the roses and tulips upon it were the work of *Nang-Fou*, daughter of the great *Chin-Chin-Fou*, who had fallen in love with the graces of his person, and sent it to him as a parting present. He assured me she was a remarkable beauty, with sweet obliquity of eyes, and a foot no longer than the thumb of an alderman. He then dilated most copiously on his silver-sprigged Dicky, which he assured me was quite the rage among the dashing young mandarins of Canton.

"I hold it an ill-natured office to put any man out of conceit with himself; so, though I would willingly have made a little alteration in my friend Wizard's picturesque costume, yet I politely complimented him on his rakish appearance.

"On entering the room, I kept a good look-out on Will, expecting to see him exhibit signs of surprise; but he is one of those knowing fellows who are never surprised at any thing, or at least will never acknowledge it. He took his stand in the middle of the floor, playing with his great steel watch-chain, and looking round on the company, the furniture, and the pictures with the air of a man 'who had seen d——d finer things in his time'; and to my utter confusion and dismay, I saw him coolly pull out his villanous old japanned tobacco-box, ornamented with a bottle, a pipe, and a scurvy motto, and help himself to a quid in face of all the company."

On seeing young Billy Dimple cross the room with a lady, he takes occasion to bring in one of his long stories.

"'A very pretty young gentleman, truly,' cried Wizard; 'he reminds me of a contemporary beau at Hayti. You must know that the magnanimous Dessalines gave a great ball to his court one fine sultry summer's evening; Dessy and me were great cronies, — hand and glove, — one of the most condescending great men I ever knew. Such a display of black and yellow beauties! such a show of Madras handkerchiefs, red beads, cocks' tails, and peacocks' feathers! — it was, as here, who should wear the highest top-knot, drag the longest tails, or exhibit the greatest variety of combs, colours, and gewgaws. In the middle of the rout, when all was buzz, slip-slop, clack, and perfume, who should enter but TUCKY SQUASH! The yellow beauties blushed blue, and the black ones blushed as red as they could, with pleasure; and there was a universal agitation of fans. Every eye brightened and whitened to see Tucky, for he was the pride of the court, the pink of courtesy, the mirror of fashion, the adoration of all the sable fair ones of Hayti. Such breadth of nose, such exuberance of lip! his shins had the true cucumber curve, — his face in dancing shone like a kettle; and, provided you kept to windward of him in summer, I do not know a sweeter youth in all Hayti than Tucky Squash. When he laughed, there appeared from ear to ear a *chevaux-de-frise* of teeth, that rivalled the shark's in whiteness; he could whistle like a northwester, — play on a three-stringed fiddle like Apollo; and as to dancing, no Long-Island negro could shuffle you 'double-trouble' or 'hoe corn and dig potatoes' more scientifically; — in short, he was a second Lothario, and the dusky nymphs of Hayti, one and all, declared him a perfect Adonis. Tucky walked about, whistling to himself, without regarding any body; and his *nonchalance* was irresistible.'

"I found Will had got neck and heels into one of his traveller's stories, and there is no knowing how far he would have run his parallel between Billy Dimple and Tucky Squash, had not the music struck up from an adjoining apartment, and summoned the company to the dance. The sound seemed to have an inspiring effect on honest Will, and he procured the hand of an old acquaintance for a country dance. It happened to be the fashionable one of 'The Devil among the Tailors,' which is so vociferously demanded at every ball and assembly: and many a torn gown, and many an unfortunate toe, did rue the dancing of that night; for Will thundered down the dance like a coach and six, sometimes right, sometimes wrong, now running over half a score of little Frenchmen, and now making sad inroads into ladies' cobweb muslins and spangled tails. As every part of Will's body partook of the exertion, he shook from his capacious head such volumes of powder, that, like pious Æneas on the first interview with Queen Dido, he might have been said to have been enveloped in a cloud. Nor was Will's partner an insignificant figure in the scene. She was a young lady of most voluminous proportions, that quivered at every skip; and being braced up in the fashionable style, with whalebone, stay-tape, and buckram, looked like an apple-pudding tied in the middle, or, taking her flaming dress into consideration, like a bed and bolsters rolled up in a suit of red curtains. The dance finished, I would gladly have taken Will off; but no, — he was now in one of his happy moods, and there was no doing any thing with him. He insisted on my introducing him to Miss Sophy Sparkle, a young lady unrivalled for playful wit and innocent vivacity, and who, like a brilliant, adds lustre to the front of fashion. I accordingly presented him to her, and began a conversation in which, I thought, he might take a share; but no such thing. Will took his stand before her, straddling like a Colossus, with his hands in his pockets, and an air of the most profound attention; nor did he pretend to open his lips for some time, until, upon some lively sally of hers, he electrified the whole company with a most intolerable burst of laughter. What was to be done with such an incorrigible fellow? To add to my distress, the first word he spoke was to tell Miss Sparkle that something she said reminded him of a circumstance that happened to him in China; — and at it he went, in the true traveller style, — described the Chinese mode of eating rice with chop-sticks, — entered into a long eulogium on the succulent qualities of boiled birds' nests, and I made my escape at the very moment when he was on the point of squatting down on the floor, to show how the little Chinese *Joshes* sit cross-legged."

We are quite at a loss how to go on. We took up the book, in order to make a memorandum of what articles to refer to as particularly good; but it was in vain, for our list was becoming nearly as long as the index, and we gave over the attempt.

Salmagundi is full of variety, and almost every thing good of its kind. Though upon an old plan, nothing can be better done than some of Mustapha's letters, particularly those upon a Military Review, and the City Assembly. The account of the Cockloft family is full of good affections; and they have not an oddity which you do not like them the better for, — their attachment to the old mansion which underwent repairs after every storm, and to the servants who had grown old in it. "The very cats and dogs are humorists, and we have a little runty scoundrel of a cur, who, whenever the church-bell rings, will run to the street door, turn up his nose in the wind, and howl most piteously." The description is so circumstantial, that you become quite domesticated amongst them; and though so queer and eccentric, they are not overdrawn.

It is one excellence of Mr. Irving, that although he has sketched so many whimsical and strange characters, they seldom say or do any thing which is against probability. — Snivers at the theatre is a sprightly draught. Will Wizard could make nothing of his face. "I might," says he, "as well have looked at the backside of his head." — The rivalry between Mrs. Toole and Madame Bouchard, intimating how far high life is made up of little things, must not be forgotten. — Wizard's visit to Ballston Springs, though forced in a small part of it, is highly entertaining. The elbowing, crowding, and scrambling at dinner, as also the philosophical discussion, which, we have understood, was quite the vogue there at the time, we shall pass by out of our respect for good company. — The paper upon Style, the same young cockney who first made his appearance at Ballston, "in gig and tandem, a pair of leather breeches, and with a liveried footman," is in true character and spirit; as is the history of the Giblets, who would up and ride, too.

That Salmagundi survived it all is a prodigy, for it must have been a true and faithful account of the birth and life of half the stylish families in New York, as it is of those of other cities. For their own sakes, to be sure, they would say nothing about Style or the Giblets, or if they did, with a forced smile and awkward compliment. But then it is so convenient, when one meets with any thing that comes home to him and makes him uneasy, to say, "Why, this is very well," and then turn to a part he cares nothing about, be highly offended, and end with declaring that "such things will never do." — As agreeable as they are, we have no room for "Straddle," nor "my Aunt Charity, who died of a Frenchman!" — The Waltz, we presume, did not long survive Pindar Cockloft's account of it to the old ladies. It is but one instance in a thousand, how feeble a safeguard of true delicacy is that which generally passes for polish and refinement. — My Uncle John is described with great delicacy; and the wit is softened down to cheerfulness by the sentiment which runs through it.

There is no truer indication of the morality and goodness of heart of a young man, than a certain reverential attachment to the old, a calm patience of their irritability, a kindly assisting of their helplessness, a giving way to their prejudices, and a greater relish for what is entertaining and instructive in them, than for the same when found in younger men. "There is a sober and chastised air of gayety diffused over the face of nature, peculiarly interesting to an old man," say the Autumnal Reflections. It is like the serenity of a good old age; and he who does not love the old while young will find himself going out into a comfortless solitude, as he travels from the crowd in which he moved in his early years. — "Autumnal Reflections," though here and there a little too youthful in expression, show a true eye for nature, and are written in a natural, moralizing strain, with a mingling of cheerfulness and sombreness, such as we feel the heart moved with when looking at the earth and sky. — The same may be said of Cockloft Hall.

Here we were about quitting Salmagundi; but recollecting that we have not spoken of The Little Man in Black, we stop for a moment to say a word of him;—for who could have the heart to neglect him? The description of his dress and person is of a piece with that of his character and situation, and distinct to the eye, though short. The mystery which begins with his introduction, and is kept up almost to the last, excites just enough of curiosity to increase the interest of the story, without interfering with the other feelings;—perfectly simple, it is one of the most delightful little tales we can call to mind. The hard opinion which the village held of the suffering man, their abuse of him, his own meekness and that of his harmless, short-legged dog, his miserable, though sublime death, the courtesy, shrinking delicacy, and humanity of old Cockloft, are all related with much pathos, and in a manner easy and natural. His turning out to be the last descendant of the renowned Linkum Fidelius, and leaving his large deal box, filled with the works of his ancestor, to old Cockloft, and bequeathing to him his dog, who became "father to a long line of runty curs that still flourish in the family," coming in at the close, eases a little the aching of the heart, and leaves one in "a most humorous sadness."

At parting company with Salmagundi, we cannot but say again, that, though its wit is sometimes forced and its serious style sometimes false, upon looking it over, we have found it full of entertainment, with an infinite variety of characters and circumstances, and with that amiable, good-natured wit, and that pathos, which show that the heart has not grown hard while making merriment out of the world.

There is but little room left to notice Knickerbocker, of which, we are glad to see, a third and neat edition has been lately published. As our remarks upon Salmagundi are, most of them, applicable to this work also, and an analysis of a story which all have read is dull matter, we less regret the want of space. Knickerbocker has the same faults and the same good qualities in its style, wit, and humour, as Salmagundi; and its characters are evidently by the same hand with the leading characters there, possessing the same freshness and originality, and suitableness to their situations. Too much of the first part of the first volume is laborious and up hill; and there are places, here and there, in the last part, to which there is the same objection. Our feelings seldom flag in the second. The sturdy old Stuyvesant, who occupies so much of it, never wearies you. The account of the author could not have been better; but our readers must go to the book for it. If they have not read the work for this last twelvemonth, and have the good fortune to be possessed of as poor memories as ourselves, they will be carried pleasantly through it.

We must leave the description of the ship Goede Vrouw, and take up that of the first governour of New Amsterdam, Wouter (or Walter) Van Twiller.

"His surname of Twiller is said to be a corruption of the original *Twijfler*, which in English means *doubter;* a name admirably descriptive of his deliberative habits. For though he was a man shut up within himself like an oyster, and of such a profoundly reflective turn that he scarcely ever spoke except in monosyllables, yet did he never make up his mind on any doubtful point. . . . . . There never was a matter proposed, however simple, and on which your common, narrow-minded mortals would rashly determine at the first glance, but what the renowned Wouter put on a mighty mysterious, vacant kind of look, shook his capacious head, and, having smoked for five minutes with redoubled earnestness, sagely observed, that 'he had his doubts about the matter,' — which in process of time gained him the character of a man of slow belief, and not easily to be imposed upon.

"The person of this illustrious old gentleman was as regularly formed and nobly proportioned, as though it had been moulded by the hands of some cunning Dutch statuary, as a model of majesty and lordly grandeur. He was exactly five feet six inches in height, and six feet five inches in circumference. His head was a perfect sphere, far excelling in magnitude that of the great Pericles (who was thence waggishly called *Schenocephalus*, or Onion-head). Indeed, of such stupendous dimensions was it, that Dame Nature herself, with all her sex's ingenuity, would have been puzzled to construct a neck capable of supporting it; wherefore she wisely declined the attempt, and settled it firmly on the top of his back-bone, just between the shoulders, where it remained as snugly bedded as a ship of war in the mud of the Potomac. His body was of an oblong form, particularly capacious at bottom; which was wisely ordered by Providence, seeing that he was a man of sedentary habits, and very averse to the idle labor of walking. His legs, though exceedingly short, were sturdy in proportion to the weight they had to sustain; so that, when erect, he had not a little the appearance of a robustious beer-barrel standing on skids. His face, that infallible index of the mind, presented a vast expanse, perfectly unfurrowed or deformed by any of those lines and angles which disfigure the human countenance with what is termed expression. Two small, gray eyes twinkled feebly in the midst, like two stars of lesser magnitude in a hazy firmament; and his full-fed cheeks, which seemed to have taken toll of every thing that went into his mouth, were curiously mottled and streaked with dusky red, like a Spitzenberg apple.

"His habits were as regular as his person. He daily took his four stated meals, appropriating exactly an hour to each;

he smoked and doubted eight hours, and he slept the remaining twelve of the four-and-twenty.

"With burghers whose minds seemed all to have been cast in one mould, and to be those honest, blunt sort of minds, which, like certain manufactures, are made by the gross, and considered as exceedingly good for the common use, the city grew like a mighty fungus, springing from a mass of rotten wood."

The speculator's huge palace of pine boards has been so often quoted, that most readers must have it by heart.

Wilhelmus Kieft, the successor of Wouter, is drawn by way of contrast. His conduct upon the taking of Fort Goed Hoop is very characteristic, and his railing against the people of Connecticut on that occasion is in as good a style of abuse as Swift would have made it.

After the death of this thin, bustling, fidgeting, noisy, do-little governour, whom the mob, — which he undertook, in a way of his own, to enlighten, — "like a knot of Sunday jockeys managing an unlucky devil of a hack-horse, kept either on a worry or a hand-gallop throughout the whole of his administration," came another kind of man, "Peter Stuyvesant, or, as he was otherwise called, Hard Koppig Piet, or Peter the Headstrong," who, taking his own course, — a terrour to his enemies, and heedless of all others, who stood agaze, — went through them with a stream of fire, like a comet, speeding onward, hot, blazing, and sputtering, through the stars.

"Dirk Schuilker (or Skulker) dubbed Galgenbrok, or Gallows Dirk," a half-Indian, who was a hanger-on at Fort Casimir, sometimes hunting and fishing all alone, day after day, and for the rest of the time employing himself in stealing, or getting drunk, alternately, or both together, as opportunity offered, has the poetical strangeness and wildness of some of the characters in Scott's novels. His making off with Van Poffenburgh's copper-bound cocked hat, and Risingh's jackboots, in the confusion of the capture of the fort, and stealing a boat to cross the river, when he carried to Governor Stuyvesant news of that event, keep up the spirit and truth of his character, in the midst of the hurry and importance of the affair, coming in like a pleasant accompaniment.

Stuyvesant's wrath upon hearing the news, his military preparations, voyage up the Hudson, the return of Poffenburgh to New Amsterdam, "with a crew of hard swearers at his heels, — heroes of his own kidney, fierce-whiskered, broad-shouldered, colbrand-looking swaggerers, — not one of whom but looked as if he could eat up an ox, and pick his teeth with his horns," must be passed over. Stuyvesant's expedition to New England is well set forth. His conduct upon his return to New Amsterdam, when blockaded by the English, and at the signing of articles of capitulation, is described with great vivacity, and quick, shifting circumstances, all good. This is one of the choicest parts of the work. But no one could form an idea of this fine-blooded old gentleman, whom we should be proud to claim as an ancestor, from any extracts we could make. His character breaks out here and there, lighting up the whole story.

We have made these few extracts and references, that Knickerbocker may be brought to the remembrance of our readers, should it have happened that they had forgotten it in the multitude of books which are daily coming out. We shall say nothing more upon it, unless we have occasion to refer to it in the few remarks which we are about making upon the Sketch Book.

It was delightful meeting once more with an old acquaintance who had been so long absent from us; and we felt our hearts lightened and cheered when we, for the first time, took the Sketch Book into our hands. Foreigners can know nothing of the sensation; for authors are as numerous and common with them as street acquaintance. We, who have only two or three, are as closely attached to them as if they were our brothers. And this one is the same mild, cheerful, fanciful, thoughtful, humorous being that we parted with a few years ago, though something changed in manner by travel.

We will be open with him, and tell him that we do not think the change is for the better. He appears to have lost a little of that natural run of style which, in his lighter writings, is so pleasing. He has given up something of his direct, simple manner and plain phraseology, for a more studied and periphrastic mode of expression, artistic, to be sure, but general and less definite. We have spoken of the defects of his former style, which are obvious enough, yet do not pervade it as a whole, and might be removed, not only without injury to the main body, but, on the contrary, leaving it firmer and more entire. It was masculine, and good bone and muscle. We do not ask for a *conversational* style in books, (except where the subject, or mode of treating it, is light and familiar,) though it is far better than that which impresses us as laboriously sought after, and cautiously put together. We shall save all trouble of defining, and be better understood, by saying, at once, that we want nothing more than a style as English and easy as that of the often-cited authority, Addison,—a style as unlike that which passes in this country, at the present day, for pure and elegant composition, as it is different from the rich, gorgeous, poetic style of Jeremy Taylor, or the less yet still poetic style of Burke.

There is in Mr. Irving's notice of Roscoe the fault we have spoken of, and he was not altogether free from it formerly in what he elaborated most; as, for instance, in his biography of Campbell. He sometimes aims at effect by a too formal inversion of sentences. Another errour, which is found principally in his serious and sentimental writings, is an occasionally inaccurate use of figurative language, which comes from connecting concrete and abstract terms, by which the picture is first presented to the eye and then blurred out. This seems to be from oversight.—Another is, that two words, both figurative, but representing different images, are brought together, and thus necessarily destroy each other.

For an instance of what may be pleasing to some, but which is not so to us, we refer our readers to the paragraph in his biography of Campbell in which he speaks of our scenery as wanting poetical associations, and the one immediately following, in which the thought is continued. They are too long to quote. In the same article he says of Campbell,—"He was left, without further opposition, to the impulse of his own genius, and *the seductions of the Muse*"; and again, he speaks of "the richer and more *interesting field* of German belles-lettres." Of Mr. Roscoe he says,—"He has planted bowers by the way-side for the refreshment of the pilgrim and sojourner, and has *established* pure *fountains*, which," &c. In The Broken Heart,—"She is like some tender *tree*, the pride and beauty of the grove;

graceful in its form, bright in its foliage, but with the worm preying at its *core*." In Rural Life in England, — "And, while it has thus banded society together, has *implanted* in each intermediate *link* a *spirit* of independence."

If a subject admits of figures, it is no matter how many a writer uses, provided he seems, without forcing himself to it, to think and feel in figure. But they must not, — indeed, then they hardly can be common. If they have been used before, there will be a novelty in their application, or in the language in which they are expressed, which will give them an air of originality.

We have made these remarks, and given these few instances, because, perhaps, it is not so much from our use of Americanisms, as they are called, as it is from defects of this kind, that we have been found fault with. They are faults, too, not easily corrected, because slowly discovered, not only by those who have fallen into them and by ordinary readers, but by others also, who have not themselves committed them. The occasional defect of vision in picture-language, if we may apply the word vision here, is more striking in Mr. Irving, as he has so good an eye for nature, and his sketches from it are drawn with so much truth and spirit. — The Sketch Book is very popular, and deservedly so; still, we think its style has been praised without due discrimination.

We have already stated why we consider Mr. Irving's former works, though more obviously faulty in places, still, as a whole, superiour in point of style to the Sketch Book. The same difference holds with respect to the strength, quickness, and life of the thoughts and feelings. The air about this last work is soft; but there is a still languor in it. It is not so breezy and fresh as that which is stirring over the others. He appears to us to have taken up of late some wrong notion of a subdued elegance. There is in his later style a too apparent elaboration, while, after all, its attained regularity of shape is not so pleasing as the easy irregularity of the former.

We have spoken of these defects in Mr. Irving, because of the influence which his name might give them. Yet it is not pleasant to be employed in pointing out the faults of a writer for whom a reader of any heart must feel a personal attachment. — We take Mr. Irving to be free from any impatience at well-meant criticism.

The Author's Account of Himself is written with simplicity; and in The Voyage, the moralizing, abstracted state of mind at sea is impressive and true. Its character of vastness and unity makes us look upon the gigantic and wild movements of the ocean as those of a tremendous existence, who, heedless of our littleness, might in a moment shake us to nothing. The account of the shipwreck is given with distinctness, though we think it enfeebled, rather than strengthened, by the reflections. The plain story told by the captain leaves a deeper impression. There is a particularity and fearful presence in the account of the storm at sea, which alarm us; and the arrival of the ship at the pier-head, and the merchant to whom she is consigned, are described with the verity of matter-of-fact. The sailor's wife would affect us more, did she not instantly bring to mind Crabbe's story of poor Sally, — which breaks over the heart, sweeping away its joys, and leaving it forlorn and wasted.

Where he speaks of Roscoe, all the kind feelings of

his heart are stirred. We have no doubt the man is worthy of it; though we think that Mr. Irving has overrated him as an author. His style answers very well to the description of his mansion. "It is not in the purest taste, yet it has an air of elegance." The early high reputation of his Life of Lorenzo de' Medici, was owing to the subject, and its being written by a banker. It has very much declined since, though it will always hold a respectable rank among the works of this day.

Mr. Irving's story of The Wife is pleasing, though the incidents are much worn, having passed through so many common novels. There is nothing mawkish, however, in the manner in which the circumstances are related. The feelings and reflections are manly and elevated, and that purity of soul shines through it, without which man can know little of what is in the heart of woman.

No man so tastes the bitterness of a lonely sorrow as does he who has one to help him bear all his other griefs. With a heart all trust, yet brooding in secret over a misery which he shrinks from making another share, and haunted by the doubt that his very forbearance may be a wrong to her that loves him, — this bears down his spring of feeling, and brings a torpor upon life, making the world seem motionless to him and without a joy. He looks upon the cheerfulness of his wife and children as a sad delusion, and closes his eyes upon it sick and weary. Where he doubts not, — in the midst of those he loves, and who are the world to him, — he sits alone in the darkness of his spirit.

The Broken Heart has passages as beautiful and touching as any that Mr. Irving has written, but they are too frequently injured by some studied, inappropriate epithet or phraseology which jars upon the feelings. The general reflections have a deep and tender thoughtfulness, and are too good for the story. It is enough to meet in life with those who can make themselves over to one man, for lucre, or something better or worse, while their hearts are with another; but in a work of sentiment it is revolting. To see those "who have had the portals of the tomb suddenly closed between them and the being they most loved on earth, — who have sat at its threshold, as one shut out in a cold and lonely world, from whence all that was most lovely and loving had departed," — to find such turning away from the grave before the grass has grown again over the broken earth, is the daily course of the world. But do not let it break in upon our visions and dreams. Let the world which the imagination makes to itself, whether sad or cheerful, be still pure and exalted, that we may come from it touched and refined, and be not wholly of the coarse matter of the earth. To read of a woman whose love death has sanctified, whose heart is in the grave with him she loves, — who talks with his spirit in the moon and the stars, — yielding up a wasted body to another man, is loathsome. We have heard talk of the affections, as if they were all reason. As reason is used by those who thus speak, it is a lie upon our mixed nature when they concern our remembrances of the dead, and when turned towards the living, is a sophistry almost as dangerous as doctrines the most sensual. We are sorry to see a mind so truly refined as Mr. Irving's thus carried away by the cant of the day.

Another fault — which is from the same false theory — is laying open to the common gaze, and common talk, feelings the very life of which is secrecy. In The

Wife: — "I have noticed the mute rapture with which he would gaze upon her in company, of which her sprightly powers made her the delight, and how in the midst of applause her eye would still turn to him, as if there alone she sought favour and acceptance."

Again, when the husband and friend reach the cottage, "a bright and beautiful face glanced out at the window and vanished." What next? Why, in the presence of this friend, who must have felt sufficiently awkward the while, the husband "caught her to his bosom, — he folded his arms around her [Mr. Irving seldom uses *round* or *about*], he kissed her again and again."

In The Broken Heart, (founded on fact, it is said,) the female carries her sorrows to show off at a masquerade, — warbles a plaintive air at the foot of an orchestra, to the no small grief of the crowd which gathers about her, — marries a man with an epaulet to each shoulder, and dies, — of what? Of disappointed love! One would have thought she had found vent for it before this.

Mr. Irving must forgive us if we are a little over-earnest at seeing a man of his delicate and sensitive cast of mind giving sanction to views and sentiments and acts so wanting in a refined reserve. He, of all men, is the last we can consent should ever lend himself to such a service. Miss Edgeworth makes one of her heroes read his love-letters, and talk of them on the street, as unmoved as he would talk about a purchase of teas or sugars. Another, in a morning ride, protests to his companions that he can never marry such a lady, for his heart is already engaged, and where his heart is, there only will he give his hand; and this very spiritedly, and all on horseback. A third declares his love upon his knees, in the presence of papa, mamma, and all the little brothers and sisters. And why should n't he? Miss Edgeworth does these things partly from her nature, we fear, and partly on system. Yet Grace Nugent is all dignity, retired delicacy, and love.

Rip Van Winkle is our favourite amongst the new stories. We feel more at home in it with the author than in any of this collection. Rip's idle good-nature, which made him the favourite of the boys, — his "aversion to all kinds of profitable labour," "thinking it of no use to work upon his own farm because every thing about it went wrong, and would go wrong, in spite of him," yet always ready to help his neighbours, — "the foremost at husking-frolics, and building stone-fences," and ready at running errands for all the old wives in the village, — and toiling all day at fishing and shooting, — these show an understanding of the apparent contradictions in character, and are set forth in excellent humour.

In his hen-pecked condition, he at one time makes a companion of his dog, who is as submissive as his master, — at another, betakes himself to the bench before the tavern door, where sit the great men of the village, and Nicholas Vedder, the landlord, "who kept his seat there from morning till night, just moving sufficiently to avoid the sun, and keep the shade of a large tree." The mountain scenery is given with much beauty; and the ghostly party at ninepins is at the same time laughable and picturesque. The author's mind is highly fanciful, and just suited to such scenes. Rip's amaze upon his return home after his long trance, the sight of his son Rip, — now full-grown and the very counterpart of himself in dress and person, confounding him utterly and making him doubt his identity, — could not have been more happily imagined. The incidents of the story are ingeniously contrived, and the whole is painted with a free, spirited touch.

Though this article is drawn to a greater length than was intended, which is apt to be the case when one is hurried, — we cannot pass over the paper upon English Writers on America, without expressing our hearty approbation of it. It is written in a just, liberal, manly spirit, worthy its author. It would be well for England would she listen to the warnings he has given her. For our own countrymen, we cannot do better than quote his own words.

"But however short-sighted and injudicious may be the conduct of England in this system of aspersion, recrimination on our part would be equally ill-judged. I speak not of a prompt and spirited vindication of our country, or the keenest castigation of her slanderers; but I allude to a disposition to retaliate in kind, to retort sarcasm and inspire prejudice, which seems to be spreading widely among our writers. Let us guard particularly against such a temper, for it would double the injury, instead of redressing it. Nothing is so easy and inviting as the retort of abuse and sarcasm; but it is a paltry and unprofitable contest. It is the alternative of a morbid mind, fretted into petulance, rather than warmed into indignation. . . . . .

"Our retorts are never republished in England, and fall short, therefore, of their aim; but they foster a querulous and peevish temper among our writers; they sour the sweet flow of our early literature, and sow thorns and brambles among its blossoms; but what is still worse, they circulate over our own country, and, as far as they have effect, produce virulent national prejudices."

We come from reading Rural Life in England as much restored and as cheerful as if we had been passing an hour or two in the very fields and woods themselves.

Mr. Irving's scenery is so true, so full of little beautiful particulars, so varied, yet so connected in character, that the distant is brought nigh to us, and the whole is seen and felt like a delightful reality. It is all gentleness and sunshine; the bright influences of nature fall on us, and our disturbed and lowering spirits are made clear and tranquil, — turned all to beauty, like clouds shone on by the moon.

Though we see in it nothing of the troubles and vices of life, we believe Mr. Irving found all he has described. If there be any thing which can give purity and true dignity to the character of man, it is country employments and scenery acting upon a cultivated mind. "In rural occupation," says Mr. Irving, (and it needs little qualifying,) "there is nothing mean and debasing. It leads a man forth among scenes of natural grandeur and beauty; it leaves him to the workings of his own mind, operated upon by the purest and most elevating of external influences. Such a man may be simple and rough, but he cannot be vulgar."

We have partial and petulant accounts of England and Englishmen from travelled gentlemen, who have bought and sold at Manchester and Birmingham, and ended with noisy politics in London coffee-houses. They have seen, what is to be seen in all great cities, the ostentatious profligacy of many in high life, and the coarse sensuality of more in low life. It is only from persons like our author, men of refined, unprejudiced, and enlarged minds, that we learn how to value the main body of the nobles and gentry of England. We need not say, that, in feeling respect and kindness towards them, neither our private virtue nor political integrity is endangered.

Upon looking back, it is with some pain that we find

how much we have dwelt upon Mr. Irving's defects. If, however, a man may trust that the feelings which lead him to his remarks will naturally appear in his manner, we have no fear that Mr. Irving will think we took any pleasure in pointing out his faults. Had we thought less highly of his powers, we should have said less about his errours; did we not take delight in reading him, we should have been less earnest about his mistakes.

The truth is, that, in this part of our notice of him, we have been more anxious for the literary character of our country, than for his fame or our own pleasure. He is a man of genius, and able to bear his faults. But then, again, he is our most popular writer, and, for aught we can see, is likely to remain so for years to come; at least, he will always be a standard author amongst us. Our literary character is said to be forming. If we have discovered talents and industry, we have, likewise, shown enough of bad taste. We cannot have a right character till this is corrected; and the sanction of Mr. Irving to some of our errours would give them a growth which would take years of our dull toiling to root out.

Here we must at last close, looking for another Sketch Book, with as pleasant articles as Rural Life in England, and other tales in the manner of Rip Van Winkle, a little longer, and no less circumstantial.

RADCLIFFE'S GASTON DE BLONDEVILLE.*

We should have been glad of a better life of Mrs. Radcliffe than the one before us. It contains but little more than is to be found in the extract in Scott's "Lives of the Novelists." Let us, however, be grateful for that little, and, in particular, for the correction of the silly stories set agoing by some small theorists, who thought to account for the operations of a mind which they should have been content to look up at in silent wonder.

Mrs. Radcliffe never was in Italy; and it now seems that all the mountain scenery of "The Mysteries of Udolpho" was laid open to the public gaze before ever she visited the Rhine, or even made the tour of the English lakes. This is fortunate for the Edinburgh Reviewers; for, as their old theory has tumbled down, they have now an opportunity to build another up. Scott, though he fell into the Rhine, has not stumbled

---

*From the United States Review and Literary Gazette for 1827.

Gaston de Blondeville, or the Court of Henry III. keeping Festival in Ardenne, a Romance. St. Alban's Abbey, a Metrical Tale; with some Poetical Pieces. By Anne Radcliffe, Author of "The Mysteries of Udolpho," "Romance of the Forest," &c. To which is prefixed a Memoir of the Author, with Extracts from her Journals. Four Volumes in Two. Philadelphia: Carey & Lea. 1826. 12mo.

on the mountains of Italy, and remarks: — "The inaccuracy of the reviewer is of no great consequence; but a more absurd report found its way into print, that Mrs. Radcliffe, having visited the fine old Gothic mansion of Haddon House, had insisted upon remaining a night there, in the course of which she had been inspired with all that enthusiasm for Gothic residences, hidden passages, and mouldering walls, which marks her writings. Mrs. Radcliffe, we are assured, never saw Haddon House; and although it was a place excellently worth her attention, and could hardly have been seen by her without suggesting some of those ideas in which her imagination naturally revelled, yet we should suppose the mechanical aid to invention, the recipe for fine writing, — the sleeping in a dismantled and unfurnished old house, — was likely to be rewarded with nothing but a cold, and was an affectation of enthusiasm to which Mrs. Radcliffe would have disdained to have recourse."

We should be glad to know where that author slept, who, in imagination, raised the grand and terrific castle in "The Romance of the Pyrenees." Likely enough, in some snug bedchamber in Manchester or Lichfield. Martin, who paints mountains with more grandeur and truth than any living artist, say his brothers in the art, was of humble origin, bred to a trade, with scarcely a common school education, and, above all, was never out of England in his life. He is a more striking instance than Mrs. Radcliffe; for, says Scott of her descriptions, (and we are pleased to have such support for our opinions,) they "were marked in a particular degree (to our thinking at least) with the characteristics of fancy portraits; yet many of her contemporaries conceived them to be exact descriptions of scenes which she had visited in person." There is a correspondence, no doubt, between the material and intellectual world, a fitness in the one for the other. There are powers in some minds, sleeping their first, infant sleep; let but a certain chord be touched in nature, and to what sweet and universal harmony do they wake! what sounds do they pour forth in unison! They need no musician to instruct them; the teacher is within! Look into your Locke, or your Stewart, and explain it if you can. You will come away little the wiser for your search, though you should come away fancying yourself possessed of all knowledge.

People were not content with making Mrs. Radcliffe lie awake all night in a chilly, damp, old house, in order to build castles in the air, but they must needs drive her mad with ghosts of her own raising; though she herself protests to us, at the end, after the manner of Snug the joiner, that they are no true ghosts, but that one is a smuggler, another an unfortunate lady, and a third a piece of wax-work. No one who has raised a sprite was ever frightened out of his senses at the sight of it. We have never heard of Monk Lewis's going mad, or of Maturin's dying out of his wits. Either of them would have been more overcome at the terrours of the other's conjuring up, than at any of his own. Writing is too serious a business; there is no leisure time to be frightened in; there are too many powers hard at work to allow of any thing more than enough of that excitement which is necessary to keep them in action. If you wish an author to feel his own production with the same kind of intensity that another does, you must let him forget it for a time, and then turn reader of his own, as if it were something that others had provided for him. "The evening was always her favourite season for composition," says the biographer of Mrs. Radcliffe, "when her spirits were in their happiest tone, and she was most secure from interruption. So far was she from being subjected to her own terrours, that she often laughingly presented to Mr. Radcliffe chapters which he could not read alone without shuddering." Not that she laughed while actually writing, or that the word "happiest" is intended to be used in its more ordinary sense.

We are not at all surprised at Mrs. Radcliffe's not going mad to oblige the world; but we cannot so well account for her doing so little to oblige it in a more agreeable way, after writing "The Italian," the best of her works. Having produced all her prose works, except the one before us, in the course of seven years, and before she was thirty-four, — an age at which few authors can be said to have reached their prime, — she seems to have sat down for the remainder of her days, satisfied with the quiet occupations and enjoyments of domestic life, and with now and then amusing herself by writing verses, or entering on her journal descriptions of the scenery she passed through in those summer excursions with her husband, of which she was so fond.

Up to the close of "The Italian," her mind seems gradually to have ascended; and perhaps she felt as if the next step might be downward. It may be that she was right. "Gaston de Blondeville," — not given to the world till after her death, and written scarcely five years after "The Italian," — though showing a surprising improvement in style, discovers, at the same time, a subsiding of those energies by which she had held us with such fearful mastery. Besides, it sometimes happens, even with minds of great genius, that, the exciting cause ceasing with the completion of a work, and exhaustion following intense action, a despondency comes over the spirits; and, instead of taking hope from the past to go on with, they are ready to stop and sit down with despair. It is true, that this state rarely lasts long, and that the mind commonly gathers strength and life again. But there may be some of a more delicate frame, who never entirely free themselves of the misgiving; and this mistrust, weakening the elasticity of their powers, brings upon them the very feebleness they feared.

It is not that critics by profession may praise a second work less heartily than they did a first, or that the crowd of second-hand talking critics and readers may declare themselves sorry at your failure, and yet take more pleasure in it than in your success, — it is neither of these, though these may mingle with it; — it is the dread of falling short of that which the mind imagines to itself, to which it looks up with tremulous delight, and longs after with all the cravings of the full, yet hungry soul.

Genius is, perhaps, not more distinctly marked out from mere talents by its originating powers, than by its delight in, and longing after, this grand and beautiful intellectual excellence, and its love of it for itself alone. He only who has had this glorious vision, and has had his spirit moved by it as the man of genius alone can be moved, — he only can know how disheartening is the fear that he may be forced to say to himself, I have failed!

Whether any thing like this had its effect upon the delicate mind of Mrs. Radcliffe is mere conjecture now. Perhaps there is something in the nature of the thoughts and passions with which, and upon which, she wrought, that exhausts itself. The terrific, in real life, is apt in time to produce indifference or stupor, and, in imaginary life, is likely, it may be, to settle away into a gentle and quieting calm. The sublime, too, besides its tenseness, may want the relief of variety in its character, to enable us to be so frequently or so long affected by it as by other emotions of the soul; and we know that the mind which has been some time forced by it above its ordinary condition becomes wearied, and is glad to loosen its hold. We are but feeble creatures here; and there are thoughts and feelings which sometimes stir themselves within us, which are too mighty for us now. If we are wise, we shall not try to strangle them in our souls, but reverently think of them as prophetic of that expanded and grander state of being which our spirits are ordained to.

Perhaps, after all, an aversion to being talked about, which seemed a striking part of this female's character; an accidental suspension of her labours breaking up the habit of application and exertion; a full relish for the snugness and quiet of home; the pleasure she took in her summer excursions with her husband, and the thousand little occupations and scarcely-observed pleasures of daily life, which so satisfy simple minds and kind hearts; and, more than these, that most absorbing of all human enjoyments, the luxurious dreaming of a creative intellect, — may have done more towards checking her after exertions than all that is contained in our notion upon the effects of the sublime and terrific. For to say that sublimity is as natural and easy to a sublime mind as wit is to a witty one, sounds very like a truism; and yet, if it be a truism, there is an end to all speculation upon the matter.

Upon her dislike to personal notoriety, and to being

stared at by the public, her biographer remarks, — "A scrupulous self-respect, almost too nice to be appreciated in these days, induced her sedulously to avoid the appearance of reception on account of her literary fame. The very thought of appearing in person as the author of her romances shocked the delicacy of her mind. To the publication of her works she was constrained by the force of her own genius; but nothing could tempt her to publish *herself*, or to sink, for the moment, the gentlewoman in the novelist."

Let the cause of Mrs. Radcliffe's silence be what it may, no one, who thinks of the new power which seems suddenly to have developed itself in "The Italian," but must feel sorry that she did not set about another work while her mind was yet glowing with the exercise of that she had just finished. We allude to the dialogues in that greatest of her works, particularly in the interview between the Marchesa and Schedoni in the church of San Nicolo; that between Schedoni and Spalatro, when the latter refuses to murder Ellena; and in the scene, also, in which Schedoni discovers Ellena to be his daughter. The deadly shrewdness, the sophistry with a mixture of emotion, in the first, — the close, abrupt, and impassioned character of the next and those following, — have been equalled by few novelists. It is this which puts life indeed into a story; and when we think what Mrs. Radcliffe might have done, had she gone on thus, we cannot but feel sad at what we have lost.

"Dialogue! dialogue! dialogue!" said Miss Edgeworth once to a sister author. It is this in which the novelist rises towards the higher rank of the dramatist; — we mean our older dramatists, when we speak of superiority; — and the closer the language, the oftener a whole train of thought or emotion is given by a sudden turn, or the peculiar use of one little word, so much the better. The best *novel* dialogues are apt to be diffuse enough.

It is well observed by the London Quarterly Review, in answer to Scott, that many have failed in the drama who have afterwards been the authors of our first-rate novels; but that we have no instance of any distinguished dramatist who has failed as a novelist. If any one should make the attempt, and fail, we should say that he failed because he had undertaken an inferiour sort of labour, and that his powers, not being fully tasked, and so not excited to their utmost, grew languid at their work. Though almost all true poets write pure prose, yet it is rarely that they ascend into high, poetic prose, we believe: in prose they do not *sing*. Sir Walter is naturally enough inclined to make the most of his own calling. But we have no belief at all, that he could write a play worthy of his reputation. Pray Heaven he do not try, and put us to shame!

We have wandered far enough, and must come back to take a look at Gaston de Blondeville. We are disappointed in it, as we feared we should be, from the kind of notices which are met with in its praise. There is a ghost, — a true ghost, and no sham; a true knight he is, too, — but he lacks "the horrours." He is, as it were, a daylight sort of ghost, and not "my father's spirit in arms," visiting the glimpses of the moon, making night hideous. Perhaps, however, we should except his first appearance, at the tomb of Geoffrey de Clinton; and his second, in the gallery, opposite the king, at the banquet. At the tournament, he is a mere parade-ghost. And the description of the tournament has this same fault, of too much getting-up; and, for the matter of that, so has Sir Walter Scott's much-praised one, notwithstanding all its splendour. Both authors should, in courtesy, have left tournaments to old Chaucer.

The merchant, on whom the story turns, weeps, and sighs, and faints, like a very woman. Now, in those days of travel and violence, it stood one of that calling well in stead to keep good heart. It is true that he begins well; but there is in this tale a want of vividness, and stir, and spirit: the fire burnt low in which this work was forged. We are not willing, after all, to think that this tameness of which we complain was owing to Mrs. Radcliffe's mind having lost its energy, but rather to her plan, her attempt to make fiction a vehicle for true history, instead of using history merely as a good ingredient to work into fiction, as Shakspeare and Scott have done. Any one, who is pleased with getting a knowledge of some of the dresses and ceremonies of those times in this way, will take a deeper interest in the work than we have done. For our part, we would rather dig in the dust of the old chroniclers. We knew a gentleman who never could bring himself to read Anacharsis, because he would not be *manœuvred* into knowledge, as the child is by the playing-map, and like trickery.

We must not be thought to say, that this work is without spirit and interest; we have intended to speak of it in comparison with what Mrs. Radcliffe had before done. In one respect, it is astonishingly superiour to her former works, — we mean in its style, which is simple, natural, unencumbered, and in good taste. Our only way of accounting for this is, that, feigning it to be an ancient manuscript, and adopting the antique phraseology, she insensibly expressed herself in the naked simplicity of former times. We find a like effect in Thomson's Castle of Indolence.

The extracts from the Journal are well worth reading. How a woman of Mrs. Radcliffe's mind could look at nature as she did, knowing that she was going straight to the inn to put it down in black and white, we cannot tell. She did it, however, and so do our lady-tourists; but our lady-tourists are not Mrs. Radcliffe. The painter sketches from nature. He tells you, "'T is my vocation, Hal!" But the poetical mind of him who is not a painter may be said to see, and not to see; all is absorbed deeply inward, and goes in mingling with emotions, and fancies of the brain, changing its shapes and relations in its very course. Perhaps there are not to be found in writing descriptions so minute and so true as those in this Journal. Light and shadow, tints of the sky, forms and hues, and positions of objects, appear to have been viewed by Mrs. Radcliffe with the minute accuracy of a painter's eye.

There follows Gaston de Blondeville a pretty thick volume of poetry. Remembering the specimens of Mrs. Radcliffe's talents in this art, scattered through her novels, we went to the volume with much misgiving. We were somewhat relieved, but not well enough satisfied to persevere. There is considerable improvement in diction, and some quite pleasing passages, which come very near being what may be called good poetry. There is nothing to which that homely saying, "A miss is as good as a mile," better applies, than to what comes under the name of second-rate poetry,— which, strictly speaking, is no poetry at all. To be sure, it may be in fashion, and be run after for a day;

for the world is more quickly taken with the false than with the true, though it will not hold to it so long. The eyesight may be dazzled, and there may be a great expenditure of the vital principle in *ecstatics;* but all comes right after a while, and people learn to distinguish between poverty and simplicity, between a superflux of words, and true passion and sentiment, and rich, original thought.

We are sorry that we cannot say more for Mrs. Radcliffe's poetry; for we would say nothing but what is well of her. There is a beauty in her mind, a gentleness, a delicacy, a retiredness in her disposition, which is wholly feminine, and which every man cannot but feel, who feels as man ought towards woman; and she who wants this disposition, though she may draw admiration, will never win and keep a true, respectful, knightly sentiment of love.

THE NOVELS OF CHARLES BROCKDEN BROWN.*

TWENTY odd years have been allowed to pass before even an imperfect edition of the works of fiction of our long unrivalled novelist is given to the public. Yet nearly all that time Brown has been alone; for no one approached the height he stood on till the author of "The Pioneers" and "The Pilot" appeared. Like his own Clithero, he lay stretched in moody solitude, the waters of the noisy world rolling blindly on around him, and a wide chasm open between him and his fellow-men. In 1815, Mr. Dunlap gave us a Life of him; an ill-arranged and bulky work, yet too meagre where it should be particular and full. To this, however, we are indebted for all we know of his life; and we owe to it also an article on Brown, which appeared in the North American Review for 1819, an article which, we fear, has left us little to say.

Mr. Dunlap's Life of our author was not of a character to be much read; and it was, after all, perhaps,

---

* From the United States Review and Literary Gazette for 1827.

The Novels of CHARLES BROCKDEN BROWN: "*Wieland*," "*Arthur Mervyn*," "*Ormond*," "*Edgar Huntly*," "*Jane Talbot*," *and* "*Clara Howard*." *With a Memoir of the Author.* Boston: S. G. Goodrich. 1827. 6 vols. 12mo.

in this case, as it has been in some others, chiefly to England that Brown was indebted for his coming into general notice at home. It is true that his stories were to be found amongst the shabby editions of works which go to make up a circulating library, and that some of them were occasionally read; but excepting his personal acquaintance, few or none knew or cared whether he was an Englishman or a Laplander; whether he was living, whether he had died a natural death, or was one of the many Browns who are regularly hanged. Even when an American edition at last appears, it is recommended to public notice by extracts from a London paper, congratulating Brown's countrymen that Boston had given them an edition of the works of a man of whom they might well be proud. We hope none will take offence. We would merely suggest to the zealous, that, whenever a man of genius appears amongst us, we should give him cordial welcome and support, and hearty praise; and not be so wanting in true patriotism as to let foreigners be the first to take him by the hand.

This edition of Brown is in six conveniently sized volumes, neat in appearance, though not so accurately printed as we could wish. The notice of him, at the beginning, gives not a single new fact, or peculiarity in his character, that we recollect. The publisher might as well have set his printer to compiling a notice out of Dunlap, as have brought such a one as this all the way from Philadelphia. We wish, too, he had taken advice before making his selections. No edition of Brown's works should be published without the Memoir of Carwin and that of Stephen Calvert. It is true, Brown did not live to finish them; but they are fine beginnings. And from the very fact that they are but beginnings, they have a peculiar and near interest in the eyes of those who feel something like a personal attachment to our author;—and what right-hearted reader does not? They connect us with him in his sickness, bring us to the side of his death-bed, and help us watch the passing of his spirit into the other world. Had any sacrifice been necessary, which we very much doubt, "Clara Howard" should have been omitted; for it has all Brown's faults, with little or none of his power. Notwithstanding these deficiencies, we hold the public to be under obligations to the publisher, and hope he will be rewarded for his praiseworthy untaking.

To the speculative mind, it is a curious fact, that a man like Brown should of a sudden make his appearance in a new country, in which almost every individual was taken up in the eager pursuit of riches, or the hot and noisy contests of party politics; when every man of talents, who sought out distinction, went into one of the professions; when to make literature one's main employment was held little better than being a drone; when almost the only men who wrote with force and simplicity were some of the leaders amongst our active politicians; when a man might look over our wide and busy territory, and see only here and there some self-deluded creature seated, harping, on some weedy knoll, and fancying it the efflorescent mount of all the Muses.

Did not the fact of Brown's having produced such works at such a time clearly show the power of genius over circumstances, we might be inclined to attribute to his loneliness of situation something of that solitariness, mysteriousness, and gloom, which surround all he wrote. But these characteristics of his writings came not of outward things. The energies of his soul were melancholy powers, and their path lay along the dusky dwelling-places of superstition, and fear, and death, and woe. They manifest themselves in the most striking manner, where he imparts to the dead-level, rectangular streets and plainly constructed houses of a freshly brick-built city, the gloom, awe, and mystery which hitherto had hung over the damp, dark, intricate passages and dread chambers of inquisitions, dungeons, towers, and hoary castles alone. The mind of such a man takes not its character from the world without, but takes out from that world what suits its nature, and passes the rest by; and what more it needs, and what it cannot find abroad, it turns for inward, and finds or creates it there. "My existence," says Brown, "is a series of thoughts rather than of motions. Ratiocination and deduction leave my senses unemployed. The fulness of my fancy renders my eye vacant and inactive. Sensations do not precede and suggest, but follow and are secondary to, the acts of my mind."

So strong was this cast of his mind, and so single was he in his purpose, that, of all men of imagination, we know of none who appear from their writings to have looked less at nature, or to have been less open to its influences. With the exception of Mervyn's return to Hadwin's, and his last journey thence, and the opening of Carwin, with one or two more slight instances, Brown seldom attempts a description of natural scenery; or where he does, and labours it most, is confused and indistinct, as, for instance, in Edgar Huntly. It is amidst shut-up houses, still, deserted streets, noisome smells, and pestilence, and death, and near the slow, black hearse and the dead man's grave, that his calling lies; and he has no time to turn aside to breathe the fresh, clear air of the country. He seems as intent in fiction upon his single purpose as ever Howard was in real life, — he who could spare no time from hospitals and prisons for statues, pictures, and palaces.

This confined purpose of the mind may be thought to be a serious deficiency in Brown's genius, yet it is curious to see how a defect sometimes takes the appearance of an advantage. The very want of variety has given such an air of truth to what he is about, showing such an earnest singleness of purpose, that perhaps no writer ever made his readers more completely forget that they were not reading a statement of some serious matter of fact; and so strong is this impression, that we even become half reconciled to improbabilities which so vex us in fiction, though often happening in daily life. This enables us, also, to bear better with his style; for, along with something like a conviction that the man who had vivacity of genius enough for such inventions could never have delivered himself with such dull poverty and pedantry of phrase, we at last are almost driven to the conclusion, that, however extraordinary they may be, they are nevertheless facts; for the man never could have made them, and things must have happened pretty much as he tells us they did.

If Brown is remarkable for having appeared amongst a people whose pursuits and tastes had, at the time, little or no sympathy with his own, and in a country in which all was new, and partook of the alacrity of hope, and where no old remembrances made the mind contemplative and sad, nor old superstitions conjured up forms of undefined awe, he is scarcely less striking for standing apart, in the character of his mind, from almost every other man of high genius. He is more like Godwin than like any other; but differs from him in making so many of his characters live, and act, and perish, as if they were the slaves of supernatural powers, and the victims of a vague and dreadful fatality. Even here his character for truth is maintained, and his invisible agencies mingle with the commonest characters, and in the most ordinary scenes of life.

It is true that these mysterious agencies are all very idly explained away, like Mrs. Radcliffe's; yet such a hold do they take upon our minds, that we cannot shake off the mystical influence they have gained over us; and even those who have practised the deceptions seem to have done it not so much from a love of deception as from a hankering after something resembling the supernatural, and an insane sort of delight in watching its strange and dreadful force over others; both he that is wrought upon and he that works seem, the one to suffer, and the other to act, as under some resistless spell. Brown's fatal power is unsparing, and never stops, and through the bitterest griefs and sufferings never draws tears or softens the heart; it wears out the heart and takes away the strength of our spirits, so that we lie helpless under it. A power of this kind holds no associations with nature; for in the gloomiest, and the wildest, and barrenest scenes of nature, there is something enlarging and elevating, — something that tells us there is an end to our unmixed sorrow, — something that lifts us above life, and breathes into us immortality. No! it is surrounded by man and the works of man, — man in his ills, and sins, and feebleness; it is there alone that we can feel what is the bitterness and weariness of unmixed helplessness and woe.

So much was gloominess the character of Brown's genius, that he does not, like other authors, begin his story in a state of cheerfulness or quiet, and gradually lead on to disappointment and affliction. Some one writes a letter to a friend who has asked him for an account of his suffering life. It hints at mysteries, and sorrows, and remorse, — sorrows and remorse to which there can be no end but in the rest of the grave. He has already passed through years of miseries, and we come in and go on with him to the end of his story. But his sorrows have not ended there; and we leave him, praying that death may at last bring peace to his sick and worn heart. There is woe behind us, and woe before us. The spirit cries, with the Apocalyptic angel, seen flying through the midst of heaven, "Woe, woe, woe, to the inhabiters of the earth!"

We know that it has become fashionable, of late years, to hold sorrow as the chiefest of sins, and the melancholy story-teller as the great seducer of men from their duties, and from the highest of all virtues, — gayety of heart. But proneness to melancholy is not the evil of our times. We live too much abroad for that; day-time and evening, we are running at large with the common herd, or are gathered into smaller flocks and folds, called societies. No one is seen ruminating alone in the still shade of his own oak or willow. The thoughtful observer, too, must have remarked, that those who are most apt to be talkative upon the duty of cheerfulness, and the danger of strong excitement, are mainly those, the depths of whose feelings a fishing-line might fathom, — those who have no dark, mysterious, unsounded places; and yet if a breeze but ruffle their placidity, one would think, from the outcry, that the mighty sea itself was heaving and tossing into fury and foam. Besides, why all this alarm? If one author is melancholy, there are hundreds who are cool and wise, or cheerful or full of fun. Be under no concern; neither college, nor the bar, nor the exchange is in danger of being changed into an Arden, nor our literati, lawyers, or merchants likely to become so many melancholy Jaqueses. But, to treat this subject rightly, we must look deeper than men are apt to look into human nature, and we have no time for that now.

But why need any man have such gloomy views, and write in so melancholy a strain always? The answer is, this was according to Brown's temperament, and whenever he tried to thwart it he failed. Of humour, Mr. Dunlap says, he "had no portion in himself, nor any adequate conception of it in others." And he himself says,—"My powers do not enable me to place the commonplace characters around me in an interesting or amusing point of view." He falls off even in the cheerful, and grows heavy.

This variety, which people so unhesitatingly ask for, as if no one could think of denying them, and it were as "good cheap" as common business talents, is in itself a mark of a high quality of genius. "Pray, Sir," one might say to Mackenzie, "I have been reading your 'La Roche' and your 'Man of Feeling,' and have been crying so! and am *so* sad!—do make me laugh now, will you?" "My dear Sir, I would gratify you with all my heart were it in my power," replies Mackenzie, "but it is not. If you wish to laugh, you must go see the Dean; or there is Shakspeare,—he will make you laugh or cry, just as you please. No; he will not make you cry; he is 'too deep for tears,' but he will make you 'as sad as night,' whenever you wish it."

Brown's genius not only wanted variety; it seemed

to be without even pliability. It was as ungainly and stiff, when put out of its ordinary track, as is an honest yeoman, when he sets himself to some act of accomplished courtesy, and for his pains gets praised for his excellently obliging disposition, and ridiculed for his awkward way of showing it.

With the exception of Constantia, in "Ormond," and Louisa, in the unfinished tale of "Stephen Calvert," there is little to interest us in the females. Perhaps we should include the Hadwins in this exception. Constantia is an excellent girl, and goes through her sufferings and the hard offices that poverty and sickness lay upon her, with all patience and perseverance. But it was not necessary, though "entire affection hateth nicer hands," to tell us that the beautiful Constantia "washed the foul linen"; or, when she tended the sick man, how she administered the medicine and watched its twofold operations: — there is a great deal which must be done by us poor mortals for one another, which it is best to say as little about as possible.

But Louisa is the most finely conceived of the female characters. Under-sized, thin, awkward, sallow-complexioned, and, O! most fatal of all to love, rough-voiced, still she is lovely. Yet she, too, must needs offend us. Brown wishes to show her frankness, and therefore, when Calvert intimates something about an early marriage, ye gods! what follows? — "My intimations were understood before they were fully expressed. They obtained not a dubious acquiescence, but a vehement assent. It was unwise to defraud herself of the happiness of wedlock by the least delay. Next week was a period preferable to the next month; to-morrow was still more to be desired. Nay, she would eagerly concur in the ratification of this contract on that very night. Domestic arrangements might follow with as much convenience and propriety as precede." — "Why tolerate a longer delay, or pass through more forms than were absolutely indispensable?" O Mr. Tremaine, thou "Man of Refinement"! which way wouldst thou have looked? and how wouldst thou have felt at such a time? and what wouldst thou have done? We tell thee what thou wouldst not have done; thou wouldst not have burnt thy fingers, and scalded thine arm, for such a *coming* fair one.

But the parson is missing; and the next day, in consequence of a conversation with a friend, Louisa tells Master Calvert that the marriage must be put off for five years, in order to give his character time to *settle*. In truth, we scarcely recollect any full-drawn and complete gentleman or lady, by an American author; and as for that nice art, love-making, — "Once, on a sudden meeting," Stephen Calvert is made to say, "she so far overstepped the customary boundaries, as to wrap me in her arms, and kiss my cheek. No self-reproof or blushful consciousness ensued this act of unguarded tenderness, though, indeed, it took place without a witness." Would he have had her kiss in company? And for our own part, we think a little "blushful consciousness" would not have made it any the less winning.

Strange things happen. Constantia has a friend, Sophia, who goes to Italy, has a lover, Courtland, and marries him; and the very next day, this Platonic lady sends him to England, and sets off herself for America, in search of her friend; and not finding her as soon as she wished, resolves, after a very flattering manner to Mr. Courtland, that she will die of grief, — that she will never know joy again this side the grave. These things are ludicrously out of nature. Besides, our author's lovers, as a matter of course, relate to their friends their love-dialogues; and the love-letters go the rounds of the family as regularly as the daily paper. Such conduct in the fair sex is extremely annoying to us sensitive gentlemen. But we have more serious charges to make against them.

There is a Mrs. Jane Talbot, who has no liking for her husband and loves another man, and yet is virtuous; sits till after twelve o' nights with him, while her husband is absent, and yet is virtuous; and when the husband dies, the experienced widow writes letters to this same friend, after a manner as girlish as one in her teens, though not always with the same delicacy, and yet she is virtuous. There is another, married, too, and living apart from her husband, and she has a friend and midnight visits, — ay, and tender embraces also, — and she, too, is virtuous. Now we have no doubts of the strength of female virtue, but a chain-cable will give way, put but enough upon it. There is not an oftener needed prayer than this, — Lead us not into temptation. These are but a few of the improprieties of the kind in these stories. Pure and delicate minds in real life never fall into them, nor will a woman of principle be apt to place herself in a situation which may have an equivocal appearance.

We believe Brown to have been one of the purest of men. The intellectual so predominated in him, and he seems so to have loathed the sensual, that perhaps he was not aware of the great strength of certain temptations over others. More than this, he had his system, or rather was caught by a system of that day, which held all distinctions in society to be but old abuses, the restraints of marriage unworthy free and rational beings, — when senate and bar-room alike rang with the bold and shallow philosophy, as it was termed, of atheists, deists, and equality-men. "Freethinkers," says Wollaston, "are half-thinkers." No one can now read the works of the time we speak of, without feeling the truth of this remark, and being amazed at the effect they produced, and the noisy notoriety they attained to. It is easy for every age to see the errours of any time but its own. We now have our systems. They may not be as full of danger, but they are almost as full of folly, as those of past ages. Brown lived to reason himself out of his errours, and settled down, as every man of fair mind and good affections will be likely to do, into a believer; but these mistakes did not quit him without doing a lasting injury to his good taste.

We have said, that even the want of variety and the defects of style in Brown have in some measure helped to the impression of the truth of his stories. He makes this impression in a better way, also, by his circumstantiality, and his careful mention of a thousand little particulars. But his characters, before undertaking the simplest act, go through a diverting process of reasoning; we have all the *pros* and *cons* that can be started; and though the reasoning has more of show than substance, still, this being the way in which the larger part of the world reasons, we are more and more convinced of the truth of his facts. He certainly has this striking characteristic of genius, the power of making his characters living and breathing men, acting in situations which are distinctly and vividly presented to our minds. To be sure, he must needs turn philosopher, and be prodigiously profound on small matters. Formal questions are put about the course to be taken, when every body sees there is but one course, and that "as plain as way to parish church." It is dark; one of his heroines has occasion to go to her chamber for a manuscript, which she wishes to read. Common folks would take it for granted, without any serious ratiocination, that the first thing would be to get a light. But softly and slowly, — there is nothing like exercising our reason on all occasions.

"To do this, it was requisite to procure a light. The girl had long since retired to her chamber; it was therefore proper to wait upon myself. A lamp, and the means of lighting it, were only to be found in the kitchen. Thither I resolved forthwith to repair; but the light was of use merely to enable me to read the book. I knew the shelf and the spot where it stood. Whether I took down the book, or prepared the lamp in the first place, appeared to be a matter of no moment. The latter was preferred, and, leaving my seat, I approached the closet in which, as I mentioned formerly, my books and papers were deposited." — Vol. I. p. 78.

Again, Constantia not only washes the clothes of the family, but makes them, too; and hear this, ye of the goose, shears, and thimble!

"Clothing is one of the necessaries of human existence. The art of the tailor is scarcely of less use than that of the tiller of the ground. There are few the gains of which are better merited, and less injurious to the principles of human society. She resolved, therefore, to become a workwoman, and to employ in this way the leisure she possessed from household avocations. To this scheme she was obliged to reconcile, not only herself, but her parents. The conquest of their prejudices was no easy task, but her patience and skill finally succeeded, and she procured needlework in sufficient quantity to enable her to enhance in no trivial degree the common fund." — Vol. VI. pp. 22, 23.

Brown's style is rather remarkable. The structure of his sentences is, for the most part, simple; but his words! they remind one of the witty M. P.'s reply, when asked what was doing in the House:—"Lord Castlereagh is airing his vocabulary this morning, that 's all." To use the happy phrase of that lord, "the fundamental feature" of the style is a most painstaking avoidance of the Saxon, wherever it is possible, and a use of words of Latin origin in such combinations as they were never put into before. Dudley's leaving New York is spoken of as "this evasion." "Her decay was eminently gradual." Constantia scarcely "retrieving her composure." "Retrieved reflection"; "extenuate the danger"; "extenuate both these species of merit"; "exclude from my countenance"; "resume her ancient country"; "immersed in perplexity"; "obvious to suppose"; "obvious to conclude"; "unavoidable to conclude"; "copious epistle"; "copiously interrogated"; "copious and elegant accommodation"; "my departure was easy and commodious"; "the barrier that severs her from Welbeck must be as high as heaven and insuperable as necessity"; "a few passengers likewise occurred, whose hasty," &c. No one, who has once read the description of Carwin as he is first introduced, can ever forget it, or the effect upon us of the musical speech of such a man,—a happy conception, and afterwards made use of by Scott, in his Rashleigh. Yet we are told, "Shoulders broad and square, breast sunken, his head drooping, his body of uniform breadth, supported by long and lank legs, were the *ingredients* of his frame." The ingredients of a pudding!

Brown is much more remarkable for putting his thoughts into the form of questions than Godwin ever was; yet *to ask* and *to question* are scarcely to be met with through the whole six volumes; but, instead of these, we have *interrogated*, *interrogations*, and even *in-*

terrogatories. It is true, that the kind of writing we speak of does not show itself equally in all his stories; some few of them are tolerably free from it.

This perverted taste is much to be regretted; for, after the excitement of a first reading, — when less attention is paid to the style of a powerful story, — we are perpetually feeling the incongruity between the strong characters and passions and terrific scenes, and the language in which they are presented to us. The distinguished novelists of this day must, by and by, suffer from defect in style, while the simplicity and truth of language of our old novelists will help to the increased pleasure they give, the more they are studied. Brown himself has said, — "The language of man is the 'intercourse of spirits,' the perfect and involuntary picture of every fixed or transient emotion to which his mind is subject." We wish he had remembered this, and left his passions and thoughts to speak their own tongue.

Though his style is never rich and idiomatic, yet, in some of his writings, it is clear and simple; and it is probable that it never would have been so wide of good English as we generally find it to be in his stories, had he received what is called a public education. It is often amusing to hear some very clever men, who have never received such an education, talk about colleges and college learning. They have most magnificent notions upon the subject; and it is a hard matter to persuade them that they can write better sense, and put it into better language, too, than can many of those who have been entered and graduated regularly. You concede that such a course of instruction is of great benefit to the industrious, and no loss to the idle, even, — that at college something is absorbed by every brain which is capable of being imbued at all with what is intellectual. But this is not enough for them. There is to these men an undefinable charm and change wrought within that circle into which they have never entered; and they conclude that they have little to do except to bear their inferiority like good Christians. They must try something, however, which shall gloss over this inferiority; and they accordingly set themselves industriously to forming modes of talking and writing such as never came from tongue or pen, learned or vulgar. They are made to suffer for all this; for what really grew out of self-distrust and humility is commonly set down to affectation and pedantry. This is the best solution we can give of the cause of Brown's style, as able a man as he was.

We cannot quit him without a word upon the inward struggle he endured in deciding between the strong tendencies of his genius, and what he seemed half persuaded, notwithstanding his scruples, to have been his duty. He was educated for the bar, and obtained some distinction in his club for his management of moot cases. We would say, in passing, that we believe, after all, these clubs are not the places to determine what are a man's powers; and notwithstanding some eminent men first distinguished themselves in these mock contests, we have great doubts whether it is not quite as well for a man to fight his first battle on the field, where nothing is allowed but keen steel and naked points. Physical and intellectual dexterity and power are very different things, and obtained by very different means. At any rate, Brown's time came, and then he hesitated, and then his friends talked, or by their marked silence pained him yet more. Unsatisfied in his own mind, and those whose good opinion he fain would have had being against him, he became harassed and dejected. There was something working within, the nature and power of which he did not then enough understand to follow without scruple. He still doubted; and when at last he did resolve, he felt not the relief and vigour of a resolved man; for he feared it might be the yielding of weakness, not the resolution of strength. It was his good fortune that the waking, instinctive energy of genius at length prevailed. Instead of living as only one of the multitude of keen and clever men at the bar, and then dying and being forgotten, he is going down with the history of our country as the earliest author of genius in our literature. Already this distinction is something; but it is to be yet greater, we trust. The writers of genius who may come up amongst us, instead of taking from his good name, will but bring to it fresh honour and reverence, for he will be called the father of them all.

Let this struggle in the sensitive temperament of Brown be a caution to parents and friends. A little more, and he would have gone to a still earlier grave, a disappointed and scarcely noted man. If a young man's bent be a strong one, so it be innocent, point out the hardships of the course he would take if you will, but let him follow it. A father talks of his experience, as if one man's experience would serve alike for all. We are not made after one pattern, or this would be no longer a world of trial and effort, of great failure and glorious success.

There are men, very kind men too, who would do good service to a man of genius, but then they must do it to suit themselves, not him. It is taken for granted that he is fantastic and wayward, merely because, as he differs in his intellectual powers, so does he in temperament and sympathies from the world at large. He must be made a useful citizen, however. Pegasus must be yoke-mate with donkey, or be turned out to shift for himself. Perhaps he submits; but, as every one might know beforehand, donkey proves the more serviceable beast, works and grows fat, while Pegasus breaks down. Nor is this all. If the man of genius declines these well-meant offers, he is sensible that he is looked upon as one who will not let you do him good if you would; and to the weight of his troubles and sorrows is added the feeling, that those who care most about him mingle disappointment and disapprobation with their concern. This is a sad and comfortless thought to visit a mind, which, from its very nature, must dwell much alone, and needs much of sympathy to take it from its solitude. There is, perhaps, no class more envied than men of genius; and it is natural enough that they should be, when estimated by their productions; and it is true, also, that they have times of high aspirations, and scenes of intellectual beauty and grandeur, seen but dimly and at a distance by others; yet could the world look into their whole souls, it would hardly envy them so.

It may be thought that we have dwelt too long upon the faults of Brown, and that we are of an ungracious temper for so doing. We have taken no delight in this part of our work, for we reverence his genius, and feel an affection for so kind and good a man. If we speak with all our hearts of what is excellent in a great man, we shall do him little harm by pointing out his defects, while at the same time we are doing good to others. We are not of those who would pull down a stone upon the head of him who is but just raising a structure for his own fame; nor of those who are glad to see the barren sands drifting over the foundation which another was beginning to lay. Brown has built up his pyramid, and laid him down to rest in it.

POLLOK'S COURSE OF TIME.*

I SHOULD be unjust to myself and to my present opinions, were I to submit this and the two following articles to the public without a word in way of explanation.

They appeared in The Spirit of the Pilgrims during the contest which the Trinitarian Congregationalists maintained against the prevailing Unitarianism of that day and of this vicinity.

In obedience to my rule, I leave the articles without any alterations that, I think, can be called material, although there are many things which I should change were I to go over the ground again.

The engrossing topics of that period left little room for other doctrines necessary to complete the circle of revealed truth. And it is not till more recently that my own mind, in common with countless others, has been led to a fuller apprehension of the faith of the visible Church, with its sacraments, powers, and ordinances, to meet the wants and fill the capacities of man's nature, — truths which are now having their return of presentation to our gradually and partially enlightened understandings.

The changes I would make are not, perhaps, so much directly in the opinions themselves, or in their relation to those in which they were in contrast, as in the point of view from which I would present them, and in the way of supplying their imperfectness by the influences and relations from which they had been severed.

Some things are sharply said. So was too much on both sides in

---

* From The Spirit of the Pilgrims for 1828.

The Course of Time. A Poem, in Ten Books. By ROBERT POLLOK, A. M. Boston: Crocker & Brewster. 1828.

that contest, as is always the case at such times. I regret that the republication of the articles obliges me to allude to any of these matters. Some of the reasons for republishing them and the other reviews are mentioned in the Preface to these volumes.

It has been said by many, who would have done well had they kept their reading to plain prose, that Cowper owed his popularity mainly, if not wholly, to the religious character of his writings. Such men, we fear, are as ignorant of the true spirit of the world as they are of the true spirit of poetry. Should we reverse the remark, and say, that the truth of his poetry made him popular in spite of his religion, we might be thought harsh; we will therefore leave his fame to the safe-keeping of men of sincere piety and just taste.

It must be acknowledged that the works of Cowper are familiar to a large class of people who might not have known so much as his name, had not his original and poetic mind been sanctified by the Gospel of his Lord and Saviour. It was because he sang by the waters of Siloa, as well as those of another stream, that there gathered to him so many of the humble and the poor; and it is because of this that we so often meet an odd volume of his works, with its worn leaves and soiled cover, in the remotest parts of the country, and in some of our plainer dwellings.

The true poet, he who sees through manners into the hearts and minds of men, will often be conscious of as grateful a feeling at finding himself in a lowly abode and in this worn dress, as in the apartment of a bookish man, and in a costlier and cleanlier attire. He knows that the seriousness which religion brings to the mind, and the tenderness which the touch of God's spirit gives to the heart, will help to his being understood and felt when he speaks simply and truly to man's better nature. He is conscious, too, that learning, instead of warming into full life the very little of the poetic temperament with which some are originally blessed, often strikes it with a death-chill; that the giddiness of fashionable life deranges the even workings of the mind, and that its frivolousness dries up the flow of the affections faster than the hurrying streams from the mountains are sucked in by the hot and thirsty sands; that learning is apt to be proud, and that the way to a true feeling and appreciation of poetry lies not through pride; that the fashionable will be thoughtless, and that thoughtlessness is a surer destroyer of those sympathies upon which poetry depends, than even poverty and toil, with their attendant ills. In defiance of the outward show of superiority and distinction which the world may make, it is the heart of man which the poet mainly regards for his subject, and with which he chiefly has to do. In this, prince and beggar are both alike to him, and all beyond it is of little concern. He looks for sympathy rather from those of plain sense and kind affections, than amongst those whose intellectual nature has been cultivated at the expense of their moral nature, or whose affections have been left to run broad and shallow, and to waste, over the surfaces of things.

No doubt, a well-cultivated intellect is essential to the full comprehension of an art which springs from the highest exercise of our faculties; but as the grand superiority of poetry consists in the due combination of our moral with our intellectual constitution, taking in not the brain alone, but the entire man, so those whom religious principle has led to self-examination, to the study of motives, and the strength and action and tendencies of the passions and affections, and to the straight or wandering courses of the thoughts, are, through this discipline, in a fairer way to receive right impressions and form true estimates of the essentials of poetry, than those of over-laboured heads, but untrained hearts.

Besides, those who have considered religion only partially would be surprised were they to observe how much it does for the intellect, and to find how well-balanced, how searching and discriminating, how quick of perception, how clear, calm, and open to intellectual beauty, may be the mind of that man who has read little else besides himself and his Bible.

No man can be truly religious without much thoughtfulness; and this quality does for the mind what a multitude of books could never do without it. Yet how many read, and how few think! How many go about showily dressed in the robes of other men, who, should they be clad in what alone they themselves had wrought, would be wretched and naked indeed! The grave and learned man, though differing widely in acquisitions, is often led to feel, and if a good man to feel with pleasure, how nearly upon an equality are his mental powers and those of the common-sense Christian. He who has read most, and at the same time thought most, sees most quickly and clearly how little, after all, is the difference between himself and him whom the world calls a plain man. If the rightly learned man perceives this, how much more clearly does the man of originality, of imagination and sentiment, the poet, — he who holds an almost supernatural communion with the minds and hearts of his fellow-men! How often has the fresh thought and homely yet strong turn of expression of those in ordinary life struck him, and how often, on the other hand, if he is wise and has learned self-control, does he sit silent and abstracted while the literary and the fashionable are retailing opinions upon master-works of the imagination! In short, how much truer and better is a simple moral education, than much learning with little nature!

Let us not be understood as taking away any thing from the culture of the intellect. We have, however, too nearly observed the mind and affections of those in middle and lower life, not to know that they have been superciliously underrated by the better sort. And we have lived too long with the educated classes, not to have felt painfully what the character often loses amidst the many acquisitions of the mind. From such a point of view of religion, morals, and intellect, we see too little improvement of the whole individual from systems of education about which we have been long wearied by the so-much talk. How beautiful, but how rare a creature, is a highly educated, yet thoroughly natural man, — one who, with all his refinement, looks with contempt upon fastidiousness; who has his purified impulses free; who not only holds, with Sir Thomas Browne, that "there is a *general* beauty in the workes of God, and therefore no deformity in any kinde or species of creature whatsoever," but has a pulse, too, that keeps time with every kind and honest heart, beat it in master or in slave!

This hasty view contains enough of truth, we trust, to be a just cause of gratification to him who takes pleasure in seeing that the distinction between the moral and intellectual state of the various classes of society, however great it may be, is often less than the outward differences and opportunities would seem to show; and that, however wide apart rank may set men, there is a common principle at work in them, which, without disturbing the differences of the social condition, may hold individuals in sympathy, and ever keep them near.

The poet, who cares less for fame than he does for that sympathy which draws the hearts of his fellow-beings to him, which moves them with his emotions, and opens the intellectual eye in them to see everywhere the beauty which he sees, finds something in this thought to bring comfort, when the sense of loneliness is heaviest upon him. He feels that when God, in giving him peculiar powers and an ardent and sensitive temperament, ordained him, in this very privilege, to peculiar pains, sufferings, and sorrows, he at the same time blessed him with that by which he might not only hold communion with all material nature, but hear, too, a brother's familiar speech throughout the tribes of his fellow-men.

We would not make it seem as if there were no order of society which does not come under these remarks. There is the utterly uninformed class, — too generally a loose and unprincipled one. There is a class of people above this, with a common school education, in comfortable circumstances and duly gainful callings, and, in the main, fulfilling decently the neighbourly duties and courtesies; but who, having their minds absorbed in such things, seldom give reach to their powers by carrying them forward into the invisible world, and by rousing them at the thoughts of its coming glories. The heart, too, clings to earth; nor is it softened by pouring itself out in supplication and thankfulness to its God. Knowing in the affairs of the world, yet self-ignorant, men of this class do nothing to prepare themselves to understand and feel the higher and more beautiful workings of the poet's spirit. They are under an insensibility of the heart and a blindness of the mind to these things, which render them as incapable of being touched by them, as if they were a race of beings made up of a distinct set of thoughts, affections, and sympathies. What heart-searchings have they? Their hearts, they think, are as well, upon the whole, as can reasonably be required of them. Why need they look to the illuminating Spirit, if indeed they acknowledge any such? Have they not a lamp to their path in the all-sufficient light of their reason? Have they not been told, — and are they not of easy faith in this matter at least, — that the earth is kindling to a blaze with the glories which come, and the greater that are yet to come, from this god which the world has set up? Why need they feel fears or repentant sorrows? Is it not in amount declared to them, that God is their good Father, that he formed them to be happy, and that, if they deal fairly and decently in the affairs of this world, it would be having hard thoughts of God not to believe that he will take care of them and deal kindly with them in the next?

And is it so? Are there no daily, no hourly duties set apart and sacred to God alone? Is there not a continuous labour needed to bring the soul into a state congenial with the things of another life, and a watchfulness required to keep it so? Is happiness something extraneous, to be given and received as we give and take the dross of this world, or is its vital principle in the character of the soul?

No man who is much in the world, and keeps his eyes and ears open, can avoid perceiving that such loose feelings and opinions as these are spreading through society, and that there is a growing disposition among men to overrate their good qualities, to lower the standard by which they should measure themselves, to lessen the requisitions of the Deity, and to lighten more and more all earnestness and concern respecting their condition in a future life; — serious and observing men see that it is so. And there is a portion of the upper classes in the same condition, who show upon system, if we may so speak, a dangerous ease and carelessness upon the subject of their responsibilities in this relation. Men delude themselves in different ways, according to their several conditions and characters. A few of the more refined substitute a vague sentimentality, and beautiful, floating, and no less vague thoughts of some ideal, in the place of the revealed God.

Those who are helping the most to work this evil in the community, probably see less of its working than any other men. Too many of them, lost in a sort of dreamy philosophizing, and as ignorant of their fellowmen as of themselves, are not conscious of it at all. But ignorance takes not from the responsibility here; and a serious responsibility it is. They may find it easy indeed to gratify man by telling him of the dignity and grandeur of his nature; but what shall afterwards prostrate him in the dust before his Maker? They may find it easy, by this soothing delusion, to rock him to sleep; but when they shall see it is the sleep of death into which they have lulled him, who shall then awake him?

Though this is cause enough for anxiety to the serious mind, yet we may still turn, and find comfort, and hope, and confidence. The Spirit of God is moving over the moral world, as it once moved upon the face of the waters. Then God divided the light from the darkness, and he is doing so now. The lights that men are lighting up, and that are flashing here and there through the darkness, though they are to flare and dazzle for a season, shall be quenched; and where they burned shall be utter darkness; and the people shall turn to the pure light, and bow before it, and it shall shine in upon their souls, — even the light of the Cross of Christ.

Here it is that the religious poet is to do his work. It is a great work, and his reward shall be great.

Several religious poems have appeared within a few years; but the one taking the widest range, and with a subject requiring the highest powers, is the Course of Time. It opens in eternity, long after the judgement. The story of the creation of the world and of man is told to a spirit from some distant sphere. The narrator describes the fall of man, its consequences, and the scheme of redemption. The ways in which the effects of the fall discover themselves in our perverted feelings and modes of reasoning are set forth, and particularly where the Gospel is brought to bear upon them. The end of the world, the resurrection, and the judgement follow in succession, and close the scene. How all this is carried out, and how relieved, we have no intention of stating, for we know of nothing so tedious, and at the same time so unsatisfactory, as a detailed account of the contents of a poem. We have answered our object, if we have laid enough before the reader to enable him to perceive, that to fill up such a plan as it should be filled up requires, not only a man earnest in his religious views, but one of profound thought, and of almost unmatched poetic powers.

The first two qualifications we believe we may grant to our author; but we cannot, in sincerity, say so much for him in the last requisite. We doubt whether his merely poetic powers are such as to make his work interesting to any poetic mind, however religious, while to render its truths palatable to the world at large would require in its poetry the magnificence and beauty of Milton himself. It is a pity that any, in their zeal for religion, should have compared our author with him the sublimity of whose mind has not been surpassed since the times of the prophets. So far from it, as a poet Mr. Pollok is neither a Cowper nor a Young. Still, his diction, for the most part, is plain;—he has not learned the art of writing without thought, or of losing himself in a smother of words; and when you lay down his poem, you have a definite notion of what you have been reading, whatever rank you may give it,—which is more than can be said of many a favourite of these days.

Wordy indefiniteness is the vice of the age; and people read on, page after page, vaguely pleased with a certain flicker and show of things, without having seen one simple and clear image, or having thought one simple and clear thought. Mr. Pollok does think; and though this may be a cause of unpopularity with the rapid readers of such books as have taught men how to read without thought, on the other hand it has led those who do think, but have not been careful, in the present instance, to bear in mind the great essentials of poetry, to over-estimate him as a whole. From his being distinguished for definite thought in plain diction, and from his having taken from the indistinct writings of others, he has made them feel as they would upon being led out from the buzz and dusty atmosphere of a factory, into the clear, still air. They had been under a half-consciousness of something like a wearying confusion before, but were not fully alive to their state, till wakened by the contrast.

Poetry is essentially more than this. A man must have something besides a taste for poetry, and a power of putting just and strong thoughts into fair verse. He must have a poet's temperament, — that in which all coming from him is first fused, and then, running into the mould of the imagination, is turned out a true form. It must not be a cold, lifeless form, however, but alive and glowing with the spiritual fire out of which it has come. Let a man be as intense with thought as he may, still the thought must appear to have arisen out of the depths of the soul; out of those depths all things must have come up, whether man, or beast, or creeping thing; yea, regions fairer than earth must rise out of them, as rose the earth above the waters, self-moved, effortless, and instinct with life. So

"Rose, as in dance, the stately trees, and spread
Their branches hung with copious fruit, or gemmed
Their blossoms: with high woods the hills were crowned,
With tufts the valleys and each fountain side,
With borders long the rivers."

Passion must utter for itself its own vehement and broken language; and sentiment and sorrow must pour forth their own soft and melancholy sounds like the flow of a fountain. Passions and thoughts should not so much be described; nor should they be so many abstractions; but rather be, as it were, living, sentient, speaking, acting beings. And when it is at any time necessary so to treat the subject as not to allow of this being the case, the poet should put you into that state of illusion, so to speak, that you shall feel as if it were some imaginary being who was revealing to your mind's eye the thoughts and emotions of his soul; or you should be so wrought upon as to become, virtually, yourself the very being who thus thinks and feels.

There must be the life-giving, the forming, and the informing principle: though the mind thinks, it must be from a feeling as if it were from some mysterious impulse communicated to it from the soul deep within; otherwise, though all may be wise and good, and in tolerable verse, it will not have in it the great and distinctive qualities of poetry.

We do not say that our author is quite destitute of these qualities, but that they are not characteristic of his poem. He appears to us to *think out* what he has written: it does not affect us as if poured through the mind from those deep and living springs within, of which we have spoken, — his images have not floated out from those invisible, spiritual waters into the mind; no, the brain furnished the material, and wrought it up by itself. His description of hell, in the first book, is the result of this process, — ingenious, not imaginative, and frightful, not poetical.

Mr. Pollok aimed at producing his effect by multiplying circumstances. But circumstances, however well fitted to move us when taken singly, by being overmultiplied lose their power, and serve only to distract us. There is something of monotony in the stronger feelings; so much of it, that the mind, not being able to relieve itself by variety in a natural way, betakes itself often to the most ludicrous images and forced conceits, thus breaking violently from one black, changeless object to which it was bound, and playing with fantastic creations, or earnestly busying itself, like a little child, with the most insignificant things imaginable. Shakspeare has frequently exemplified this in his characters when under intense grief; and the critics, ignorant of the action of mind, and more ready to make a show of their own acuteness and taste than to learn humbly of this philosopher, have set it down to his ignorance of the fitness of things, and a fondness for conceits.

Besides, Mr. Pollok's particulars, when taken singly, too often fail of the intended effect from want of peculiarity, — that which gives individuality. Now, one may go on for ever multiplying particulars, but while each has this air of generality he will not only come short of his object, but produce weariness, too. Take, as a favourable specimen of our author, his character of Lord Byron. Surely, no thoughtful man can read it without being made more thoughtful. It contains many exceptions to our remarks, and some fine reflections, yet, before getting through it, we catch ourselves casting an eye forward to see where it will end; while reading it, we wish it was not quite so long; when we have finished, we wish again that it had not been so long; we leave it with self-dissatisfaction that we were not more affected by what we cannot pronounce to be without a certain merit, and we wish we could like it better than we do; in truth, with whatever there may be to praise in it, it lacks the absorbing power.

It is not alone the want of that peculiar poetic vitality upon which we have said so much, nor the multiplying of particulars and the dwelling too long upon a subject, that weakens the effect; — the language gives it a certain heaviness. We have said that there is no want of plainness in Mr. Pollok, that he writes with meaning, and that we take his thought at once. But his style is not poetic. We do not mean that it is not sufficiently ornamented. Ornamental terms are well-nigh *used up;* and the poet, now-a-days, must trust almost solely to the happy combination of the simplest terms. No poet, however great he may be, will again appear in that Asiatic gorgeousness in which Milton robed himself, his costly drapery lying full and rich, fold over fold. But the simple terms of our language never can grow old. Taking endless changes of combination, they will ever have in them the complexion, life, and vigour of the thoughts and feelings that gave them birth.

This brings us round again to the same cause with that of the former-mentioned defects of our author, — a want of the poetic temperament in all its warmth and vitality. We have acquitted him of a certain kind of fashionable wordiness; but we cannot of another kind. He abounds in epithets; and these too often of a character so general, that they might almost as well be applied to any other object as to that to which they are attached. This remark belongs in a degree, and as far as can be consistently with an intelligible expression of strong thought, to his style generally. Select any of Shakspeare's better passages, and try to take out a word from one of them; so closely is his work joined together, so exactly proportioned and fitted is each part to each, and each to the whole, that, should you attempt to remove one timber, the building would come tumbling down upon your heads. There is a commonness in Mr. Pollok's style, and, with all his plainness, diffuseness. If we allow him to be a strong man, his bulkiness gives him a heavy movement. The same bone and muscle in a compact frame would indicate energy and action. But nature formed him thus; and you might as well try to make that painter a colourist who wants an eye for colour, as to mend a defect like this: Language, though it is something besides, is the poet's colour.

Mr. Pollok cannot be so easily excused in another

particular, — a fault which is hardly to be accounted for in a man of his good sense and independent thinking, — we mean in his imitations. In the first two books we met with so much of Milton's structure of sentences, and so many of his favourite turns of expression, that we had no expectation of finding Mr. Pollok so manly a thinker as he turns out to be. He works himself pretty free of this fault as he gets used to his labour, though occasional imitations occur, and these so close, that you cannot but smile now and then in the most serious passages.

He sometimes affects certain words; these, however, are few; such as, —

"The frothy orator who *busked* his tales."

"His lures, with baits that pleased the senses, *busked*."

"How happily
Plays yonder child, that *busks* the mimic babe."

We have "eldest hell," "eldest energy," "eldest skill," and often the old word "whiles." The sentences frequently end with an adjective brought feebly in to fill up the measure. Violence is mistaken for strength; and where he attempts sarcasm after the manner of Cowper, unlike Cowper, he not seldom misses his aim. In the bad taste of Young, he occasionally introduces conceits into the more serious passages; and we find him aiming at impression by repeating an emphatic word, which, in the main, is little better than trick in oratory, and very bad in poetry.

Having seen Mr. Pollok extravagantly and indiscriminately praised, we have dwelt the longer upon his faults and deficiencies, being aware that nothing so endangers a man's reputation as excessive commendation. Our author has already reaped some of the natural consequences of this conduct in his admirers; and we know of no surer way to secure to him his fair deserts, than by freely giving up what we are not satisfied he is entitled to.

His main defects were probably radical, and such as would have gone with him through life, though he had lived to be old. Time and culture may improve a man in what he hath, but cannot give him what he hath not.

Let us not be too sweeping. We would not deny that there are passages which may be called poetical. The poem is virtually without machinery, — and so long a work will almost of necessity go sluggishly without it. Had it a more dramatic form, it may be that qualities which we have considered the author as wanting, and more vividness, energy, and closeness, would have been imparted to it. If he had in him the power of conceiving a character sufficiently individual, and of possessing himself fully of it, the character, as always in such a case, would have taken possession of him in turn, and have spoken through him as though he had been its mere organ. — But had he this power? Mr. Pollok, also, chose blank verse, — which tasks a man severely, inasmuch as, of all forms, it least endures diffuseness.

Taking these difficulties into consideration, and recollecting that a man never can put forth all his strength when he has a misgiving at heart that what he is attempting may be beyond his strength, no one can say Mr. Pollok might not have shown more poetic power had he undertaken a work requiring less. He appears to have been a truly religious man, and it may be that the very awfulness of his subject subdued rather than aroused his energies; that he felt himself a mere mortal setting his foot upon holy ground.

His mind was meditative; and he must in his early years have devoted to meditation no small portion of those hours which are usually spent by the young in amusements. His work is not a mixture of youthful crudities and clever thoughts, but is characterized by maturity of thinking. He writes like an old observer of men, one who had looked enough upon the world to have seen just what all its glosses are worth. He was not to be deceived into a false estimate of human nature, either by the pride of his own heart, or by short and disconnected views of the hearts of others. He had independence and clear-sightedness enough to look quite through the fallacies of his own day, and to see, moreover, that most of the boasted discoveries in what is styled the philosophy of religion were little better than old errours in new dresses; that many of the schemes, so vaunted of for their originality, were but modified forms of those which moved in the twilight, when the old revelation was set upon nigh all the world, and the Sun of Righteousness was not yet risen to bless it, — schemes which floated in that light to darken it when it did at length arise, and which would overshadow it now, were not God more than man.

There are men who have a certain acuteness at detecting a fallacy, and an activity and clearness of intellect, which work very well within a particular sphere; but who want largeness of thought to enable them to follow out the many and far-reaching relations of a great scheme, and to comprehend it as a whole. But Mr. Pollok was not without something of this comprehensiveness of mind, and he brought the exercise of it to the greatest of all subjects, — the relation of man to God and a future state. He appears to have wrought with it, clear of the perversion of human vanity, and with a sincere and humble reliance upon his Maker for aid. We believe his prayer, in the last book, came from the heart, and that it was one which often went up from him during his labour: —

> "Jehovah! breathe upon my soul; my heart
> Enlarge; my faith increase; increase my hope;
> My thoughts exalt; my fancy sanctify,
> And all my passions, that I near thy throne
> May venture, unreproved."

He seems to have been led to this theme from a love of it, and to have been sustained by the hope, that he was labouring in the cause of God, and for his fellow-men. Notwithstanding what we have said of his deficiencies, we trust his labour will not be in vain. The cast of thought which pervades his work from beginning to end, the manner in which he sets forth man's fall from holiness, and the evil of sin, not only as it is discovered in our acts, but in its perversion of our reason, in its pollution of the secret springs of our hearts, and in our littleness and folly, compared with that grandeur and wisdom to which God ordained us, — these, and what else he has written, make the book a monitor to go to when we are getting light-minded, or growing into a good conceit of ourselves from comparing ourselves with others, or from hearing eulogies upon human nature when we should be listening to admonitions upon our faults, and warnings against our dangers. There is, likewise, so much thinking in the book, that a serious, plain-sense man will find it so in accordance with his own mind as to awaken sympathy, and give it a hold upon his attention.

That comprehensive view of God's government to which we have alluded adds value to this work in these days of bold assumptions grounded on careless, imperfect notions of the nature of sin, and partial and half-way reasonings upon the character and providence of God,— days of daring doubt, too, as to the woes pronounced against sin, because, forsooth, they sort not with our notions of benevolence. Would that he who thus speculates would remember the words of Baxter, that "self-discovery is not the least part of illumination"; then might his eyes be opened to what he is, and what he should be; then might he "perceive, that it is not possible for the best of men, much less for the wicked, to be competent judges of the desert of sin"; then might he understand that benevolence itself may require what had before so shocked his perverted reason, and be ready to say to himself, in the language of the same writer,— "Alas! we are all both blind and partial. You can never know fully the desert of sin, till you fully know the evil of sin: and you can never fully know the evil of sin, till you fully know the excellency of the soul which it deformeth, and the excellency of the holiness which it doth obliterate; and the reason and excellency of the glory which it violateth; and the excellency of the glory which it doth despise; and the excellency of the office of reason which it treadeth down; no, nor till you know the infinite excellency, almightiness, and holiness of that God against whom it is committed. When you fully know all these, you shall fully know the desert of sin." Believe the Word, then, and in thy present ignorance be humble:—

"Be content;
It will seem clearer to thine immortality."

In the mean time ponder the words of our author:—

"Though God should stoop,
Inviting still, and send his only Son

To offer grace in hell, the pride, that first
Refused, would still refuse; the unbelief,
Still unbelieving, would deride, and mock;
Nay more, refuse, deride, and mock; for sin,
Increasing still, and growing, day and night,
Into the essence of the soul, becomes
All sin, makes what in time seemed probable —
Seemed probable, since God invited them —
For ever now impossible."

And again: —

"The form thou saw'st was Virtue, ever fair.
Virtue, like God, whose excellent majesty,
Whose glory, virtue is, is omnipresent.
No being, once created rational,
Accountable, endowed with moral sense,
With sapience of right and wrong endowed
And charged, however fallen, debased, destroyed;
However lost, forlorn, and miserable;
In guilt's dark shrouding wrapped, however thick;
However drunk, delirious, and mad,
With sin's full cup; and with whatever damned,
Unnatural diligence it work and toil,
Can banish Virtue from its sight, or once
Forget that she is fair. Hides it in night,
In central night; takes it the lightning's wing,
And flies for ever on, beyond the bounds
Of all; drinks it the maddest cup of sin;
Dives it beneath the ocean of despair;
It dives, it drinks, it flies, it hides, in vain.
For still the eternal beauty, image fair,
Once stamped upon the soul, before the eye
All lovely stands, nor will depart; so God
Ordains; and lovely to the worst she seems,
And ever seems; and as they look, and still
Must ever look, upon her loveliness,
Remembrance dire of what they were, of what

They might have been, and bitter sense of what
They are, polluted, ruined, hopeless, lost,
With most repenting torment rend their hearts.
So God ordains their punishment severe,
Eternally inflicted by themselves.
'T is this, this Virtue hovering evermore
Before the vision of the damned, and in
Upon their monstrous moral nakedness
Casting unwelcome light, that makes their woe,
That makes the essence of the endless flame.
Where this is, there is hell; darker than aught
That he, the bard three-visioned, darkest saw."

If such views as these are so held as not to limit the power of the Almighty over his creatures, or to call in question retributive justice, — if they are taken as acting with his power and justice, and not superseding them; as being issues of his laws, and not necessities above them; as instruments to carry out his purposes, and not forces of spiritual natures checking or turning those purposes aside, — we are glad to find them becoming more prominent. We do not speak of this so much for the sake of the humble believer, who, having once felt assured that the Bible is the word of God, receives without questioning whatever that word reveals, — though it must be a help to him to catch glimpses of the reasons for all that God has ordained, — but because it serves to counteract the influence of those who set aside the authority of the Bible where convenience requires it, or, professedly admitting it, torture its meaning, or render it unmeaning, that it may not speak contrary to their notions of what God should do and God should be. Such treat the denunciations of eternal woe as if they must necessarily be the mere arbitrary threatenings of a severe judge; and therefore, with them, eternal woe cannot mean eternal woe, and God still be merciful. They have but superficially considered the effects of purity presented to an impure, or holiness to an unholy mind. "Horrible doctrine," they cry, "that God should condemn man to eternal misery for the sins of time!" Just as if, through all eternity, God would not suffer man to be happy!

There is a vague impression, that men would not go on for ever enduring unmixed misery, if the soul could by any effort free itself and find joy. But God, in his benevolence, has ordained that the joys of eternity shall spring from holiness alone; and who is prepared to say that measureless suffering will drive man to pray for *that* with all the heart? And if the evil passions are never to be satisfied in the other world, will man, therefore turn away from them? How is it in the present world? Are not unsated lust, and ungratified envy, and hate, causes of misery? Needs he who lusts, and envies, and hates be informed that they are? Is not his spirit stretched hourly upon the rack; and needs he be told who they are that bind him there? If hate has no opportunity to avenge itself, nor envy to rejoice over the fall of the envied, nor lust to satiate its longing, will telling the man this cut his cords, and set him free from the torture? Does not the very despair give a blind and wild energy to his passions? Does he not cling closer and closer to his torment? Though it sounds of paradox, does not his very torture make a kind of diseased delight? If those who, to rid themselves of hard thoughts of God, are ready to give up the plain meaning of the Bible, would but substitute the terms holiness and unholiness for happiness and misery, there is a possibility that, in good time, they might be able to reconcile God's goodness and the truth of his Word. Let them take along with them the principle, that, in the future world, mixed character and mixed happiness and suffering will be at an end; that man, assimilated either to his God or to evil spirits, will be conscious of happiness as an effluence of holiness, or of misery as an effluence of sin; and then they may come to the conclusion, that all the incongruity had been in their own brains, and each be at last ready to say, in the language of one who scarcely acted up to his profession, — "I have no ambition to be a philosopher in opposition to Paul, or to postpone Christ to Aristotle."

In speaking of the passages which have given rise to these suggestions, we cannot but regret that the principle held in them does not discover itself more in the tenth book. Let us again say, that we would not have it the sole pervading principle; for we read of God's anger against the wicked, and his direct punishment of them hereafter; and though we may not be able fully to comprehend the natures or modes or reasons of these, we will not fall into the very errours to which we have been objecting, and, to rid ourselves of difficulties, resolve the whole into mere necessary self-torture. We believe the terms to have a distinct meaning from that, and a fearful one, too; and suppose it the part of justice, that punishment should follow on the heels of crime, and that if a being will go on for ever making war, though a vain one, against an all-holy and happy state, it is right that he should suffer evil from without for his rebel pride and hate of goodness.

The principle of benevolence may be here acting along with that of justice; and it may be one of the means of maintaining beings of free will steadfast in virtue, that, where crime is obdurate, they should not only witness self-paining sin, but also the direct displeasure of God turned against it. The fact, that he who dies in his sins will voluntarily persevere in them for ever, under all their evil consequences, may likewise be used to the same end; and thus sin, which had set itself in array against God's scheme of mingled holiness and happiness, be brought to thwart its own evil intent, and made to give stability to that government which it would fain overthrow. Let the bright angel now standing by God's throne see the evil spirits restored, as some dream they will be, and who can tell that pride would not arm him against his Maker, and the standard of sin be again lifted in the heavens, and uproar and shoutings of revolt be heard ringing through the joyous and glittering hosts that are now sending up the cry, Glory to God in the highest? Then would the firm state of heaven be shaken, revolt crowd upon revolt, and pardon on revolt, and then revolt, and the shoreless universe be left heaving through eternity, a restless, ever-surging sea. Would this be benevolence?

We have not time to pursue this speculation further now, though it might be presented in a variety of lights, and be multiplied many fold. If our faith took hold upon nothing more in eternity than that of which we could explain the shape and purposes, we would cut loose at once, and let the current of time drift us whither it would.

In the following address to the sea, in which all should be simple and massive, we have a heaping of epithet upon epithet, as if, by accumulation, there was a hope of rising to mountain grandeur, while, in truth, we are left with little else than a sense of weariness at the cobbled ascent; and yet the passage is much relieved by our omissions of the poorest parts.

"Great Ocean! too, that morning, thou the call
Of restitution heardst, and reverently
To the last trumpet's voice, in silence, listened.
Great Ocean! strongest of creation's sons,
Unconquerable, unreposed, untired,
That rolled the wild, profound, eternal bass,
In Nature's anthem, and made music, such
As pleased the ear of God! original,
Unmarred, unfaded work of Deity, —

. . . . .

Unfallen, religious, holy sea!
Thou bowedst thy glorious head to none, fearedst none,
Heardst none, to none didst honor, but to God
Thy Maker, only worthy to receive
Thy great obeisance! Undiscovered Sea!
Into thy dark, unknown, mysterious caves,
And secret haunts, unfathomably deep,
Beneath all visible retired, none went,
And came again, to tell the wonders there.

. . . . .

Self-purifying, unpolluted Sea!
Lover unchangeable, thy faithful breast
For ever heaving to the lovely moon,
That, like a shy and holy virgin, robed
In saintly white, walked nightly in the heavens,
And to the everlasting serenade
Gave gracious audience; nor was wooed in vain.
That morning, thou, that slumbered not before,
Nor slept, great Ocean! laid thy waves to rest,
And hushed thy mighty minstrelsy. No breath
The deep composure stirred, no fin, no oar;
Like beauty newly dead, so calm, so still,
So lovely, thou, beneath the light that fell

From angel-chariots, sentinelled on high,
Reposed, and listened, and saw thy living change,
Thy dead arise."

The vain endeavours of man to escape death and the thoughts of death are thus described, with many repetitions:—

"He turned aside, he drowned himself in sleep,
In wine, in pleasure; travelled, voyaged, sought
Receipts for health from all he met; betook
To business, speculate, retired; returned
Again to active life, again retired;
Returned, retired again; prepared to die;
Talked of thy nothingness, conversed of life
To come, laughed at his fears, filled up the cup,
Drank deep, refrained; filled up, refrained again;
Planned, built him round with splendour, won applause,
Made large alliances with men and things,
Read deep in science and philosophy,
To fortify his soul; heard lectures prove
The present ill and future good; observed
His pulse beat regular, extended hope;
Thought, dissipated thought, and thought again;
Indulged, abstained, and tried a thousand schemes,
To ward thy blow, or hide thee from his eye;
But still thy gloomy terrours, dipped in sin,
Before him frowned, and withered all his joy.
Still feared and hated thing! thy ghostly shape
Stood in his avenues of fairest hope;
Unmannerly and uninvited, crept
Into his haunts of most select delights.
Still, on his halls of mirth, and banqueting,
And revelry, thy shadowy hand was seen
Writing thy name of—Death."

The following is the gentle call of nature to man:—

"The seasons came and went, and went and came,
To teach men gratitude ; and as they passed,
Gave warning of the lapse of time, that else
Had stolen unheeded by. The gentle flowers
Retired, and, stooping o'er the wilderness,
Talked of humility, and peace, and love.
The dews came down unseen at evening-tide,
And silently their bounties shed, to teach
Mankind unostentatious charity.
With arm in arm the forest rose on high,
And lesson gave of brotherly regard."

As an accompaniment, we give part of the lament over the general decay of nature : —

"Ye flowers of beauty, pencilled by the hand
Of God, who annually renewed your birth,
To gem the virgin robes of Nature chaste,
Ye smiling-featured daughters of the sun !
Fairer than queenly bride, by Jordan's stream
Leading your gentle lives, retired, unseen ;
Or on the sainted cliffs on Zion hill
Wandering, and holding with the heavenly dews,
In holy revelry, your nightly loves,
Watched by the stars, and offering, every morn,
Your incense grateful both to God and man ; —
Ye lovely gentle things, alas ! no spring
Shall ever wake you now ! ye withered all,
All in a moment drooped, and on your roots
The grasp of everlasting winter seized !
Children of song, ye birds that dwelt in air,
And stole your notes from angels' lyres, and first
In levee of the morn, with eulogy
Ascending, hailed the advent of the dawn,
Or, roosted on the pensive evening bough,
In melancholy numbers, sung the day
To rest ; — your little wings, failing, dissolved,

In middle air, and on your harmony
Perpetual silence fell!"

The following description is given with some touch of tenderness: —

"Wrinkled with time,
And hoary with the dust of years, an old
And worthy man came to his humble roof,
Tottering and slow, and on the threshold stood.
No foot, no voice, was heard within. None came
To meet him, where he oft had met a wife,
And sons, and daughters, glad at his return.
None came to meet him; for that day had seen
The old man lay within the narrow house
The last of all his family; and now
He stood in solitude, in solitude
Wide as the world; for all that made to him
Society had fled beyond its bounds.
Wherever strayed his aimless eye, there lay
The wreck of some fond hope, that touched his soul
With bitter thoughts, and told him all was passed.
His lonely cot was silent, and he looked
As if he could not enter. On his staff,
Bending, he leaned; and from his weary eye,
Distressing sight! a single tear-drop wept.
None followed, for the fount of tears was dry.
Alone and last, it fell from wrinkle down
To wrinkle, till it lost itself, drunk by
The withered cheek, on which again no smile
Should come, or drop of tenderness be seen."

We close our extracts with one from the most natural, simple, and touching passage in the poem, yet with many of the writer's defects. It is supposed to describe his own early hopes and disappointments.

"One of this mood I do remember well.
We name him not, — what now are earthly names? —
In humble dwelling born, retired, remote;
In rural quietude, 'mong hills, and streams,
And melancholy deserts, where the sun
Saw, as he passed, a shepherd only, here
And there, watching his little flock, or heard
The ploughman talking to his steers; his hopes,
His morning hopes, awoke before him, smiling,
Among the dews and holy mountain airs;
And fancy coloured them with every hue
Of heavenly loveliness. But soon his dreams
Of childhood fled away, those rainbow dreams,
So innocent and fair, that withered Age,
Even at the grave, cleared up his dusty eye,
And, passing all between, looked fondly back
To see them once again, ere he departed:
These fled away, and anxious thought, that wished
To go, yet whither knew not well to go,
Possessed his soul, and held it still awhile.
He listened, and heard from far the voice of fame,
Heard and was charmed; and deep and sudden vow
Of resolution made to be renowned;
And deeper vowed again to keep his vow.

. . . . .

"Thus stood his mind, when round him came a cloud,
Slowly and heavily it came, a cloud
Of ills, we mention not. Enough to say,
'T was cold, and dead, impenetrable gloom.
He saw its dark approach, and saw his hopes,
One after one, put out, as nearer still
It drew his soul; but fainted not at first,
Fainted not soon.

. . . . .

"He called philosophy, and with his heart
Reasoned. He called religion too, but called

Reluctantly, and therefore was not heard.
Ashamed to be o'ermatched by earthly woes,
He sought, and sought, with eye that dimmed apace,
To find some avenue to light, some place
On which to rest a hope; but sought in vain.
Darker, and darker still, the darkness grew.
At length he sank, and Disappointment stood
His only comforter, and mournfully
Told all was passed. His interest in life,
In being, ceased; and now he seemed to feel,
And shuddered as he felt, his powers of mind
Decaying in the spring-time of his day.
The vigorous weak became; the clear, obscure.
Memory gave up her charge, Decision reeled,
And from her flight Fancy returned, returned
Because she found no nourishment abroad.
The blue heavens withered, and the moon, and sun,
And all the stars, and the green earth, and morn
And evening, withered; and the eyes, and smiles,
And faces of all men and women withered:
Withered to him; and all the universe
Like something which had been appeared; but now
Was dead and mouldering fast away. He tried
No more to hope, wished to forget his vow,
Wished to forget his harp; then ceased to wish.
That was his last. Enjoyment now was done.
He had no hope, no wish, and scarce a fear.
Of being sensible, and sensible
Of loss, he as some atom seemed, which God
Had made superfluous, and needed not
To build creation with; but back again
To nothing threw, and left it in the void,
With everlasting sense that once it was."

Now, few will deny some merit to these passages, and fewer still, that you are not impatient for them to end much sooner than they do. You read on, thinking at first that you are advancing; but you find you go a little forward only to retrace your steps, — that there is a perpetual return to the same words. Yet we think that we have selected passages most favorable to Pollok. We have spoken of the injury done to him as a poet by the indiscriminate and excessive praise of his admirers; we hope and believe, that, in avoiding their errour, we have not fallen into an opposite one, or if so, that, by having made our selections from the better portions of his poem, all will be set right. Aside from the question of its poetic qualities, and for those who think and feel differently about it from ourselves in this respect, we would add, that there are principles set forth in it which may furnish help to the meditations of the serious, and a corrective for those who are fully enough prone to think well of themselves and human nature as it is, and lightly enough of what is required of us all. There is, we fear, a too strong tendency towards both these errours; — indeed, they are necessarily coupled in the vain fancies of this preëminently vain and self-confiding age.

We are becoming more and more creatures of society. The increasing facilities of intercourse, with other circumstances, are helping to make us so. The tendency of this state of things is to give us what the world calls good-natured views of our fellow-men, or, in other words, to make us less scrupulous concerning their points of moral conduct, and indiscriminately familiar with the good and the unprincipled, and ready enough, perhaps, to expend upon ourselves something of this same good-nature which we are bestowing so liberally upon the world at large. Thus much, at least, is true: the retired man, when occasionally amongst those living much with the world, is conscious of a depressing sensation at the absence of a certain sensitiveness where he feels quickly, a want of earnestness and deep seriousness about that which he believes to be connected with what is most important to our natures, and a disposition to pass lightly over that which lies closest to his heart.

Should men of the world, and those holding to a certain indifferentism, think the moral and religious character of this poem overstrained, they will at least find all urged without bitterness or severity, and pressed upon them with a spirit of love; and they may be led, also, to reflect how differently things have all along appeared in their eyes from what they did in those of a deeply religious mind.

We learn from the Christian Review, that Robert Pollok was born at his father's farm, Muirhouse, parish of Eaglesham, in 1798, — was graduated at Glasgow, and studied divinity at the United Secession Divinity Halls under the care of Dr. Dick, — was licensed to preach by the United Secession Presbytery of Edinburgh, in 1782, — was soon disabled by illness, and, on his way from Scotland to Italy for his health, died at Southampton, at the age of twenty-eight. He is represented as having been a man of more than common acquirements; and although the Course of Time was long a subject of meditation, it must be thought that he possessed too great a facility in writing, as he produced the last four books at the rate of nearly one thousand lines weekly. He wrote much besides, and destroyed a good deal.

How many, like Pollok, have died of consumption in early life, who have discovered an extent of acquirements, and a development of the intellectual powers, which have led us to say of one and another of them, "Had he lived, what a man he would have made!"

It is probably a mistake. This disorder often operates like a forcing system, and could it be stopped, and the subject of it be allowed to live on, there would most likely be little further growth. It would seem as if God had, in fatherly kindness, thus early opened to the wonders of his world here the minds of those so diseased, seeing that the days appointed to them on earth are few. Often, too, they are blessed with a clearness and calmness of spirit which make us look upon them as half-celestial creatures, passing by us on their way to a better world. He of whom we have been speaking, in truth, passed quickly, yet not without leaving something meant for our good.

It may be gathered from what we have said, that we think a great religious poem in our language is something still to be desired, rather than something already attained; and that we are yet left to exclaim, with the longing of Cowper, and, we trust, with somewhat of his hope, —

> " 'T were new, indeed, to see a bard all fire,
> Touched with a coal from heaven, assume the lyre,
> And tell the world, still kindling as he sung,
> With more than mortal music on his tongue,
> That *He* who died below, and reigns above,
> Inspires the song, and that his name is love."

Yes, we cannot but have the hope, let us say the faith, that from the earth will yet go up strains that shall mingle with the harps of hymning angels in the heavens.

If we are not to look for another poem so appalling, so magnificent, and yet of such paridisiacal loveliness as Milton's, still the Christian must feel that Paradise Lost is not of a character to answer the great religious end in view. One is dead who, furnished by God with celestial arms, too often, in his bitterness and scorn, turned them against man, and sometimes, in his recklessness, against his Maker too. There still lives one who might build up a temple into which all might enter with wonder and awe;—it is Coleridge.

Whatever he may think of his poetic powers, we believe we are not rash in prophesying, that, with the course of thought which his mind has long held, and with the feelings with which he would enter upon such a work, he would leave behind him a poem worthy of such a cause, and second only poetically to that Epic which he so reverences.

In speaking of Mr. Coleridge's intellect, we are reminded of Mr. Pollok's passage upon the poet; and it is not his only one on that theme.

"Most fit was such a place for musing men,
Happiest sometimes when musing without aim.
It was, indeed, a wondrous sort of bliss
The lonely bard enjoyed, when forth he walked,
Unpurposed; stood, and knew not why; sat down,
And knew not where; arose, and knew not when;
Had eyes, and saw not; ears, and nothing heard;
And sought—sought neither heaven nor earth—sought naught,
Nor meant to think; but ran, meantime, through vast
Of visionary things, fairer than aught
That was; and saw the distant tops of thoughts,
Which men of common stature never saw,
Greater than aught the largest worlds could hold,
Or give idea of, to those who read.
He entered into Nature's holy place,
Her inner chamber, and beheld her face,
Unveiled; and heard unutterable things,
And incommunicable visions saw."

We are not wholly free from hesitation in thus

speaking of Mr. Coleridge. Men of original minds, in stretching off in their flight after truth, have so pleasurable a consciousness of intellectual vigour in the exercise of their higher powers, that they sometimes, unawares, pass by that calm, clear-shining orb, and lose themselves for a season amidst mock suns. If, however, such men sincerely love truth, they are of use to us in the end. They rouse the mind, give it a longer reach of thought, and here and there open to it a scene so glorious, that the light which comes from it detects the very errours to which they themselves had given life, and which shall at last fade and die in that light, while the light itself shall shine on, growing brighter and brighter, and spreading more and more.

We must not be impatient because we cannot make every mind just what we would have it; but should rather reflect upon our own imperfections, and lament, while we consider what it is which gives a certain truth to the words long ago uttered, — "Nothing is less in a man's power than his own mind."

It seems to be a law of our fallen natures, that evil should be connected with every great power in man, if in no other way, at least in the very excess of that power; which must needs be, for in whom but in Him who made us are all the powers in even balance? Amongst the great ones of the earth, who, for instance, is there, of all the reformers, who has not carried overthrow beyond the bounds of errour? This should render the great meek; but let it not make the little conceited. Let them remember that they have their weaknesses, too, unnoticed, because they have no grand points in contrast to set them off.

Mr. Coleridge's proneness to deep speculations upon things spiritual, and the character of his philosophical reading, have led him into some opinions which we cannot think sound. No one will suspect, that, when we desire him to take a religious subject for a poem, we at the same time place him amongst those who make up their minds beforehand as to what the Word of God should mean, and then go to it with little other purpose than to distort it till it takes the shapes of the deformed progeny of their own brains. Mr. Coleridge is too well known to endanger his being numbered with these; but we do apprehend, that, in his fondness for speculating and refining, he sometimes runs off upon a course that leads him away from the simple meaning of the Bible, though he makes that book his starting-point. Other religious men have fallen into like errours through this same propensity.

We believe Mr. Coleridge has so deep a reverence for God's Word, that, could he but catch a glimpse of danger in the path in which, if we do not err, he is sometimes seen wandering, he would shun it as he would the way of death; knowing, as he does, that errour can never be harmless, and, however insignificant in itself, where connected with a great truth, never trifling.

May he, with the full sense of his responsibility in such an undertaking, mature well the plan of a poem, and give these his latter days to the work, having, for the strengthening of his spirit through his labours, the sanctifying dew of which Pollok speaks, —

> "Coming unseen . . . . .
> Anew creating all, and yet not heard;
> Compelling, yet not felt."

In his *own* words to that Mountain made sacred by his noble Hymn, we would call upon him, —

> "Awake,
> Voice of sweet song!"

NATURAL HISTORY OF ENTHUSIASM.*

If we look about us, we find the principal part of mankind made up of those whose pursuits, thoughts, and desires, whose whole moral and intellectual being, move round this material world, and are brought to bear upon the circumstances of life, just as if existence here were our only existence, and our powers were given us for the single purpose of ransacking this physical world, to administer to the comforts and luxuries of our physical nature; as if man's chief advantage over other animals lay in his being more knowing than they, and better able to make more of the world he lives in.

There is another and a smaller class, who lead a sort of speculative existence, who would etherealize this gross world, and its homely concerns, and the eternal relations and forms of being with which they are connected, into a universal spiritualism, of which these are accounted as but so many presentations.

---

* From The Spirit of the Pilgrims for 1830.

Natural History of Enthusiasm. [By Isaac Taylor.] Boston: Crocker & Brewster. New York: J. Leavitt. 1830. p. 302.

The reader is referred to the heading of the article on Pollok's Course of Time, p. 344.

Here their minds may go at large, with nothing to restrain or humble, pain or offend; here they become what their fancies may shape them to, and they and all around them in harmony, for all things are what they will them: — in such speculation they now live, and in such they seem to dream they shall live for ever.

The various forms which these two systems take, and the modifications which they undergo, according to the characters of the individuals who adopt them, can hardly be stated here. It may be shown, however, that, though seemingly so opposite, they spring from one principle, and in the course of time have one result; that they are equally in contradiction to the constitution of man, and, with the various opinions more or less nearly connected with them, stand no less opposed to direct revelation itself, than to the mode in which that revelation is made in the Word of God.

The Bible has regard to man in his twofold character, a creature of body and spirit; and while it speaks to us of mysteries that both humble us for our ignorance and excite us to know more, it meets us in our common walks, and is a rule and help in our daily concerns; and, at the same time that it treats of the Infinite Unseen, it takes sensible possession of the heart, and modifies the affections, as well in relation to the persons and affairs of this life as in connection with invisible things beyond. It does not compel us to keep our faculties on the strain, in order that our conceptions of God should retain their hold, for He comes to us "manifest in the flesh"; while He is seated far above spiritual principalities and powers, the train of His robe sweeps this temple. Nor are we held in a state of abstraction, for the affections to grow cold and our apprehensions dim, and then left to return to earth for something at the sight of which our hearts may glow again, and our minds clear and brighten. God has mercifully considered us, not only as we should be, but also as we are. Our spiritual vision being darkened, He draws near to us in his Son, visits our hearts in the Holy Spirit, lifts the eyes of the groveller to Himself, calls in our shapeless imaginations from abroad, and imparts to them form and purposes and practical uses for time and eternity. Christianity does indeed make itself our household god, and domesticates itself with us to give spirituality to our sensible natures, and reality and truth and object to our vague imaginations and misguided reason.

It is remarkable how this principle pervades the whole word of God. The Bible does not simply contain a mixture of certain intimated mysteries, and great spiritual revelations, and plain moral rules of conduct; but the narrative of startling mysteries, blended with common actions, runs on as naturally and unpretendingly as if it were a tale of the mere ordinary occurrences of life. Thus, the hand, as of a man, is mysteriously put forth; Daniel, the inspired of God, reveals what it writes; the shaped light vanishes, and, goes on the narrative, — "In that night was Belshazzar, the king of the Chaldeans, slain; and Darius the Median took the kingdom, *being about threescore and two years old.*"

Thus is the Bible adapted to the condition and two-fold nature of man. We are struck with this most forcibly, when considering man in the different states of society; that in which the Word of God has never been set before him, and that in which he rejects it, and shuts out its influence. Where, in a state of ignorance and sensuality, he comes nearest to the mere brute, and makes the world but a larger sty, a strong principle within forces itself out through all his fleshliness, and he whom we had coupled with the fed and lazy swine is found superstitiously peopling infinitude with wild and giant shapes of terrour and awe, at the sight of which his soul trembles. There is an intensity of strength and action in this principle in man, which makes the scoffer's heart beat quick; for he feels that there is a meaning in it, and a dreadful meaning. Call it imagination, or what he may, it is not so to be passed by; there it is, a reality in it to himself as well as to him he would despise. It may take other forms, — as those of beauty, and of a cheering, enticing nature; it is still the same restless power at work, striving after something beyond the visible and tangible, and by its blind, uncertain efforts warning man that there is something beyond.

What is there beyond? He cannot rend the veil that sin has hung between himself and heaven. Thus, he sees not the glory of God, nor does he hear his voice. He grows weary of these gropings after something, he knows not what, and sinks back once more into the senses. But as he cannot rest in these, he makes them minister to his spiritual desires, and forms from them images of wood and stone; and these are his gods before which he bows down, as things in which dwelt life. In these visible bodyings-forth of the perverted cravings of our being, the senses soon in turn become the taskmasters, and the higher power within is made to toil for the flesh; and every loose appetite is symbolized, and borne in triumph as a garlanded deity, and the mad rout dance and sing before the image that does but give back the shape and pressure of their own fallen nature.

Here we behold the senses and that inward principle gradually wrought into one; the soul, weary of its earthiness, giving form and an image of life to the dull and shapeless clod, and the earthy part of man polluting with its foulness and dust the creations of the soul. Thus man ever has worked, and thus he will again sooner or later work, unless he humbly receive God as he has, in adaptation to man's twofold state, mercifully seen fit to reveal Himself in Jesus Christ. Man cannot annihilate one portion of his nature, and the other live in health. The mystery of God manifest in the flesh is great; but he who denies it because of its mystery is blind to the mystery and wants of his own being, and denies his own nature no less than the revelation of God.

There are periods in society when the inward principle here spoken of seems to lose its energy and die away; when the whole man is turned towards physical objects, not as in any way representatives of the spiritual, but simply as materials of physical science, and as administering to physical enjoyments and wants. Man in such periods ceases to be superstitious, without learning to be religious. Having just enough of the light of knowledge to scatter the shadowy creations of other times, he begins to suspect that all which is not tangible is unreal, and so surrounds himself with material things that the light of revelation is shut out; his spiritual appetences perish for want of use, and he ceases to take pleasure in the exercise of faith. At most, he is possessed but by a wavering, half faith; bearing the name of a Christian, he is a skeptic at heart: in short he believes in steam, and in his five senses, and these are about all in which he really does believe.

This practical materialism, if we may so term it, is, in another way, as fatal to a full spiritual belief as is theoretical materialism; for it makes man forgetful of his weakness and conscious of his power; while, in relation to another world, if he feels at all, he must feel himself to be only a dependent creature, and about which, to know a little, he must believe much. But, treating the material world as its master, he likes not to become a child before the mighty invisible powers of the spiritual; and he turns back again to the world of sense, where he has visible proof of his sagacity and strength; and hope, and imagination, and the complacency of success hurry him along the road of those physical discoveries to which he can see no end. Over this world he feels himself to be the lord, and dreams that here, to the operations of intellectual powers, well applied, there are no bounds. Knowledge, not wisdom, becomes his god; and to be beyond his possible knowledge, and not to be, are with him the same. Man is all in all. Man discovers, and man uses and applies. The detection of the errours of past ages, instead of making him diffident of human intellect, does but raise a feeling of self-gratulation, which is both father and child to high notions of the superiority of his own times. His is not the age of superstition; and therefore, he argues, it is the age of reason. The Bible, so far as suits this reason, and God, when moulded by this reason, he may admit; but mysteries past its solving are an insult and an offence. The moral beauty of Christianity may be taken, for a time, to set off a modified deism; but having no close hold upon the heart, and making but few and weak demands upon his moral nature and his faith, it becomes, at last, a mere creature of the intellect, employed to wind up the machinery of the universe, and keep it in motion.

As no leading principle operates long in a single class of society, but soon runs into all, we find this same principle at work in the order of imaginative men; and there, God becomes the soul of man, the beauty and the perfume of the flower, the glory of the sun, and the spirit of the ever-moving sea. He who makes himself a mere creature of the sciences, and brings his whole nature to bear upon the material world alone, and what are called its laws, and he who leaves all these for the invisible, and philosophizes upon God and the soul of man, and reasons upon revelation, and not from it, are both moved by the same main principle, and, however contrary the ways they take, must both finally come to the same result. Whatever apparent difference there may be, both are in fact going on without faith; both are at war with that principle of dependence which is the law of all that is created; both striving to act as if self-formed, — the one lording it over the material world, as if no God created and sustained it, and the other, in opinion, looking through all spiritual existences and relations, as if no revelation were needed wherewith to behold them. The one, a creature of matter, and the other, a sort of spiritual abstraction, are equally engaged in the vain endeavour to annihilate a portion of their natures. And were it not that Christianity, which meets the wants of the whole man, must accomplish the work given it to do, both would move surely, though slowly, forward, and those who had refused to receive "God manifest in the flesh" would end, the subjects either of a gross idolatry, or of an idolatry more fanciful and refined. The man of matter must needs satisfy longings which will arise in his soul, and must endue his dull substances with life; while the man of abstraction, to fill his painful void, must have material forms, around which the fleecy drapery of his idealism may be thrown: So far as their self-working goes, idolism of some sort must be their common end.

Though this may seem to some to be pushing a principle to the extreme, it is nevertheless sure; for it is in the very nature of the soul thus to act; and it has always taken this course, and always will, when it leaves its revealed God. When the old world departed from the revelation of God, and worshipped stocks and stones, creeping things, and the lights of heaven, and peopled earth and air with deities, it was not because there were no sciences in the world and no mighty intellects. Every day is making better known to us how much in the arts and sciences, and in the philosophy of mind, has floated down to us out of the wrecks of former times, and how many of our discoveries are but rediscoveries. "Verily," may the man say who reads the philosophy of this day, "there is nothing new under the sun." It is forgetfulness, or ignorance of the intellectual advancement of those times, which has helped so much to the self-complacency of our own, and begotten that dangerous and presumptuous confidence, that man's reason is sufficient to itself, and treats with scorn the thought that the now enlightened man should again wander back into darkness. Yet the history of man is not that of an originally ignorant and savage being. Go back, age beyond age, and call upon him, and each time he will answer thee, I am fallen! I am fallen! Where he first set his foot, the strong trees root themselves amidst mighty ruins, and from between leaning columns and shattered arches comes a voice of warning, — Stand not up in thine own strength, O man, lest thou be brought low; nor trust alone to the light of thine own reason, lest thick darkness encompass thee."

What else could be looked for? What poorer philosophy than that which supposes the imperfect can, of itself, keep in steady advance, till it results in perfection? Yet thus, virtually, argues the rationalist. And it is the great principle of a popular philosophy, that the created contains an all-sufficient power within itself; and hence it is that we hear so much more of the light of reason than of the light of the Word, of the power of the soul than of the Holy Spirit; and for this it is that, when God comes mysteriously near to us in his Son, we reject Him, and put Him afar off. Setting no limits to our own powers, we refuse to contemplate God, except in his infinitude; and stretching forth our finite faculties after the infinite, and searching after the invisible, we become weak and wandering, and are lost. Our God is made an abstraction, and our hearts grow cold, and the heavens void. "I beheld the heavens," says the prophet, "and they had no light . . . . . and all the birds of the heavens were fled . . . . . and the heavens above be black." So cheerless, so empty, so dark and still are the spiritual heavens, to him who looks up to them through any other than that path, all light, along which Christ ascended to his glory.

To fill this void in the soul, a religious sentimentality is substituted for religion of the heart, and a sort of atmospheric divinity breathes around us like a balmy day, and, like a Claude sky and light, wraps heaven and earth in soft transparency. A mawkish love takes place of the wise and just benevolence of God; and our Creator and final Judge is fairly idealized and sentimentalized out of his own creation, providence, and rule.

Creation, and not the Creator, is the life and the spirit to us, and must needs be so; for the Creator not being presented to us in the Son, nor felt in the heart, through the Spirit, and being without impersonation for our apprehension, the mind must somewhere seek a reflex action; and it finds it in the objects of the natural world. It would exhaust itself by its continual efflux through infinitude after such an abstraction as that to which the rationalist would give the name of God; and so it turns out that Nature, however idealized, and however shrouded in metaphysic mist, becomes, at last, man's God, and his only God.

Another effect is to make man assume to himself something of the character of Creator. Not receiving God as he has presented himself in his Revealed Word, and denying what is called experimental religion, he has nothing to fall back upon, on which to rest as a plain, matter-of-fact reality. So the imagination goes busily to work; and, with the help of a little philosophy, sentiment, and poetry, and a due mixture of Christian morality, a religious system is made up perfectly rational, — for how can it be otherwise, being the product of his own reason? — and the man becomes a pleased and constant worshipper; and well he may, for his God is the issue of his own brain, and from out himself he worships himself. Behold the progeny of human pride, — the Creator the creature! the creature the Creator! Yes, enter into the temple of his worship, and see man setting up there the work of his own hands, and bowing before it as his God. The walls of that house do but reflect back his own image; the spirit that fills it is Pride; its Shechinah is Self.

What a result is here! A creature of sin and knowing nothing, born yesterday and to die to-morrow, virtually having no God to whom his thoughts and affections can run back; but seeing, feeling, believing, — no, here is no place for belief, — only what he puts forth from himself. This floats before his mind as his Deity: here are his angels, archangels, principalities, and powers: here is the world that he has made unto himself, in the midst of which he sits the crowned sovereign, and which the sceptre of his imagination sways as he may will. But he must die, and must awake again. Awake to what? The creation with which he surrounded himself, angels and powers, are all vanished; his very God is gone; and he is left a poor spirit, — infinitude around him, and he alone. Not even the influence of the all-pervading Spirit touches him there; no light from out the throne visits him there, — eternity, eternity, and no God! There his rejected Saviour and final Judge need not say to him, "Depart from me." From the solitary depths of his own soul the words are for ever and ever ascending, — "Without God!"

There are those of whose religion this is the sum, though they cannot bear to be told of it. They have found for themselves a most pleasing substitute for the "things hard to be understood," and for doctrines which it requires the teachable disposition of a child to learn, and a renewed heart to obey. They see great moral beauty in the character of the Saviour; and the contemplation of moral beauty, even without conformity to it, is a pleasurable employment. Most of them profess the belief, and many of them, without reservation, might say, with Nicodemus, "Rabbi, we know that thou art a teacher come from God." But when Jesus, instead of commending their faith, immediately replies, "Verily, verily, I say unto you, Except a man be born again, he cannot see the kingdom of God," they do not, in their straits, ask, "How can these things be?" but say in their hearts, "These things cannot be," and straightway leave Him. John says unto them, "Behold the Lamb of God that taketh away the sin of the world!" "What!" they reply, "is God Moloch, that he should require innocent blood?"

It is hard for him who has found this substitute for religion in philosophic chimeras or poetic visions, to give all up, and come and sit humbly at the feet of Christ. The sensations which he experiences are so pleasing; the mind is taken up and floated off, in its dreamy, discursive course, into regions so magnificent and beautiful; the man, in his own esteem, is so elevated with the grandeur of that nature which can imagine these things; and they are withal, as he deems them, so pure, and so intellectual, that they must be truth, — and, above all, truth not bestowed, but gained by the great, unaided intellect itself. Such a man, it may be, has his hours of despondency and misgiving, and is sore when the truth of God touches him; yet he will, perhaps, say to the very last, as, in the course of his life, Jacobi once said, "With your complaints about the unsatisfactory nature of all our speculations I most heartily, though sorrowfully, agree. I know, however, no other course than to speculate and philosophize right on." A melancholy warning and confession indeed.

Some of this order, having no settled truth to start from or to refer back to, that they may ascertain whether the opinions and schemes which they have formed can be logically deduced, are left without a regulator to the movements of their mental machinery, and the reasoning faculty acts under a disturbing, uneven force. The imagination, necessary in reasoning for furnishing objects and conditions, becomes the dominant power, and reason is swept round and round, as in an eddy, and judgement goes to the bottom.

Another class of narrower and drier, though of acute minds, perhaps, speculate upon some detached point, not rightly apprehended because not seen in its relations. A single attribute of God may be the subject of their thoughts, — His benevolence, for instance, which, severed from His attribute of justice, is made to sink into a quality little better than human weakness; and thus the completeness and harmony of the Divine character are lost.

> "A God all o'er, consummate, absolute,
> Full-orbed, in his whole round of rays complete:
> They set at odds heaven's jarring attributes;
> And with one excellence another wound;
> Maim heaven's perfection, break its equal beams,
> Bid mercy triumph over — God himself,
> Undeified by their opprobrious praise:
> A God all mercy is a God unjust."

Such men not only make a perverted use of their own powers, but are sometimes the occasion of a wrong bent in the minds of those who receive the Bible as divine authority. In order to meet the rationalists in their objections, and perhaps, too, from an unobserved fear of not being held quite so enlightened as they, believers become excessively anxious to account for all that is contained in that book, to show that every thing is upon perfectly rational principles, and adapted to the real nature of things, and that all objections arise from the want of fair, clear, and comprehensive views in the objectors. In doing this, they sometimes seem to be under great fears for the reputation of the Bible, and to be unconsciously possessed by a misgiving, that, were it not for their intellectual efforts on its behalf, it might turn out at last not quite wise and philosophical enough for advancing reason, and that the ingenuity of man was in a fair way to circumvent the wisdom of God.

To be able to refute opposers, and to show the rationality of the scheme of revelation to an age vain of its reason, and consequently skeptical, may be well; but there is danger of its unawares forming in the believer's mind a habit of resorting too much to his own argumentation for the strengthening of his faith, and to find a place of rest for his belief more in that which his own sagacity has enabled him to account for, than in the simple declaration of the Word itself, and for the single reason that it is God's Word. Notwithstanding he holds the Bible of divine authority, he slides into the habit of making his own processes of reasoning the resort of faith, rather than the single fact that God has said it. Now this process of arriving at or confirming faith is not faith, and the believer who resorts much to it is in peril of losing something of his thorough, home conviction of the truth; his belief will not be so a portion, as it were, of his consciousness, the element of his existence, — his belief will not be faith, not the faith of which the Apostle speaks. He too faintly considers that revealed truths are not mere intellectual truths, or to be sought intellectually alone, and that man cannot have a mere intellectual knowledge of them, — that, in fact, (let the rationalist sneer if he will,) without the life of religion there can be no true knowledge of the highest and most glorious truths of religion.

This mode of treating upon religious concerns is, also, not without its unfavourable effects upon those to whom it is addressed. It leads them to look upon the great Book of God's law rather like judges who are set to put their own constructions upon it, than like criminals whom it condemns; rather as if they were to see whether it were worthy their acceptance, than to find through it a way of pardon for their transgressions. Something like a feeling of intellectual superiority arises in the heart, as if it were a matter of favour for beings such as they to accept it; — they will think of it; they will make up their minds about it.

The Apostles did not go thus round about to persuade men by long argumentation. They took man as he is, a sinner; with this they went directly to his heart. They compelled him to turn his eyes inward, and look at the prison there; to behold how dark it was; to hear the mutterings of wrath; to see Sin, the jailer, with his chains, and bars, and instruments of torture; and then they would open the door of hope, and let in the soft, still light from above, and man would look out through it, and, lo! the revealed glories of the heavens and the splendours of the Cross: — then man saw and felt the truths of the Word of God. This was the plain apostolic way of dealing with man; and let this wise age learn that it was and is the truly philosophic way. Man must have a sense of what sin is before he can perceive the harmony of the great doctrines of condemnation under it and restoration from it, and learn their adaptability to his desires and needs.

If unbelief, under its various modifications and names, would be wise against what is written, have there not been, from the first, believers who would be wise beyond what is written? From what else proceed the speculations with which Evangelical Christendom has been kept astir for ages? Is there not enough lying within the light of revelation, that men must needs be for ever passing out beyond its borders, and holding sharp contest with the shadows hovering in the twilight there?

Men deceive themselves in supposing they do all this for truth's sake. It too often has its origin in an unwillingness to acknowledge practically that there are limits to the intellectual powers, or, at least, in an ignorance or forgetfulness of the fact. When we shall have learned that the remedy for this lies in childlike humility, we shall have discovered that its origin was in pride. Or if we suppose it to arise in part from a fondness for intellectual effort, it grows to a disease, which spreads from our own to other minds, and, what is more, lays upon the Bible the burden of our errours, presumption, and extravagances. When we see a scheme set up by one man only to be pulled down by another, and two theories in battle array both overthrown by a third, and system after system coming up, and passing off, to return with a new name, and pass off again, we cannot but apply to their authors the words spoken of a less harmless race of men:—"These ingenious and hard-working people toil incessantly to draw up Truth from her deep well. After unceasing efforts, by many turns of the windlass, and having eagerly watched scores of fathoms of dripping rope, instead of bringing to light a naked goddess, they very carefully land another bucket of water."

May there not yet be educed from the Word of God a philosophy more widely applicable to the diversified nature and relations of man, than has been hitherto well developed? Not that in certain words and passages in it there are wonderful powers shut up in a sort of hieroglyphics, to which another Young or Champollion is to discover the key, and lay open mysteries to the astonished world;—nor, on the other hand, that what in it we have humbly bowed before, as among the hidden things of God, some complacent rationalist is to unlock, and, by the shining of his own mind, relieve us of our awe, by letting us see there was nothing there, or nothing but what reason, of itself, might have found out; — but that we shall go to it, not only as the source of all moral and spiritual truths, but to be imbued by it also with a wider apprehension of material things in their forces, and the mysterious relations of these with man and all spiritual beings; that, as both have one Creator, and One ordained the laws by which both were to move, and appointed the purpose of their motions, analogies, relations, harmonies, deeper than the surfaces of things, must intertwine by living chords, running in among both and all.

When this truth shall be received, not speculatively, but practically, into the very life of the mind, man's researches into soul and matter will be regulated upon the principle, that truly to learn one in its varieties, energies, and completeness, he must learn both in their strange and divine sympathies, — remembering that there are influences common to creatures and things unendowed with will, and to him whose will, misused, became his condemnation, — that the earth felt man's fall, and "that the whole creation groaneth and travaileth in pain together until now," and, in the restoration of man, looketh for its own return to the beauty and calm of paradise again. And as the light of revelation is now spreading through the dark places of the earth, so shall it not spread through the twilight places in the partially enlightened religious mind, permeating the workings of every power of man, and teaching him how to think and know? Then will a dim, shadowy, fantastic philosophism, the hallucination of many a fine mind, vanish away, and cold and almost soulless systems be reformed and quickened into a new life.

From one cause or another it has been too much a matter of course to shut the doors and windows of certain intellectual apartments from the light of revelation, and to light up candles, and kindle a new fire, before men went about their work. These doors and windows are, however, yet to be thrown open, and into these abodes revelation is yet to shine; and by its fires and with its light the noblest labours of men are yet to be performed. Men are not for ever to gather their knowledge and make up their systems of philosophy from any thing and every thing rather than the Bible, and then to bring that book to their preconceived notions. It is to become the great source whence man's philosophy is to be drawn. When this shall be the case, the moral character and the intellectual will move together in an harmonious advancement. Man will learn, that to be wise in philosophy he must be wise unto eternal life. The Holy Spirit is to be the great Teacher; abstract philosophy is to become, as it were, experimental philosophy, — in other words, true philosophy will be learned through experimental religion and the Bible. We believe that out of the fall of man, and through his restoration, God is not only carrying on a great moral plan, but also exhibiting a wonderful intellectual process for man's study and joy and steadfastness, and that He is about showing more clearly than He has yet done, that receiving his Word in faith, being renewed in his image, living obedient to his law, and being regulated in all our affections by the love of Him, are to lead to a glorious display of the powers of man, and that this intellectual world is to move on with the even energy and splendour of the spheres. System after system has come up and shone, and men have gazed at it, and then it has rolled far off into the darkness, to be wondered at no more. But that which God will make manifest, to vindicate his own mind, shall have his revealed Word for its central light, and planets shall move round it, in sweet obedience to its influence, till these heavens shall pass away, and then shall they circle his throne for ever and ever, and drink in for ever of his light.

That which man goes through to come into his proper communion with God opens depths in the soul, down which not only had he never looked before, but which till then had been unthought of regions. The stillness which had brooded there is broken; far, far down, deep is calling unto deep, and the waters of the dead sea move. O, if man would know something of that truly shoreless ocean, the soul, something of those caves which no line has fathomed, and feel the power of the spirit that is moving there, let him see and feel himself a sinner before Almighty God! If thou wouldst know the infinite capacity of thy nature, man, feel thyself a worm, and less than a worm, before thy God! To hear one prate of the light of reason, and the dignity and perfectibility of his nature, who has never felt the searchings of conviction and the throes of sin, — how gaudy, how poor, how sad it is! What does such a man know of those depths out of which a redeemed one is come, or of the height and grandeur to which he is ascending?

This experience in the life of man gives him a wonderful knowledge of himself, not only by calling into vivid action powers that had slept within him, but by bringing them into action as he and all within him stand related to God, the source of all knowledge, wisdom, and power, and helping him to see himself as he is, a dependent being, and not, as he once esteemed himself, sufficient to himself in his own reason, independent and unrelated. But to see one's self in one's true relation is the better part of self-knowledge. More than this, when the world rouses us, and the soul is up with the stir of the passions, the mind is looking outward, and fastening upon something there, and it then takes little note of what is within. And when it afterwards philosophizes about its emotions, it is through the memory, which brings back the past faintly and partially. But when man is conscience-stricken before his God, and would fain turn to Him and live, the mind is set inward; and as the workings of the soul wax stronger and stronger, and he sees into himself with a power of vision almost, nay, perhaps indeed supernatural, — not to philosophize about himself, not even, it may be, with a purpose to know himself, — he feels driven, as it were, to search himself through and through; so that the passions are working and the self-examination going on with an almost simultaneous movement, and the man observes and examines his emotions while they are in full life and fervid action.

When man shall form his philosophy, not by wandering to the ends of the earth after his God and to become acquainted with himself, but shall learn that the Life and Light come from God's Spirit, and must be within himself, or cannot be to him at all, that which will teach him this so distinctly requires of him the humility of a child, and so surrounds him with its solemn mysteries, that it will call up with his first thoughts a consciousness of his short-sightedness, and will show him on all sides how closely the limits of his earthly vision press upon him. But to learn early what things they are that are not to be understood is the surest way to understand aright that which is knowable. To be ever reaching forth after the indefinable gives exaggerated proportions to the distant, and diminishes the near; while to make the distant and undefined nothing more than the present and obvious, exaggerates the near, and robs the distant of its glory. In the one case, imagination seats itself on the throne of reason; and in the other, reason would stretch its rule where even imagination can catch but glimpses. The endeavour to subject to reason what lies beyond its control obscures its clearness of vision, disturbs its precision of action, and turns it off from truth in its results. The strength which sometimes appears imparted is unnatural energy, followed by a weakness which can be again forced into action only by being forced out of its natural and just movements. The several powers of the man get into each other's places, and thus objects are seen through false mediums, and come to the mind under changed and false aspects; so that nothing is perceived as it is in itself, but becomes the embodied presentation of the illusion within. To such a one the impossible first becomes possible, next probable, and then true, and he ends in believing a lie.

> "O hateful Errour! . . . . .
> Why dost thou show to the apt thoughts of men
> The things that are not?"

There is a beautiful influence in mystery as it comes to us from the Scriptures, exalting our imagination through our faith. It is not like the mystery evolved from our own minds, as smoke of incense to our pride, but like clouds around God's throne, luminous with the permeating glory from within, suffering us to draw near to that which no man could look upon at full and live, humbling us with the thoughts of what we now are, while lifting us above angels with thoughts of what we shall be: We ascend, and bow and adore as we ascend. Yes, he whom the Cross has humbled may bear to look on its mysterious splendours and not be proud; for his heart within him is like a little child's, while the mind is filled with images of surpassing glory, and might, and love.

When Christianity shall have had its foretold influence on society at large, and its vitality shall not be confined to scattered individuals, or to a flock folded here and there, then its principles, as connected with the intellect, will be brought out. It will then be settled, that the intellectual powers can be justly and thoroughly developed through the moral and religious character alone. — Of its effect upon the physical nature, and the reaction of that upon the spiritual, when all move upon the principle and by the power of God's law, we will not now speak. — As we are social beings, in the proportion that numbers are multiplied unto God man will find a helper in his brother man, and to be in the world will no longer be, as it now is, little else than a temptation to overcome, but an excitement to holy affections, and a strengthener of our hope and faith. The man of piety is not to find all his enjoyment, or all his aid to holiness, in the direct contemplation of God and the scheme of redemption, or in dwelling at seasons in solitary pleasure upon nature as the work of God's hands. Multitudes in all classes and occupations, the high as well as the low, and minds of greatest reach, are to become sons of God on earth and followers of the Cross. Poetry under all its forms, whether of words, colour, shape, or sound, is to be dedicated to Him who made us and all things, who gave us its spirit, and set all things in order before it for its use; and thus all our knowledge and all our pursuits are to be of and for God, and we God's.

Then will that glorious display of the powers of man, of which we have spoken, come. It is coming, it is already near, even at the door. Look at the world. The great mass is heaving; for the Spirit of God is putting forth its power. The old temples of errour, and those whose cement is not yet hardened, are beginning to sway. A little more, and they will be like Babel. France is giving out rays of the breaking day; in Germany an increasing number of learned and intellectual men are arraying themselves under the Cross; and from the laity of England, of all professions and ranks, works are appearing on the side of Evangelical truth which would be creditable to studious divines. Of our own country we need say nothing as yet. When the secret or open enemies of God's Word shall have had their brains intoxicated with something better than the neglected dregs which German and English schemers left standing to grow stale in the sun, it will be time enough to speak about the friends of Truth here, and what they are doing and have done. [Alas for the critic's prophecy! — Enough of overthrow indeed, but by what a Power!]

Of the religious works lately put forth in England, that before us is one of the most able, and best adapted to oppose the forms in which errour and the spirit of unbelief are showing themselves in this our day. If we were asked what was its characteristic, we would reply, generally enough to be sure, but emphatically, Wisdom. And let us add, that Coleridge, though differing in many points from the writer, has said, — "It is evidently the work of a mind at once observant and meditative; and I willingly give to his genius that respect which his intentions without it would secure for him in the breast of every good man." We have kept our readers from it too long, without even the apology that what we have been saying has a direct bearing upon it. But it put us into a somewhat thoughtful humour, and we, as well as others, have our humours in which we like sometimes to indulge.

The Natural History of Enthusiasm — a somewhat quaint title, perhaps — treats, under several heads, upon Enthusiasm, secular and religious, — in Devotion, — in perversions of the doctrine of Divine Influence, — as the source of Heresy, — in Prophetical Interpretation, — in abuses of the doctrine of a Particular Providence, — in Philanthropy, — of Enthusiasm as it appeared in the Ancient Church and in Ancient Monachism, — and closes with Hints on the Probable Spread of Christianity, submitted to those who misuse the term Enthusiasm.

As the reader enters upon this work, he feels that he is passing into a calm, clear, temperate atmosphere, in which objects are beheld in their true size, proportions, and colours, and every plant seems healthy and growing. The author's mind evidently rests upon well-laid principles of sound doctrine. He has not chosen these to set his building upon because he was ignorant that there were materials enough, and to spare, from the demolished temples of other times, wherewith he might have put together his foundation and have raised his superstructure; nor has he endeavoured to ascertain how much of that foundation, of which Christ is the corner-stone, might be taken away, and the house yet stand. He evidently has too much good sense for either of these follies; too much clear-sightedness to be so deluded himself, along with too much honesty to practise the delusion upon others. The habit of his mind is rather an unusual one for these days. He seems to have reflected much upon God, as he is revealed to us in the Bible, and upon the doctrines of the Bible, and then to have sat down and composed himself to meditate slowly and carefully upon men and their affairs, in connection with the representations, doctrines, requirements, and promises of that book, — in short, our author is a thinker, and not a dreamer. How few are there who make the distinction! and last of all, the dreamer himself. He dreams that he thinks, and he makes intellectual idlers dream so too, while he is nothing more than a better sort of voluptuary. A thinker! why he is the hardest worker in all man's heritage.

Our author has the characteristics of a select reader; one who has gathered in his materials, not from a silly love of accumulation, nor from the poor ambition of display, but as matter for reflection. With a mind made to look beyond the times, he considers the coming times in relation to the present, and these, again, in relation to them. He seems to be under the conviction, that God is beginning the broad unfolding of the millennium, and that the work now going on in so much of the world as may, in the strict sense of the word, be called Christian, is a making of the highways straight, exalting the valleys, and bringing low the hills. He has firm faith in still unfulfilled prophecy; yet, though by no means cold concerning it, with all its exciting motives, he treats his subject with the calmness and freedom from mysticism and schemes with which he would write upon the history of ancient times. He is the very first man whom you would go to, in straits, for advice. Whether the subject of your doubts were one of intricate and extended relations, or of few and confined ones, whether it had been familiar to him, or had lain out of his track, you would be sure that the result of his meditations upon it would be just. He unites exactness with comprehensiveness, neither losing sight of the whole in its particulars, nor of particulars in the whole. With the faculty of imagination strong enough to enable him to look up into the higher regions of thought, he has a judgement that will not suffer him to take illusions there for realities. Yet this man has no sneers for regeneration by the Spirit, nor does he turn his back upon his wounded Saviour and the mysteries of the Cross. What a rebuke his calm, comprehensive, obedient mind is to the presumptuous sophistry of inflated men! They seem to stand before his steady judgement like schoolboys taken to task. Some, we trust, will be made better by it, but not all, perhaps not many; for unbelief is all rank with self-complacency, superciliousness, and scorn. Look at it! The Liberal scoffs the Orthodox, the avowed Deist the Liberal, and the Atheist makes jest of them all.

Making allowance for a parade term now and then, the author's style is plain and manly, and sometimes ascends to grandeur. And, with the exception now and then of a word out of place in the figurative passages, he has followed pretty well Swift's definition of good writing. As a whole, no book has lately been published in which thought is brought out with more clearness and directness. There is no misty medium between the author and his readers. His mind comes directly in contact with theirs.

We have left ourselves room for only a passing remark upon a few extracts. There is but little need, however, of our saying much upon a work which every reading man will read, and which will commend itself to every religious, and, we hope, to every thinking man. It is a book to be meditated upon, not to be run over and forgotten.

"Enthusiasm," says our author, "is not a term of *measurement*, but of quality." — "Where there is no errour of imagination, no misjudging of realities, no calculations which reason condemns, there is no enthusiasm, even though the soul may be on fire with the velocity of its movements in pursuit of its chosen object." This will suffice to explain the sense in which the writer uses the term.

We quote the following, not that it is altogether novel, but because it is clearly expressed, and may serve to awaken a class of intellectual men who are dreaming out a life of sad delusion.

"The religion of the heart may be supplanted by a religion of the imagination, just in the same way that the social affections are often dislodged or corrupted by factitious sensibilities. Every one knows that an artificial excitement of all the kind and tender emotions of our nature may take place through the medium of the imagination. Hence the power of poetry and the drama. . . . . . Whenever excitements of any kind are regarded distinctly as a source of luxurious pleasure, then, instead of expanding the bosom with beneficent energy, instead of dispelling the sinister purposes of selfishness, instead of shedding the softness and warmth of generous love through the moral system, they become a freezing centre of solitary and unsocial indulgence ; and at length displace every emotion that deserves to be called virtuous. No cloak of selfishness is in fact more impenetrable than that which usually envelopes a pampered imagination. . . . . .

"A process of perversion and of induration precisely similar may have place also among the religious emotions. . . . . . Whoever disaffects the substantial matters of Christianity, and seeks to derive from it merely, or chiefly, the gratifications of excited feeling; whoever combines from its materials a paradise of abstract contemplation, or of poetic imagery, where he may take refuge from the annoyances and the importunate claims of common life; — whoever thus delights himself with dreams, and is insensible to realities, lives in peril of awaking from his illusions when truth comes too late. The religious idealist, perhaps, sincerely believes himself to be eminently devout; and those who witness his abstraction, his elevation, his enjoyments, may reverence his piety; meanwhile this fictitious happiness creeps as a lethargy through the moral system, and is rendering him continually less and less susceptible of those emotions in which true religion consists."

In a period of society when prayer is so much neglected, when even females, bearing the name of Christian, are tainted with an unbelieving sophistry as to its need, the following extracts may not be inappropriate.

"To err in modes of prayer may be reprehensible; but not to pray is mad. And when those whose temper is abhorrent to religious services animadvert sarcastically upon the follies, real or supposed, of religionists, there is a sad inconsistency in such criticisms, like that which is seen when the insane make ghastly mirth of the manners or personal defects of their friends and keepers. The very idea of addressing *petitions* to Him who 'worketh all things' according to the counsel of His own eternal and unalterable will, and the enjoined practice of clothing sentiments of piety in articulate forms of language, though those sentiments, before they are invested in words, are perfectly known to the Searcher of hearts, imply that, in the terms and the mode of intercourse between God and man, no attempt is made to lift the latter above his sphere of limited notions and imperfect knowledge. The terms of devotional communion rest even on a much lower ground than that which man, by efforts of reason and imagination, might attain to. Prayer, in its very conditions, supposes, not only a condescension of the Divine nature to meet the human, but an humbling of the human nature to a lower range than it might easily reach. The region of abstract conceptions, of lofty reasonings, of magnificent images, has an atmosphere too subtile to support the health of true piety; and in order that the warmth and vigour of life may be maintained in the heart, the common level of the natural affections is chosen as the scene of intercourse between heaven and earth."

"Every ambitious attempt to break through the humbling conditions on which man may hold communion with God, must, then, fail of success; since the Supreme has fixed the scene of worship and converse, not in the skies, but on earth. The Scripture models of devotion, far from encouraging vague and inarticulate contemplations, consist of such utterances of desire, or hope, or love, as seem to suppose the existence of correlative feeling, and of every *human* sympathy, in Him to whom they are addressed."

The uses of the discipline of Providence in giving a sense of reality and importunacy to prayer is thus well expressed.

"The dispensations of the Divine Providence towards the pious have the same tendency to confine the devout affections within the circle of terrestrial ideas, and to make religion always an occupant of the homestead of common feelings. 'Many are the afflictions of the righteous,' and wherefore, but to bring his religious belief and emotions in close contact with the humiliations of animal life, and to necessitate the use of prayer as a real and efficient means of obtaining needful assistance in distress? If vague speculations or delicious illusions have carried the Christian away from the realities of earth, urgent wants or piercing sorrows presently arouse him from his dreams, and oblige him to come back to the importunacy of prayer, and to the simplicity of praise. A strange incongruity may seem to present itself, when the sons of God, the heirs of immortality, the destined princes of heaven, are seen implicated in sordid cares, and vexed and oppressed by the perplexities of a moment; but this incongruity is only perceived when the great facts of religion are viewed in the false light of the imagination; for the process of preparation, far from being incompatible with these apparent degradations, requires them; and it is by such means of humiliation that the hope of immortality is bound down in the heart, and prevented from floating in the region of material images."

And now one word to those who pray.

"If the language of humiliation is at all admitted into the enthusiast's devotions, it must be so pointed with extravagance, and so blown out with exaggerations, that it serves much more to tickle the fancy than to affect the heart: it is a burlesque of penitence, very proper to amuse a mind that is destitute of real contrition. That such artificial humiliations do not spring from the sorrow of repentance is proved by their bringing with them no lowliness of temper. Genuine humility would shake the whole towering structure of this enthusiastic pietism; and therefore, in the place of Christian humbleness of mind, there are cherished certain ineffable notions of self-annihilation and self-renunciation, and we know not what other attempts at metaphysical suicide. If you receive the enthusiast's description of himself, he has become, in his own esteem, by continued force of divine contemplation, infinitely less than an atom, — a very negative quality, — an incalculable fraction of positive entity: meanwhile the whole of his deportment betrays the sensitiveness of a self-importance ample enough for a god."

For those who look with cold scorn upon the strong workings of the soul in view of its state of sin, and who treat conviction and conversion as little better than slang terms, we quote the following: —

"In witnessing, first, the entreaties, and supplications, and tears of a convicted, condemned, and repentant malefactor, prostrate at the feet of his sovereign, and, then, the exuberance of his joy and gratitude in receiving pardon and life, no one would so absurdly misuse language as to call the intensity and fervour of the criminal's feelings enthusiastical; for however strong, or even ungovernable, those emotions may be, they are perfectly congruous with the occasion: — they spring up from no illusion; but are fully justified by the momentous turn that has taken place in his affairs: — in the past hour he contemplated nothing but the horrours of a violent, and ignominious, and a deserved death; but now life and its delights are before him. It is true that all men in the same circumstances would not undergo the same intensity of emotion; but all, unless obdurate in wickedness, must experience feelings of the same quality. And thus, so long as the real circumstances under which every human being stands in the court of the Supreme Judge are clearly understood, and duly felt, enthusiasm finds no place: all is real; nothing illusory. But when once these unutterably important facts are forgotten or obscured, then, by necessity, every enhancement of religious feeling is a step on the ascent of enthusiasm; and it becomes a matter of very little practical consequence, whether the deluded pietist is the worshipper of some system of abstract rationalism, or of tawdry images and rotten relics; though the latter errour of the two is, perhaps, preferable, inasmuch as warm-hearted fervour is always better than frozen pride."

We have not room for the remarks upon the Roman Catholic doctrine of the mediatorial office of Christ, and what our author considers the substitution of a kind of worship addressed to the imagination with the most consummate art, — this, of course, resulting in Enthusiasm. For he observes, that "when, either by the refinements of rationalism, — a gross misnomer, — or by superstitious corruptions, the central facts of Christianity are obscured, no middle ground remains between the apathy of formality and the extravagance of enthusiasm."

The section on "Enthusiasm the Source of Heresy"

should be read with care. We scarcely know how to select from it; for if we pitch upon one part, we feel as if we were leaving a better behind. There is a solemn veracity in the following passage. We look around us as we read it; and we behold it an embodied, living truth. There go the throng. We could point out one and another in it for a warning; but it would be invidious. Perhaps, too, this is no longer needed.

"In like manner as the passion for travel impels a man to perambulate the earth, and then makes him sigh to think that he has not other continents to explore, so the constitutional enthusiasm of speculation urges its victim to traverse the entire circuit of opinions; and even then leaves him insatiate of novelty. It is not caprice, much less is it the excessive solicitude of an honest mind, always inquiring for truth, but rather the impetus of a too highly wrought intellectual activity, which carries the heretic onward and onward, from system to system, blazing as he goes, until there remains no form of flagrant errour with which he has not scared the sober world. Then, though reason may have forgotten all consistency, pride has a better memory; and as this passion forbids his return to the centre truths he has so often denounced, and denounced from all points of his various course, nothing remains for him, when the season of exhaustion arrives, but to go off into the dark void of infidelity.

"The sad story has been often realized. In the confirmation of the *heretic by temperament* there is more of intellectual mobility than of strength: a ready perception of analogies gives him both facility and felicity in collecting proofs, or rather illustrations, in support of whatever opinion he adopts. So copious are the materials of conjectural argument which crowd upon him, and so nice is his tact of selection and so quick his skill of arrangement, that, ere dull sobriety has gathered up its weapons, he has reared a most imposing front of defence. Pleased and even surprised with his own work, he now confidently maintains a position which at first he scarcely thought to be seriously defensible. Having convinced himself of the certainty of the new truth, and implicated his vanity in its support, deeper motives stimulate the activity of the reasoning and inventive faculties; and he presently piles demonstration upon demonstration to a most amazing height, until it becomes, in his honest opinion, sheer infatuation to doubt. In this state of mind, of what value are the opinions of teachers and of elders? Of what weight the belief of the catholic Church in all ages? They are nothing to be accounted of; — there seems even a glory and a heroism, as well as a duty, in spurning the fallible authority of man; — modesty, caution, hesitation, are treasons against conscience and heaven!"

We make the following extract without applying it, leaving it to the good sense and just observation of others.

"We have spoken of the enthusiasm of mysticism. But there is also an enthusiasm of simplification. The lowest intellectual temperature, not less than the highest, admits extravagance, and sometimes even admits it more; for warmth and movement are less unnatural, in the world of matter or of mind, than congelation;—what so grotesque as the coruscations of frost?"

"Driven from the inclosures where the demonstrable sciences hold empire, the enthusiasts of speculation turn off upon ground where there is more scope, more obscurity, more license, and less of the stern and instant magistracy of right reason. Some give themselves to politics, some to political economy, and some to theology; and whatever they severally meet with that is in its nature, or that has become, concrete, complex, or multifariously involved, they seize upon with a hungry avidity. The disease of the brain has settled upon the faculty of analysis; — all things compound must therefore be severed, and not only be severed, but left in disunion. It cannot but happen, that, in these zealous labours of dissolution, some happy strokes must now and then fall upon errours which wiser men have either not observed, or have spared: mankind owes, therefore, a petty debt of gratitude to such eager speculatists, for having removed a few excrescences from ancient systems. But these trivial successes, which are hailed with a din of applause by the vulgar, who delight in witnessing any kind of destruction, and by the splenetic, who believe themselves to gain whatever is torn from others, inspire the heroes of reform with unbounded hopes of effecting universal revolutions; and they actually become inflated to so high a degree of presumption, that, at a time when all the great questions which can occupy the human mind have been thoroughly discussed, — and discussed with every advantage of liberty, of learning, and of ability, — they are not ashamed to adopt a style of speaking as if they thought themselves morning stars on the verge of the dark ages, destined to usher in the splendours of true philosophy upon a benighted world."

We will make one more extract, and then close.

"The great principle of vicarious suffering, which forms the centre of Christianity, spreads itself through the subordinate parts of the system, and is the pervading, if not the invariable, law of Christian beneficence.

"The spontaneous sympathies of human nature, when they are vigorous enough to produce the fruits of charity, rest on an expectation of an opposite kind; for we first seek to dispel the uneasy sensation of pity; then look for the gratitude of the wretch we have solaced, and for the approbation of spectators; and then take a sweet after-draught of self-complacency. But the Christian virtue of beneficence takes its stand altogether on another ground; and its doctrine is, that whoever would remedy misery must himself suffer; and that the pains of the vicarious benefactor are generally to bear proportion to the extent or malignity of the evils he labours to remove. So that, while the philanthropist who undertakes the cure only of the transient ills of the present life may encounter no greater amount of toils or discouragements than are amply recompensed by the immediate gratifications of successful benevolence, he who, with a due sense of the greatness of the enterprise, devotes himself to the removal of the moral wretchedness in which human nature is involved, will find that the sad quality of these deeper woes is in a manner reflected back upon himself; and that to touch the substantial miseries of degenerate man is to come within the infection of infinite sorrow."

We wished to give some passages in connection with the above, for the strengthening of those whom the peculiar state of the times has called to great endurance of contumely and injustice from high and low; but we have no room. They have this consolation, that a rest remaineth. And how is strength put into their hearts when they reflect, that though they may have much to bear, and may meet with particular disappointments in their course, the great cause in which they are engaged will move surely and steadily on! God has said that the wrath of man shall praise Him, and that the remainder of wrath He will restrain.

In furnishing these extracts, we have, perhaps, done as well as if we had gone into a particular analysis of the work. There are many books of good reputation, of which the substance might be given within a small compass. But beside the fact that this work treats upon several distinct subjects, an analysis of it would have run us out to a tedious length, so compact is it, and so made up of striking and intimately connected thoughts. There is no loose work in it, — one scarcely sees where to drive in a wedge.

It is a consolation to us, that this work is likely to fall into the hands of certain readers who stand much in need of it, — we mean men in the literary and professional orders, and others in a class less literary, yet well informed, who are in various ways associated with them. We have opportunities of knowing that many of these are not quite at ease respecting the opinions of their teachers. They have misgivings that all may not be well, not quite so well as it would fain be made outwardly to appear. When opinions which they know not how to reconcile with their own old-fashioned, yet half-forgotten, notions of faith are somewhat boldly thrown out, they are startled into the question, Is this the Christianity which we used to read of in the Bible? and they are alarmed for the moment, to think how far they have been gradually and unconsciously drawn away from their old belief; and ask themselves, Where must all this end?

Their situation is a critical one; for they allow themselves to be quieted by some plausible excuse, — such as that the opinion was loosely expressed, or was intended to be understood with such and such qualifications, or that it came from one generally held to be adventurous and indiscreet; or their attention is called off and directed to some part which is of a more serious character. Thus, what with a sprinkling of Scripture phrases, and a mixture of some truth with much errour, they are gradually wonted to a system of unbelief. They begin with doubting, and doubt turns to denial, till they are finally in danger of ending in the disbelief of almost every thing but that they themselves are very exemplary believers.

If, instead of looking at the subject occasionally and detachedly, they could be brought to examine it in reference to first principles, and the operation of these, and their necessary results, they would discover that loose opinions in point of belief no more come of accident, nor spring less from fixed causes, than do those of the most thorough and firm faith. Would they then go a little farther, they would also find, that, if the same principles by which this qualified, half belief has been reached were fairly carried out, they would infallibly bear men far out of the bounds of Christianity.

When men are far gone in unbelief, this effort is hardly to be expected of them. Many a man who has been finally lost in infidelity might have been brought back from it, and have stood firmly in the faith, if, upon first doubting a doctrine of the Gospel, he could have been prevailed upon immediately to try all the other doctrines by the same principle upon which he questioned that one. Then he would immediately have seen the justice of Good's remark, — that "there is no intermediate ground upon which a sound reasoner can make a fair stand, between that of pure deism and that of moderate orthodoxy, as held by the evangelical classes both of Churchmen and Dissenters"; and the fearful truth would have come upon him whole, and before the mind had formed the ruinous habit of half closing its vision, or of turning away from necessary conclusions.

There is much, however, to hope for from the men of the classes we are speaking of; for here and there may be seen one and another coming out of the by-paths of errour into the open paths of truth. They may have to forego expectations of distinction and power; they may have hard things to encounter, — coldness on the part of old acquaintance, — sneers, which have a sting often out of proportion to the size of the insect, — and with these, and harder than these, they may have to endure false surmises as to their motives, cast on them by their intimates, too, and made to stick the closer by an adhesive varnish of smooth extenuation laid on in feigned charity and love. But all these things are easily borne after a time. And who would not bear them, for the sake of that strengthening conviction of the sincerity of one's faith and love which the endurance of evil for the truth always gives a man?

Sacrifices such as these will be met more generally and quickly than they have for a long time been; for motives to do so are pressing more and more. The hues of truth and of errour are fast separating; the doubtful twilight breaking; truth brightening, and errour darkening. Soon there will not be a spot for the hesitating man to stand upon, nor a shred left out of which the timid man shall weave his cloak of charity to hide his own selfishness, while he is bringing odium on the open, hardy soldiers of the Faith. The two sides will soon be marked off plainly enough; the distance between them will become wider and wider, — too wide for the voice of parley with errour to be heard across it; the way of faith will be made more and more plain, and the sin of unbelief be stripped bare of excuse. The great question, as our author says, is speedily to be, Have we a revelation from God? And as each man decides this for himself, so will he reject the Word for once and all, or honour the Son even as he honours the Father.

May God grant us the spirit of self-sacrifice in this his cause, teach us to contend earnestly, yet meekly, for the truth, and pardon our infirmities when we forget his teachings!

MEMOIR OF HENRY MARTYN.*

No man, it has been said, ever put pen to his diary, without a side glance at his window. A close examination of our own state of mind so well satisfied us of this, that we committed to the flames every scrap of the records of our feelings and thoughts, being unwilling to seem to have written under an assurance of secrecy, while there was a lurking misgiving at heart. We should have been content with this general direction, — " To be burnt unread," — had we not learned, that even writing in cipher and throwing away the key was no security, as nearest friends would forge a key and unlock our secrets to the public; that indeed, short of extinction, there was no security against publicity. We have witnessed with our own eyes the burning of our scroll, have seen the faint traces of the lines

---

* From The Spirit of the Pilgrims for 1831.

A Memoir of the REV. HENRY MARTYN, B. D., *late Fellow of St. John's College, Cambridge, and Chaplain to the Honourable East India Company.* By the REV. JOHN SARGENT, M. A., Rector of Lavington. *From the tenth London Edition, corrected and enlarged. With an Introductory Essay and an Appendix by the American Editor.* Boston: Perkins & Marvin. 1831. pp. 432.

The reader is referred to the heading of the article on Pollok's Course of Time, p. 344.

in the blackened mass, repeating as we looked on, the humorous couplet of the melancholy Cowper, —

> "There goes the parson, O illustrious spark!
> And there, no less illustrious, goes the clerk."

And with these bright personages went our record, — a record such as must make up the life of even the most favoured of the sons of earth, — a record of sinning and repenting, of much sorrow and of little joy.

Whether it be best for a man to keep a secret journal of his states of mind cannot now be a matter of discussion. There is no longer any such thing as secrecy in this world. In that graceless article upon "The Evangelical School," in a late number of the Edinburgh Review, are some clever remarks upon the evils that must result from the breaking in upon all a man's retirements. And it is now well understood, that if a man gains a battle for his country, or writes a book for its entertainment, the penalty he must pay for it is the vulgar exposure of every emotion that he had ever written down for one nearest his heart, and of every treasured thought and feeling that he had recorded for his soul's good. This is the most awful form of bondage; for it holds the mind enslaved. It is a weight upon the free spirit, and shuts up in dead stagnation those waters which might have flowed out from the heart, and blessed the man himself and those he loved. In proportion to a man's refinement is his sensitiveness on this point; and as is the beauty of the spirit, so is the withering power of his distrust upon it. He who has made the world his debtor becomes thereby its bondman. He can treasure up no little testimonies of the love of those who are gone, lest, when he too is departed, the rude palm of the public should handle and soil them. He must part even with these also; and the dead must speak to him only in memory any more. A letter to a close friend must be written as under the public eye;—in short, the throng possess themselves of every secret outlet of his soul. This begets a habit of reserve, and that, in time, brings coldness and hardness upon the gentlest spirit. There are fibres of the soul too delicate to be thus felt and probed. We recollect having read, in an account of the inmates of a hospital for the insane, of one who formed a head-piece out of a pewter basin, which he fitted close to his skull, complaining that his neighbours were in the habit of sending little spirits in at his ears, who, after coursing his brains and getting information of his embryo inventions, flew back to their masters with their stolen knowledge. We much doubt whether a man who should appear in a like head-piece, now-a-days, ought, on that account, to be held a proper subject for Bedlam.

A sensible man cannot now keep a diary, under a reasonable expectation that it will never meet the public eye; and if he is an honest man, and one in whose account of himself we may put trust, he will not affect to do so,—he will not talk in soliloquy loud enough to be overheard by his neighbours. Whatever he writes in this way he must regard, not only as property for his own particular use while he lives, but as a legacy to the public when he dies. Let writer and reader henceforth understand each other, and the world will be better able to judge what allowance to make in these records of one's self, and the man himself be less likely to be deceived as to the sincerity with which he sets them down.

With respect to the particular kind of diary of which we have been speaking, it is well, perhaps, that things have come to this definite result. For to write under an equivocal state of feeling, at any time, must endanger the clear integrity of the mind, and make it liable, at all times, to a subtle bias which will warp the plain truth. Had the honest man any distinct apprehension of his state, he would turn away from his work. It is but the more dangerous for its secret and unobserved character, and before one is aware may spread like weather-stain over the mind, and change its whole hue: It is difficult to suppose an indirectness of mind in one particular, which may not infect its sincerity and weaken the strength of its uprightness in all.

And, especially, will a misgiving of exposure, when setting down the results of self-examination, not only lead to a false view of some part of one's character, but throw the whole out of its true proportions also. No one can look into a diary of the mind, without observing, that no mention is made of some of those evil propensities which would have been the subjects of long and sorrowful consideration in hours devoted to such reflections as were never intended to be put upon record, — that a self-examiner, with pen in hand, is a very different creature from a self-examiner empty-handed.

But how does a tolerably honest man make amends to his own conscience for this partial view of things? Why, one way is, by so wrapping the vice up in general and indefinite terms, that neither he nor any one else shall be able clearly to distinguish what it is, and then calling it by the hardest names he can think of. He lays on the most violent blows; but the folds are so thick, he might as well have spared himself the labour of the beating. But this leads to self-delusion, for vague terms react, and produce vague perceptions in him who uses them, — his sins gradually fade into indistinct shadows to him, and then his compunctious visitings become feebler and feebler, and he seems less a criminal to himself standing before his thus recorded sins, for he has so talked about himself as to have talked himself out of a knowledge of himself. Or, what has a like or no better result, he passes by one sin and lays a double load on the next, which has to bear the twofold weight of reprobation, — its own and its neighbour's; and thus, excess in one point answering for deficiency in another, and the *whole* man receiving his due share of self-reproof, conscience is quieted, as the amount of evil in the character is made up, and the world (for it is thoughts of the world that lead to all this) is not deceived in the sum total.

But the world is deceived, and, what is worse, the man himself is deceived, and, saddest of all, is encouraging a spirit of self-deception. Every time he goes to his task, a secret principle is at work in him, which is blinding him more and more to one fault, and bringing out another in monstrous and exaggerated proportions. In certain diseased states of the senses, parts of the body will appear to the patient to be swelling to an enormous and horrid size; his fingers, for instance, will seem to him to be growing to the size of arms and legs, while he takes no notice of his other members, nor looks to see whether they also are undergoing this fearful change. Now, could the character wrought out in the process of self-examination of which we are speaking assume a body, and stand up in its uncouth deformity before the examiner, when in his right mind, how horridly unlike himself would its aspect be, and how would he flee from it, in terrour and amaze! Yet here would be made visible to him the product of his own well-meant labour; here would be the result of self-examination, — here, self-knowledge!

A false aspect is also given to the character, by a proneness to dwell upon the compunctions of conscience and the gloomy and agonizing thoughts that sin occasions, rather than upon the cheerfulness and serenity that religion imparts to the soul. To record the former savours of humility to us, while to set down the other in black and white has a cast of self-commendation. So that if a man should look back upon the history of his past life merely through his diary, he would by and by be persuaded that he had all his days been the most miserable of men, when, after all, he had lived the life of a tolerably happy Christian. Now this is one way in which a man deceives himself into an unfortunate view of himself, and leads others into a false estimate of his character, and a very unfavourable and gloomy view of his religion; and it comes of his secret misgiving of exposure, with a commendably honest fear, perhaps, that, if he should speak the whole truth, the world might think better of him than he deserves.

In his intercourse with the world, the honestest man is too much of his time a double character. There is an outer and an inner machinery, a set of processes of thoughts and feelings for his fellow-men, and another set for himself. Without any fixed purpose at assuming to be that which he is not, — on the contrary, with a full dislike of all forms of hypocrisy, — unless he is willing to lay his heart bare to the common gaze, he must be content to be thought other than he is. This he does, not by assuming the false, but by concealing the true. O, how has the upright man been humbled, when praise for some known good has set before him those infirmities which no earthly eye but his own ever saw, and which the most censorious never guessed to be within him! A man's refinement, his very love of purity, his sense of propriety, his abhorrence of sin, all render him, if we may be allowed the expression, but a better sort of dissembler: There is a shameless honesty found only in the lowest recklessness of vice.

How does such a man feel the need of getting away from the world, and of acquainting himself in solitude with his own heart! and how does he hurry to strip it bare, and see it just as God sees it! — that God who

> "spares all beings but himself
> That hideous sight, a naked human heart."

Let such a man beware how he takes the world with him into his closet. The door and the window must be barred, and every little crevice stopped; not the smallest gleam must come in from abroad; there must be an absolute certainty, a perfect rest of the mind, that no human being knows, or can by any possibility ever know, what passes in this his communion with himself. Let him be thoroughly honest with himself, then, and throw away his tablets, if he would truly and entirely know himself. Let him be his own master, a freeman, for once. The world, at best, has but too much dominion over us, biasing our opinions as to what is without, and what is far worse, warping our judgements of what is within.

If this diary of the inner man is more or less attended by a secret mistrust that it will one day betray us to the world, — if this misgiving infects our reflections, and insensibly sways the mind, — there are also some lesser evils waiting upon it. It has a tendency to make the act of recording partially a substitute for the act of close and deep examination. A man has a little time at the close of the evening for meditation; and the question is, "What entry shall I make in my diary for this day?" The mechanical process comes into the mind; and "What shall I say of myself, and how shall I say it?" though it would seem only to lead to another and prime question, "What have I been and done?" does more than merely lead to it; it enters into and interferes with its simplicity and directness, and its thorough, unsparing search. And not only is this preparatory process of meditation interfered with; but when the man comes to make his entry, there is another subtile, but no less injurious, influence upon the mind. The man is writing *about* himself, and by this very act he *about* whom he writes becomes to him, in a sense, a third person; he in some measure, without wholly losing a secret, unobserved partiality, sets himself off from himself; the pungency of his convictions is weakened; conscience, shame, remorse, are more or less dulled; and though he applies all the language of those passions to this outer self, the inner self, the real man, is not so pierced by them to the quick, has not that vivid, sharp sense of them which he would have felt, had he simply given himself up to self-examination and reflection.

And here we are half inclined to ask the question, whether, by this process, conscience does not, as it were, write, in black and white, a sort of partial discharge; and whether a man gets up from making an entry in his diary with that same sense of unworthiness accompanying him and abiding on him, as would have gone with him had he simply arisen from meditating upon his heart.

Once more, what we commit to paper, we are very

apt to free the mind from the burden of carrying about. One man makes it a rule never to rely upon a memorandum for what he has to do. Another trusts to his memorandum; and it will be well for him if he does not forget what he has to do and his memorandum also. The same principle applies to this diary-keeping. The only difference is, that the latter concerns things infinitely more important. And it is much to be doubted, whether occasionally turning over the leaves of such a journal will compensate for what is lost by keeping one at all.

Some may question these views altogether; others may think we are over-refining. We advise the latter to study the workings of the mind a little more closely. And if any are ready to ask us, whether we mean to apply our remarks to such men as Brainerd, and Martyn, and Payson, we must be allowed to reply, in those much abused terms, "Principles, not men"; and to add, that, elevated Christians as these men were, we believe they might have been just as good Christians if they had never put down a line for a record of their thoughts; and we think it probable that they would have known themselves more truly, and have been all the happier. Not that the habit of recording their states of mind was the main cause of their partial self-ignorance and consequent sufferings; it only performed a kind of under service in continuing and increasing these. The great cause lay far deeper. And here we are naturally led to another subject, — the self-inflicted sufferings which they, and many other excellent Christians like them, have endured, and the principal causes of these sufferings.

We are aware that this is a difficult, not to say dangerous, matter to treat upon. Were we writing for the deeply religious only, we should not fear that our meaning would be misunderstood, or be put to an evil use. But where there is quite enough of nominal, with so little of real Christianity, we are sensible how delicate a thing it is to point out the faults or mistakes of the religious, and not bring disrepute upon them and their cause with "your easy Christian"; and how impossible it is to show that the renewed in heart have endured unnecessary self-infliction, without its being made an occasion to question the depravity of man, and the whole plan of grace and salvation growing out of that awful truth. But, on the other hand, the misery that many holy men have endured, and the serenity and cheerfulness of which they have deprived themselves, through erroneous views of their duties and relations, have led to as much skepticism respecting the true Gospel as any unsound speculations of its friends, not to say any attacks of its enemies.

There is an extreme scrupulosity in some minds about bringing the failings or mistakes of a good man before the world. This is being wiser than the Bible. When God permitted the crimes of David to be published to all generations, he knew that it would make David the jest of the thoughtless and unregenerate through every age. But his purpose was to teach men not to depend upon themselves; to save his backsliding children from despair, and to point out to them the way of repentance; and He did not refrain from this, though He foresaw that it would be made an occasion by the sinner of scoffing at his Word, of hardening the unrenewed heart, and leading to a heavier condemnation. There are also very honest men, who are sometimes as much afraid of letting out a particular truth upon a sinful world as they would be of setting loose a wild beast, as it must tend to the destruction of so many. And what truth has not? "There is a soul of goodness in things evil"; and so, to sin, there is a soul of evil in things good. No truth can be brought fully out, nor its virtue proved, till it has undergone every experiment to which perverted ingenuity can subject it, and every modification which the mistakes of its friends can give to it. God is using this world as the great laboratory of his universe; and every truth, as well as every errour, is undergoing moral processes enough to make the most knowing chemist stare. There will be dross enough; but when the work is done, and the laboratory shut up, there will be no more mistakes as to what is dross and what gold. The metals that come out of that fire will have no base mixture; it will be all smelted out.

For eighteen hundred years, the great truths of the Gospel have been operating upon portions of the world, and the same principles have been acting upon the same natures. As man was when Christ appeared, so is he now; in his natural state an enemy to God, and in his renewed state still a sinner; and the Gospel is a system of mercy and salvation for him, and the Holy Spirit the regenerating power. These great truths admit of no change, and every man must have received them who is born of God. But with these and other leading principles of the Gospel may be connected minor principles and modes of operation, and diversities of relations and influences and bearings and appliances, which many a saint now in heaven either never thought of or misunderstood. As in the material world developements have been taking place and all things maturing for ages, so in the moral world the leading principles of the Gospel, in themselves unchanged, have been gradually working upon the individual and social man, and opening out secret relations and bearings, which, in principle, they have always stood connected with, but with which they have been slowly coming into contact in act. In the mind of God, the union must always have existed; but He did not make his mind fully known at once. Gradual developement, if not necessary in the very nature of things, has, at least so far as we are allowed to see, always been the mode of God's working, and must therefore be the right mode. His purposes are both particular and universal, and in these He may be said, in a certain sense, to be represented in man, considered in his combined individual and social characters. And as He does not regard the particular independent of the universal, neither the universal independent of the particular, so He has not as yet set forth all the bearings and purposed influences of the Gospel in any individual, but is gradually bringing them more and more into action and manifestation in the individual and in society at the same time. A few simple principles thus operating upon subjects single or in masses, or closely or slightly related, are unfolding cheerful varieties, healthful freeness, and beautiful dependences, going to make up a whole full of harmony.

Is it an over-excited and exaggerating spirit which leads to the expectation that Christianity, as a social system, is beginning to be better understood? Has it not been looked upon too exclusively as a system by which individuals were to be converted, while it was forgotten that it was further intended to shine upon and permeate society in the mass, and so to change it as to bring out into a clearer light the obligations of this social body, and the right and wrong of its enjoyments, labours, and purposes? And must not those who have philosophy enough to perceive how necessarily one truth bears upon another, apparently remote, also see, that, if society in the mass becomes indeed enlightened by Christianity as to what concerns itself, the individual is at the same time let into a better apprehension of the bearing of religion upon the character and uses of his individual attributes, and into an enlarged knowledge of the attributes, purposes, and acts of the Deity? — that with the advance of what surrounds the individual, he himself advances in self-knowledge? — and that, though not a more religious man at heart, perhaps, he is led to a more enlightened view of things and to juster action, and his mind filled with a more expansive wisdom than may have belonged to those of earlier times?

The more objects to which a man sees religion applied, and the more purposes which he finds it fulfilling, the better will he understand the nature of it when brought home to himself, as the laws of light and its beautiful effects are perceived, not by looking upon one object, but by seeing it as it falls on all the varieties of form, and is thrown back in shifting hues from things around him. The taking of this view of religion has led to the discovery of the sinfulness of many a deed which good Christians once never questioned; and it will lead, also, to the conviction, that many a practice from which they now refrain as sinful may be indulged in, not only without harm, but with benefit. Newton did not feel the criminality of the slave-trade, while he was scrupulous about some things which may now be held innocent and healthful. Christians deny themselves many things, because of the perverted uses to which the evil-minded put them; but will not the time come when, the influence of Christianity having spread far and wide, this motive to restraint will become less and less, and religion will be found to be a regulating and subordinating system in these particulars, as well as one of self-denial?

It is the character of sin, not only to love what is sinful, but to pollute whatsoever it touches; to make that which is in itself pure seem impure to the conscientious, and thus to deprive a good man of many an innocent enjoyment. It is probably in part from this, that some scrupulous people have cut themselves off from the pleasures of music, and that others look upon the taking of delight in the fine arts as a questionable indulgence; and that from poetry, painting, and sculpture some have turned off their eyes, as if they were the works of the Man of Sin, or, at best, the products of laborious idleness. Dress, too, comes in for a share of condemnation; and no distinction is made between gaudiness and extravagance, and a becoming tastefulness of costume, till confined views produce sour feelings, and a perception of the beautiful is almost lost to the mind. But outward nature and our inward being are in correspondence. External beauty awakens in the healthful mind a pleased internal sense of the beautiful; and as, by its own law, the mind seeks to produce what is within, it becomes generative of the beautiful, and, as it does so, more perfectly realizes its own idea and what is without. To be scrupulous, then, about the beautiful in any of its forms as the production of man, people, to be consistent, should go a little further, and doubt whether it would not have been as well had the Creator been less prodigal of beauty in his universe; and when they see a bright flower perched upon the peak of some rough shore-cliff, should cast an eye of half contempt upon the idle thing, as it dances in the morning air on the very edge of danger. God's works and Word are both in opposition to such views, and we read from both their condemnation, in language of surpassing beauty and simplicity, uttered by our Saviour: — "Consider the lilies of the field, how they grow; they toil not, neither do they spin; and yet I say unto you, that Solomon, in all his glory, was not arrayed like one of these." What a personification is here! What living, fair creatures!

Our senses were given us for something more than the plainer uses of life; and our pleasurable perceptions through them were meant for other than mere temptations. They were designed to administer, under every form, to the health and fulness of the soul. We were once at table with a man who said that he ate from a sense of duty. We could not but admire the exemplary manner in which he fulfilled the obligation laid upon him, and wished in our hearts that we could as faithfully follow the law which bade us refrain, as he did that which bade him do.

It is a false view of the subject to consider our pleasurable perceptions as merely pleasurable. The soul would "cream and mantle like a standing pool," were not these bright, rippling streams continually running in and out and freshening its waters. You might as well deprive certain animals of their feelers, as the soul of these uses. What exhilarating variety they give to the mind! and how they quicken the soul's sensations, and brighten up the thoughts! If the love of God flows into the heart, it may flow out through these, enriching what it passes through, and reflecting itself back from all those differing and modified forms with which He has kindly diversified the world.

There is no one power which the mind exercises that has not an intimate and frequent relation to all its other powers; and to cut it off from its natural uses, as well as to use it in excess, is an injury to the general constitution of the soul. The application to higher purposes of those powers which act through the senses enriches the mind with new conceptions of beauty or grandeur in sound or sight; the mind is filled with fair or magnificent ideas, our contemplations and reflections become indefinitely multiplied as we look upon that mysterious inner world of the soul, and those spiritual regions are relieved from a flat and wearisome sameness, and broken up into all that invigorating variety of hill and valley, wood, rock, and stream, which we find in the outer world.

The soul, to say the least of it, must be as complicated as the body; and it is with the former as with the latter, its very strength depends upon its antagonist powers, — its oppositions make its oneness. When it was created with the power of abstraction and of turning inward upon itself, it was at the same time provided with appetences to allure it outward, that, amongst other reasons, it should not be kept too tense at one hour, to become lax and feeble the next, thus living between joyless lassitude and over-working effort. It was constituted with this great multiplicity, not only because the multiplicity would give pleasurable sensations, but that through a variety of moving powers there should be no over-strain upon one, and that all should play easily and without forcing. There was no one part provided save in wisdom, and serving, in its turn, to relieve every other part, and going to make up a perfect whole.

Besides keeping the mind fresh by such means,

another purpose with our Creator may have been to render it healthful, vigorous, cheerful, and benevolent, by drawing it forth into action, putting in motion the social principle, and thus relieving the individual from a diseasing introversion, and alluring him to lose self at times in his acts. The religious individual then becomes a part of the religious community, and is not all self-absorbed while doing for others; and society and the individual working sympathetically, each upon each, by mutual impartation are modifying and improving one another. But we are ever tending to extremes; and if, through the action of this social principle, comparatively few religious minds now suffer under delusive and paining self-infliction, from the individual having become more a portion of the religious community, is he not in danger of becoming individually characterless, and of being resolved into an indistinguishable part of the mass? and are not meditation, self-examination, and a care of self, all too likely to be lost in over-busy activity, and a meddling concern for others?

Nevertheless, as turning the mind long inward upon itself, though for the examination of its religious condition, puts it into a more abstract state, and deprives it, in a measure, of help from those faculties which keep the feelings more easily in play, to feel becomes an effort; and then we grow impatient, and fall to condemning ourselves and to stirring up remorse for our insensibility, and finally, to making ourselves miserable by miscalling our superinduced exhaustion our sin. In this morbid state, too, we prefer being miserable to being lifeless; and are in some danger of mistaking a craving after excitement for the emotions of repentance.

To know ourselves, we must be content, sometimes, to go out of ourselves. It is a vain struggle to endeavour to feel much or justly a long time together, with the intellect under the strain of abstraction, and with but one power of the soul in action, and that too upon a narrow circle of subjects. The mind becomes monotonous under such a system, and this must produce insensibility, from which the only escape is into exaggerated and short-lived excitement, to fall back again into insensibility. Take up the diaries of the best men that ever lived, and if you find them speaking of the "happy frame" they had been in through the day, you will feel absolutely certain of seeing it followed by three or four days of sufferings, and these, again, by a course of self-upbraiding for great stupidity of soul. Now, this series of extremes is not at all necessary to a religious life; it grows out of our confined views of our duties, and our ignorantly warring against those laws of our nature which God has established in us. Instead of the Christian living with a deep sense of blessedness within him, he becomes his own tormentor, and if he is not very careful, may be so from an unobserved feeling stealing upon him, which may involve in it something of the notion of the merit of works; and while talking of the Roman Catholic scourging the body, he may be inflicting upon himself a spiritual flagellation. What work sin, and the remainder of sin, make in the mind, as well as heart! In what woful ignorance, — self-ignorance, — does it involve us! See the feeble Martyn, worn down with the excess of toil through the day, and with spirits exhausted, in bitterness because he cannot *feel* more in his protracted devotions at night; whereas, had he commended his soul to his Saviour in quiet prayer, and laid himself to sleep upon the arm of his God, he would have endured no anguish, and have awaked in the morning cheered and filled with love.

Brainerd, Payson, and some others, lived long enough to lament these errours, and to be sensible that much which they had endured neither sprang from a right cause, nor tended to a good end. We must remember, however, that these men were of peculiarly delicate and sensitive frames, — that, from their constitutions, life in them might be said to be a state of intensity for the little while it lasted, and that, if they unnecessarily suffered much from mistaken views, their sufferings might have been past enduring, and they themselves have been swallowed up quick, had not religion possessed their hearts.

After all, we cannot measure the how much one good man needs to feel, by what another, equally good, may feel; the degree must depend upon relations about which we can know little or nothing; but this we know, that every religious man must, from a sense of his sins, have his times of suffering. The more the purity of God's character opens upon him, the more clearly must he see and abhor his own pollution; and the more he feels what Christ has done for him, the more he must sorrow that he should have wounded him in the house of his friends.

But are we wrong when we say, that, unless the mind is affected by bodily disease, or by erroneously gloomy views, no true Christian's sufferings can be so unmixed as, at times, appear to have been those of the men to whom we have so often referred? It appears to us that a Christian's sorrows and a Christian's remorse for sin have blended with them an alleviating sense of good; that in the darkest hours and darkest places of his mind, rays of light are stealing in with cheering influences; and that these influences make the heart tender, melt, and comfort it. A sense of forgiven sin is somewhere in his heart, and the thought is not wholly lost, that the time will come when he shall sorrow no more, neither sin any more.

Let us not, then, attempt to be wiser than God, or think that he has been mistakenly indulgent in bestowing upon us so many faculties for intellectual culture and bodily enjoyment. As that body is the most perfect in which not only each part is beautifully formed in itself, but each bears a due proportion to the others, and is most completely developed when every part is brought into exercise, just so is it with the intellectual and moral man. With the love of God in our hearts, we need not fear to use freely those powers He has bestowed upon us, or to find refreshment and delight in any thing He has condescended to make. With all allowances for the mistakes of different periods of the world, much of this scrupulosity is being righteous overmuch; and this, in the mildest form of it, is sad self-deception. And there is no little danger in the endeavour to annihilate the variety of our occupations and enjoyments; there is a perpetual risk of some awful outbreak; whereas, let the thoughts and feelings of a sanctified man run gently, and they will become purer and purer as they flow along. Why! out of "a pestilential congregation of vapours," what glories has God spread over the skies! And yet there are persons, who, if they could have had the making of the world, and have carried out into creation the principles they apply to men, instead of a sky piled up with clouds of dazzling whiteness, or a sun setting in gorgeous yet solemn pomp, from one end of the heavens even unto the other they would have had one dull, heavy cope, of a cold, melancholy, leaden hue. It is as weak in this case as it is in all others, to reason against the use of these things from their abuse. And when we have learned that the grand purpose of religion upon a sanctified heart is to keep our faculties and affections in well-subordinated action, and not to put one half of them into fetters, the Christian's mind and heart will be much healthier, and that serenity which comes from on high will not be so often driven from his soul.

But beside the sorrowful hours that we must pass on account of our own sins, it may be said, "Is not the world all around us lying in wickedness, and how can we talk of being happy?" We will tell you how. Set immediately about making the world better. When a man is in earnest in God's work, he has very few spare minutes to be unhappy in. It is that sluggishness of "waiting God's time," which breeds melancholy and every unclean thing. Men had much rather mope over the world than labour for it. But this will no more carry on the work of sanctification and peace and joy in the soul, than it will convert a soul. God's time is now; and he who waits for it never sees it. Then act. And while you do your part, depend upon it, God will do his. And along with this, take care that there be an absorption of your will into his will. Learn to rejoice with all your heart and mind in his glorious sovereignty; then will you see the wrath of man praising him, and the remainder of wrath restrained. Do you think the angels in heaven are made miserable by the thought of their fallen compeers, or by the folly and madness of men? Strive, then, to live near God's throne, as they live; be, as they are, his swift messengers, and be happy.

Those who have but dim views of the evil of sin, who would sink God's justice in his mercy, and bring down that mercy from a wise and universal benevolence to the partial and weak fondness of humanity, must not endeavour to draw encouragement from what has been said, or affect an approval of it. For have they not cause to go mourning the day long, and while the song is yet in their mouths, "To enjoy is to obey"? If unconcern for their spirit's welfare, if vague thoughts of accountability, of the laws of God, and of what He will require of those who have disobeyed, and not repented and turned to our Mediator, have left them to find their chief enjoyments, the coarser or the more refined, in the world, — if the sciences and the arts are their graven images, and Nature another God to them, — if, by misusing God's bounties, they have driven the mistaken Christian from their right uses, — let them not make his errour bring their sins in recoil upon their own heads, nor, in deriding him, make mock at their own state and all that is fearful in eternity: — If their sin has occasioned his errour, may not his errour prove their madness?

Perhaps in some things here they may be led to see that these men's sufferings came of human infirmity, and are not the legitimate offspring of the great doctrines in which they believed; and they may take home this one thing, — it was not so much the mere fear of God, nor alarm at the penal consequences of sin, as it was the sense of guilt, which weighed upon their souls. With all their errours, is there not something heroic in this? Is not the Christian hero a glorious being by the side of the world's paragon? We must consider, too, that diaries, as we have said, give the reader a very imperfect notion of the man, and a very imperfect notion of the man even to himself. Says one, "I have read my journal, though I can hardly identify myself with the person it describes." And though we might read

Martyn's entries, and conclude that he was always bent down with sorrow, yet his English editor says, " They also with me can aver, that Henry Martyn was not less cheerful as a companion, than he was warm-hearted and constant as a friend." — " Those who imagine that a smile scarcely ever played upon his countenance, that his manner was cold and forbidding, would have been startled at hearing his hearty laugh, which still sounds in my ears, and in seeing little children climbing his knees, affording him a pleasure as great as they themselves received." And one who knew Payson well in conversation has also exquisitely said of him, — " His thoughts flew from him in every possible variety of harmony and beauty, like birds from a South American forest."

Poor Henry Martyn, too, — how, after all, did he love nature! " A dried leaf, or a straw, makes me feel myself in good company." It was not long after saying this, that his leaf withered. But he is gone now where there is no more decay for ever.

THE END.

www.ingramcontent.com/pod-product-compliance
Lightning Source LLC
LaVergne TN
LVHW021134110826
845150LV00005B/1028

9781425548766